AF361551

THE HISTORY OF AL-ṬABARĪ

AN ANNOTATED TRANSLATION

VOLUME XVI

The Community Divided

THE CALIPHATE OF ʿALĪ I

A.D. 656–657/A.H. 35–36

The History of al-Ṭabarī

Editorial Board

Ihsan Abbas, University of Jordan, Amman

C. E. Bosworth, The University of Manchester

Franz Rosenthal, Yale University

Everett K. Rowson, The University of Pennsylvania

Ehsan Yar-Shater, Columbia University (*General Editor*)

Estelle Whelan, *Editorial Coordinator*

Center for Iranian Studies
Columbia University

SUNY

SERIES IN NEAR EASTERN STUDIES

Said Amir Arjomand, Editor

*The preparation of this volume was made possible in part
by a grant from the National Endowment for the
Humanities, an independent federal agency.*

Bibliotheca Persica
Edited by Ehsan Yar-Shater

The History of al-Ṭabarī
(Ta'rīkh al-rusul wa'l-mulūk)

VOLUME XVI

The Community Divided

translated and annotated
by

Adrian Brockett

State University of New York Press

Published by
State University of New York Press, Albany
© 1997 State University of New York
All rights reserved
Printed in the United States of America

For information, address State University of New York Press,
State University Plaza, Albany, N.Y. 12246

Library of Congress Cataloging-in-Publication Data
Ṭabarī, 838?–923.
    [Tārīkh al-rusul wa-al-mulūk. English. Selections]
    The community divided / translated and annotated by Adrian
Brockett.
        p.   cm. — (The history of al-Ṭabarī = Ta'rīkh al-rusul
wa'l mulūk ; v. 16) (SUNY series in Near Eastern studies)
(Bibliotheca Persica)
    Includes bibliographical references and index.
    ISBN 0–7914–2391–3 (alk. paper). — ISBN 0–7914–2392–1
(pbk. : alk. paper)
      1. Islamic Empire—History—622–661. 2. ʿAlī ibn Abī
Ṭālib, Caliph, 600 (ca.)–661. 3. Camel, Battle of the, 656.
I. Brockett, Adrian. II. Title. III. Series. IV. Series:
Ṭabarī, 838?–923. Ta'rīkh al-rusul wa-al-mulūk. English ;
v. 16. V. Series: Bibliotheca Persica (Albany, N.Y.)
DS38.2.T313 1985 vol. 16
[DS38.1]
909'.1 s—dc20   96–17177
[909'.097671]   CIP

Preface

THE HISTORY OF PROPHETS AND KINGS (*Ta'rīkh al-rusul wa'l-mulūk*) by Abū Jaʿfar Muḥammad b. Jarīr al-Ṭabarī (839–923), here rendered as the History of al-Ṭabarī, is by common consent the most important universal history produced in the world of Islam. It has been translated here in its entirety for the first time for the benefit of non-Arabists, with historical and philological notes for those interested in the particulars of the text.

Al-Ṭabarī's monumental work explores the history of the ancient nations, with special emphasis on biblical peoples and prophets, the legendary and factual history of ancient Iran, and in great detail, the rise of Islam, the life of the Prophet Muḥammad, and the history of the Islamic world down to the year 915. The first volume of this translation contains a biography of al-Ṭabarī and a discussion of the method, scope, and value of his work. It also provides information on some of the technical considerations that have guided the work of the translators.

The *History* has been divided here into 39 volumes, each of which covers about two hundred pages of the original Arabic text in the Leiden edition. An attempt has been made to draw the dividing lines between the individual volumes in such a way that each is to some degree independent and can be read as such. The page numbers of the Leiden edition appear in the margins of the translated volumes.

Al-Ṭabarī very often quotes his sources verbatim and traces the chain of transmission (*isnād*) to an original source. The chains of transmitters are, for the sake of brevity, rendered by only a dash (—) between the individual links in the chain. Thus, "According to Ibn Ḥumayd—Salamah—Ibn Isḥāq" means that al-Ṭabarī received the report from Ibn Ḥumayd, who said that he was told by Salamah, who said that he was told by Ibn Isḥāq, and so on. The numerous subtle and important differences in the original Arabic wording have been disregarded.

The table of contents at the beginning of each volume gives a brief survey of the topics dealt with in that particular volume. It also includes the headings and subheadings as they appear in al-Ṭabarī's text, as well as those occasionally introduced by the translator.

Well-known place names, such as, for instance, Mecca, Baghdad, Jerusalem, Damascus, and the Yemen, are given in their English spellings. Less common place names, which are the vast majority, are transliterated. Biblical figures appear in the accepted English spelling. Iranian names are usually transcribed according to their Arabic forms, and the presumed Iranian forms are often discussed in the footnotes.

Technical terms have been translated wherever possible, but some, such as "dirham" and "imām," have been retained in Arabic forms. Others that cannot be translated with sufficient precision have been retained and italicized, as well as footnoted.

The annotation aims chiefly at clarifying difficult passages, identifying individuals and place names, and discussing textual difficulties. Much leeway has been left to the translators to include in the footnotes whatever they consider necessary and helpful.

The bibliographies list all the sources mentioned in the annotation.

The index in each volume contains all the names of persons and places referred to in the text, as well as those mentioned in the notes as far as they refer to the medieval period. It does not include the names of modern scholars. A general index, it is hoped, will appear after all the volumes have been published.

For further details concerning the series and acknowledgments, see Preface to Volume I.

Ehsan Yar-Shater

To
Fiona and Andrew
with love

Contents

The Caliphate of the Commander of the Faithful ʿAlī b. Abī Ṭālib

The End of the Account of the Battle of the Camel

Abbreviations

EI[1]: *The Encyclopaedia of Islām*, 1st ed., 4 vols and Supplement, Leiden and London, 1913–42

EI[2]: *The Encyclopaedia of Islam*, 2nd ed., Vol. I–, Leiden and London, 1960–

EIr.: *Encyclopædia Iranica*, Vol. I–, Costa Mesa, Calif., 1985–

IA: Ibn al-Athīr, ʿIzz al-Dīn Abū al-Ḥasan ʿAlī, *al-Kāmil fī al-taʾrīkh*, ed. C. Tornberg, repr., Beirut, 1965, Vol. III

IJMES: *International Journal of Middle East Studies*

IQ: *Islamic Quarterly*

JESHO: *Journal of the Economic and Social History of the Orient*

RSO: *Rivista degli Studi Orientali*

Editors' Foreword

The section of al-Ṭabarī's *History* dealt with in the present volume covers pp. 3066–3256 of the Prima Series in the Leiden edition, which was prepared under the general direction of M. J. de Goeje. It deals with the events of the latter part of the year 35/656, beginning with the election of ʿAlī b. Abī Ṭālib as caliph after the assassination of ʿUthmān, and the events of ʿAlī's reign in the greater part of 36/656–57. The chronicler then passes on to an account of the confrontation between ʿAlī and Muʿāwiya b. Abī Sufyān at Ṣiffīn on the upper Euphrates, the Khārijite secession, and the murder of the caliph by a Khārijite assassin.

The events during this single year or so were momentous and were to have resonance through much of subsequent Islamic history. In dealing with them al-Ṭabarī was almost exclusively concerned with the heartland of the caliphate, that is, northern and central Arabia (including the original centers of the new faith of Islam, Mecca and Medina) and southern and central Iraq, where, during the reign of the second caliph, ʿUmar b. al-Khaṭṭāb, the Arab *muqātilah*, or warriors, had defeated the might of Sasanian Persia and driven the Sasanian ruler and his demoralized forces east across the Iranian plateau. It was along the fringes of the Mesopotamian lowlands and the northern Arabian desert—from which access to reserves of fresh Bedouin manpower was easy— that ʿUmar had set up the two great military encampments (*miṣr*) for his warriors, al-Baṣrah and al-Kūfah. ʿAlī was eventually to move his capital to al-Kūfah from Medina, the home of the Prophet Muḥammad for the ten years before his conquest of Mecca and the capital of the first three Rightly Guided caliphs; the political capital of the Islamic world was never again to return to the Arabian peninsula, which became increasingly a backwater, often held by sectarian groups like the Khārijites and, nearly three centuries later, the radical Shīʿite Carmathians.

Although al-Kūfah, with a strongly, but not exclusively Yemenī, or southern Arab, tribal element in its population, proved generally sympathetic to ʿAlī and, at various points in the following Umayyad and early ʿAbbāsid periods, to his descendants, al-Baṣrah speedily became the epicenter of resistance to ʿAlī's claim to the caliphate after ʿUthmān's murder. A rebellion of anti-ʿAlid forces took shape there, under the leadership of two veteran Companions of the prophet, Ṭalḥah b. ʿUbaydallāh al-Taymī and al-Zubayr b. al-ʿAwwām al-Asadī, both from aristocratic clans of Quraysh and former members of the *shūrā*, or consultative council, that ʿUmar, on his deathbed, had appointed to regulate the succession. They thus considered themselves to have as valid a claim to become Commander of the Faithful as did ʿAlī. These two leaders had the backing of ʿĀ'ishah bint ʿAbī Bakr, the Prophet's favorite wife and daughter of the first caliph. Although ʿĀ'ishah had supported the opposition to ʿUthmān, she had had no hand in the tragic events leading to his death and had come to regard ʿAlī as at least a passive accomplice in the killing. All three rebel leaders feared that the infant Arab state would be dominated by anarchic and uncontrollable Bedouins in al-Kūfah and elsewhere, who were becoming ʿAlī's main supporters. There was thus a distinct possibility that the more aristocratic and conservative elements of Quraysh, which these leaders represented, would be relegated to a less powerful role in the state.

The outcome of this clash of interests was the Battle of the Camel on 10 or 15 Jumādā II 36/4 or 9 December 656, in which Ṭalḥah and al-Zubayr were killed; ʿĀ'ishah was subsequently deported under escort to retirement in Medina by the victorious ʿAlī. In the present volume al-Ṭabarī gives a highly detailed account of the events leading up to the battle, from the *bayʿah*, or giving of allegiance to ʿAlī in Medina (accounts vary as to whether Ṭalḥah and al-Zubayr gave their allegiance to the new caliph willingly, grudgingly, or not at all), and ʿĀ'ishah's raising the call for "vengeance for ʿUthmān." Then there is a lengthy account of the battle itself, which took place outside al-Baṣrah, the center of support for the rebels, in which ʿĀʾishah, in an armored howdah on her camel, was the insurgents' rallying point and the real instigator and inspiration of the troops. Ṭalḥah and al-Zubayr were quarrelsome and somewhat indecisive leaders, both laboring under the handicap of accusations that they had broken their oath of allegiance to ʿAlī.

This volume ends with the triumphant caliph precariously in control of Arabia and Iraq and sending governors to such provinces as Egypt and Khurāsān. He had to accept a de facto division of the Islamic lands, with his rival Muʿāwiya b. Abī Sufyān as governor of Syria and the Byzantine marches and the latter's influential supporter ʿAmr b. al-ʿĀṣ al-Sahmī as governor of Egypt. The remainder of ʿAlī's rather brief caliphate was to be spent in an ultimately unsuccessful attempt to humble the much more experienced and sagacious Muʿāwiya, to restore the unity of the caliphate under his own leadership, and to combat the violent and irreconcilable Khārijite secessionists from his own army, who would, in fact, bring about his death.

All these events left a legacy of dissension that was to resound through Islamic history for centuries to come, involving such basic political and religious questions as how the caliph or imām was to be chosen, what should be his qualifications for office, and what should be the basis of the *ummah*, the community of true believers? Above all, these events were part of the prehistory of the Shīʿite movement in Islam, which came to involve such vexed points as the position of ʿAlī and his descendants: Should they be regarded, as Shīʿite partisans were to assert, as the rightful spiritual and political heirs of ʿAlī's cousin Muḥammad and the Prophet's daughter Fāṭimah, possessors of a divine light of guidance for the faithful implanted in all the ʿAlids by God? Or had their political and military incompetence disqualified them from leadership of the community in favor of the much more capable Umayyads and ʿAbbāsids? The debate continues today.

For this section of al-Ṭabarī's text the editor was the Bonn scholar Eugen Prym. For the earlier part of the preceding section on ʿUthmān's caliphate Prym had at his disposal as many as four manuscripts (see R. Stephen Humphreys, "Translator's Foreword" in Volume XV *The Crisis of the Early Caliphate*, pp. xviii–xix), but for the latter part of that caliph's reign he had only the Berlin manuscript Springer 41 (*siglum* B). This manuscript was also the only one available for the present volume, and Prym had to seek elucidation of difficult passages and readings in the works of the later historians Ibn al-Athīr, in his *al-Kāmil fī al-taʾrīkh*, and al-Nuwayrī, in his *Nihāyat al-arab fi funūn al-adab*, supplemented by occasional references to such historical and biographical works as al-Dīnawarī's *al-Akhbār al-ṭiwāl*, al-Masʿūdī's *Murūj al-dhahab*, Ibn al-Athīr's *Usd al-ghābah*, Ibn Ḥajār's *Iṣābah*, al-Dhahabī's *Mīzān al-iʿtidāl* and *al-Mushtabih fī asmāʾ al-rijāl*, and Ibn Taghrībirdī's *al-Nujūm al-zāhirah*, as well as to such geographical works (primarily for place names) as al-Bakrī's *Muʿjam mā istaʿjam* and Yāqūt's *Muʿjam al-buldān*.

Translator's Foreword

This volume of al-Ṭabarī's history deals with the traumatic breakup of the Muslim community following the assassination of the caliph ʿUthmān. It begins with the first seriously contested succession to the caliphate, that of ʿAlī, and proceeds inexorably through the rebellion of ʿAʾishah, Ṭalḥah, and al-Zubayr, to the Battle of the Camel, the first time Muslim army faced Muslim army. As such, it deals with the very first violent response to the two central problems of Muslim history: Who is the rightful leader? Which is the true community? It is therefore a section with the most weighty implications for the Muslim interpretation of history, wide open to special pleading. There are the Shīʿa who depict ʿAlī as a spiritual leader fighting against false accusation and the worldly ambitious. Conversely, there are those who would depict him or his followers in a negative light, and there are the ʿAbbāsid historians, who, while anti-Umayyad, have to balance reverence for the Prophet's household (*ahl al-bayt*) with a denunciation of ʿAlid antiestablishmentarianism. All these points of view, and more, are represented in al-Ṭabarī's compilation, illustrating the difficulty the Muslim community has had as a whole in coming to terms with these disastrous events.

Acknowledgment

Many thanks to my friend, Muhammad Munir ʿAbd al-ʿAziz, for many enjoyable discussions about the text.

Adrian Brockett

The Caliphate of the Commander of the Faithful ʿAlī b. Abī Ṭālib

The
Events of the Year

35 (cont'd)
(655/656)

'Alī b. Abī Ṭālib was given allegiance[1] as caliph in Medina in this year.

An Account of the Allegiance—Who Gave It and When

Earlier biographers give different accounts. According to some of them, the Companions of the Messenger of Allāh asked 'Alī whether he would accept investiture on their behalf and on behalf of the Muslims, but he declined. When they refused to accept his decision, however, and asked him again, he did accept.

Details of this account and its authorities.

According to Ja'far b. 'Abdallāh al-Muḥammadī[2]—'Amr b. Ḥammād[3] and 'Alī b. Ḥusayn—Ḥusayn—his father[4]—'Abd al-

---

1. Done with a handclasp, as in any contractual agreement; see Lane, 285a–b; *EI²*, s.v. Bay'a.
2. For this informant, see also I, 2983, 2986, 3004.
3. Ibn Ṭalḥah; see I, 2986.
4. 'Īsā; see I, 2986.

Malik b. Abī Sulaymān al-Fazārī[5]—Sālim b. Abī al-Jaʿd al-Ashjaʿī[6]—Muḥammad b. al-Ḥanafiyyah:[7] I was with my father when ʿUthmān was killed. He got up and entered his house, and the Companions of the Messenger of Allāh came to him and said, "This man has been killed, and the people must have an imām. We know of no one at this time more suitable for this, of greater precedence in Islam, and of closer relationship to the Messenger of Allāh than yourself." He said, "Don't do this. It's better that I be a wazīr than an amīr." They replied, "No, by Allāh! We will go no farther until we have given allegiance to you." He said, "It should be done in the mosque then. Allegiance must not be given secretly or without the approval of the Muslims."

[3067]

According to Sālim b. Abī al-Jaʿd—ʿAbdallāh b. ʿAbbās:[8] I did not like the idea of ʿAlī's going to the mosque because I was afraid there would be a commotion around him, but he insisted on going there. When he went in, the Muhājirūn and the Anṣār[9] went in too and gave him allegiance, and everyone else followed suit.

According to Jaʿfar [b. ʿAbdallāh al-Muḥammadī]—ʿAmr and ʿAlī—Ḥusayn—his father—Abū Maymūnah—Abū Bashīr al-ʿĀbidī: I was in Medina when ʿUthmān was killed.[10] The Muhājirūn and the Anṣār gathered, among them Ṭalḥah[11] and al-Zubayr,[12] and they came to ʿAlī and said, "Abū Ḥasan, let us give you allegiance." He said, "I have no need to be caliph; I am with you anyway and whomever you choose, I will be satisfied. So just make your choice." They replied, "We'll choose no one but you." They came and saw him a number of times after the murder of ʿUthmān, and on the last visit they said to him, "The people's interests are not served except by a single authority, and things

---

5. D. 145/763; U. Sezgin, 192–93.

6. D. 100/718; known as a *muḥaddith*; U. Sezgin, 193.

7. Son of ʿAlī b. Abī Ṭālib. Cf. the similar report with a different lower *isnād*, p. 5, below; Caetani, VIII, §370.

8. ʿAlī's famous first cousin, *EI²*, s.v. For this report, cf. Caetani, VIII, 371.

9. In the Qurʾān these twice form a pair. The Muhājirūn were Meccans who had performed the *hijrah*, or emigration, to Medina, and the Anṣār were Medinan allies, or helpers.

10. For this report, cf. Caetani, VIII, 372.

11. Ibn ʿUbaydallāh; *EI¹*, s.v.

12. *EI¹*, s.v.

have taken too long."[13] He replied, "You have come to see me a number of times, and here you are again, so let me make a suggestion. If you accept it, I will agree to take command; but, if you don't, I'll be quit of it." They replied, "Whatever you say we will accept, Allāh willing." So he mounted the *minbar* (pulpit), and the people crowded around, and he said, "I was unwilling to take command of you, but you insisted that I should. You must be aware, however, that I ask for no authority from which you are excluded, other than to hold the keys to your treasury. Know also that I would never take a dirham from it without your permission. Is this acceptable?" They agreed. So he said, "O Allāh, bear witness against them!" and he accepted their allegiance on this condition. Abū Bashīr added, "I was standing that very day by the Messenger of Allāh's *minbar*, and I heard his words."

According to 'Umar b. Shabbah[14]—'Alī b. Muḥammad[15]—Abū Bakr al-Hudhalī—Abū al-Mulayḥ:[16] On Saturday, 18 Dhū al-Ḥijjah (June 17), when 'Uthmān was killed, 'Alī went out to the market. A crowd followed him and hurried up to him,[17] so he went into the courtyard of Banū 'Amr b. Mabdhūl[18] and said to Abū 'Amrah b. 'Amr b. Miḥṣan,[19] "Lock the door!" The crowd then came and knocked at the door, and Ṭalḥah and al-Zubayr entered with them and said, "Stretch out your hand, 'Alī!" and the two of them gave allegiance to him. Ḥabīb b. Dhu'ayb[20] was

[3068]

---

13. Caetani, VIII, 372 n. 1, rejects these accounts of delay and says that 'Alī allowed himself to be proclaimed on the very day of 'Uthmān's murder, as in 'Umar b. Shabbah's report, and al-Ṭabarī's remark, (p. 15, below) that people reckon 'Alī's caliphate from 'Uthmān's murder.

14. D. c. 259/873; Petersen, 92 n. 45; Nagel, 230–33. For this report, cf. Caetani, VIII, 375.

15. More usually called Abū al-Ḥasan al-Madā'inī, from Baṣrah, b. 135/752, d. 215–31/830–45; EI², s.v. al-Madā'inī. See also Petersen, 92–99, esp. 98.

16. Following Ibrāhīm's vocalization.

17. *Wa-bahashū fī wajhihi. Al-bahsh ilā* "hastening to get something"; Ibn Manẓūr, VII, 155.5; cf. Hava, 49; p. 100, below. Glossed *irtāḥū ilayh;* "pleased with him," in 428 n. 1.

18. A tribe of the Anṣār (Caskel and Strenziok, I, 186).

19. Bashīr, who fell by 'Alī's side at Ṣiffīn (Caskel and Strenziok, I, 186, II, 225).

20. Al-Balādhurī calls him Qabīṣah b. Dhu'ayb al-Asadī but is probably confused. Qabīṣah b. Dhu'ayb al-Khuzā'ī was the well-known secretary to 'Abd al-Malik (Caskel and Strenziok, II, 454; VIII, 329) but is not known to have had a brother Ḥabīb (Caskel, table 199).

looking at Ṭalḥah when he gave allegiance and said, "It is a withered hand that first gave allegiance. No good will come of this!"[21] ʿAlī then went out to the mosque and ascended the *minbar*, his sandals in his hand, wearing a waist wrap and a cape[22] and a silk turban, supporting himself on a bow. All those there gave him allegiance. Then they brought Saʿd,[23] and ʿAlī said, "Give allegiance." But he replied, "I won't do so until the people have, but, believe me, you've nothing to fear from me." ʿAlī said, "Let him go." Then they brought Ibn ʿUmar,[24] and ʿAlī said, "Give allegiance." And he replied, "I won't do so until the people have." "Bring me a guarantor,"[25] ʿAlī said to him. "I don't see why I should,"[26] replied Ibn ʿUmar. "Let me cut his head off," said al-Ashtar,[27] to which ʿAlī replied, "No, leave him alone! I'll be his guarantor. I knew it; you[28] are as rude as a man as you were as a child."

According to Muḥammad b. Sinān al-Qazzāz—Isḥāq b. Idrīs—Hushaym—Ḥumayd—al-Ḥasan: I saw al-Zubayr b. al-ʿAwwām give allegiance to ʿAlī in one of the palm gardens in Medina.

According to Aḥmad b. Zuhayr—his father[29]—Wahb b. Jarīr—[3069]   his father—Yūnus b. Yazīd al-Aylī—al-Zuhrī:[30] The people gave

---

21. *La yatimmu hādhā al-amr*, as also p. 14, below. "This affair will not finish well"; (Caetani, VIII, 324).

22. Perhaps sleeved like a *ṭaylasān*; cf. Lane, 1894c, 1886c.

23. Ibn Abī Waqqāṣ (cf. p. 9, below), the famous Meccan general and governor of Kūfah. He is said to have retired from politics at this time; hence, "you have nothing to fear from me" (*EI*[1], s.v.). He was a member of the electoral council that elected ʿUthmān; see p. 10, below.

24. ʿAbdallāh, son of the caliph preceding ʿUthmān (and therefore especially esteemed). He was a nonvoting adviser to the electoral council and at the election of other caliphs is said to have conformed to the will of the majority, as here (*EI*[2], s.v.). See also Caetani, IX, 22 n. 4.

25. *Ḥamīl*, glossed *kafīl* in IA, 191, and in an editor's note in Ibrāhīm, 428 n. 3.

26. A rude reply; cf. p. 34, below.

27. Mālik b. al-Ḥārith al-Nakhaʿī, an early comer to Kūfah and one of the *qurrāʾ* or paratribal elements (Hinds, "Alignments," 357ff., esp. 360), a persistent agitator against ʿUthmān and the ruling elite and a supporter of ʿAlī. He is said to have been one of those who besieged ʿUthmān's house (I, 2989–90) and regarded as one of his murderers (Hinds, "Murder," 460). For his threats against those reluctant to give ʿAlī allegiance, see also pp. 12–14, below; al-Dīnawarī, 152. See also *EI*[2], I, 704. He died in 37/658.

28. I.e., Ibn ʿUmar; cf. IA, 205, where ʿAlī says it to him after trying to persuade him to join him against ʿĀʾishah. See *Glossarium*, CCXXXI; p. 34, below.

29. Zuhayr b. Ḥarb.

30. ʿUbaydallāh b. Saʿīd? (Wellhausen, 5). See also Juynboll.

allegiance to ʿAlī b. Abī Ṭālib, so he sent for al-Zubayr and Ṭalḥah. He then invited them to give allegiance, but Ṭalḥah delayed.[31] Unsheathing his sword Mālik al-Ashtar then said, "By Allāh! You had better give allegiance, or else I will strike you through the forehead." "There is no way out of this," said Ṭalḥah, and he gave allegiance, followed by al-Zubayr and everyone else. Ṭalḥah and al-Zubayr then asked ʿAlī to give them the governorships of al-Kūfah and al-Baṣrah. "You are to stay with me. I need you to share the burden," he replied. "I would be lost without you."

According to al-Zuhrī: There is another report according to which he said to them, "If you wish, give allegiance to me, or, if you wish, I'll do so to you." They replied, "We'll give allegiance to you." A little later they explained, "We only did it out of fear for our lives, since we knew that he would never give us allegiance." Four months after ʿUthmān's murder, they went down[32] to Mecca.

According to ʿUmar b. Shabbah—Abū al-Ḥasan [al-Madāʾinī]—Abū Mikhnaf[33]—ʿAbd al-Malik b. Abī Sulaymān—Sālim b. Abī al-Jaʿd—Muḥammad b. al-Ḥanafiyyah: The evening ʿUthmān was killed I was with my father [ʿAlī] until he withdrew to his house. A group of the Companions of the Messenger of Allāh then came to him and said, "This man has been killed, and the people must have an imām." "Maybe there should be an electoral council," he replied. "You are our choice," they replied, to which he said, "To the mosque then! For it must be all the people's choice." So ʿAlī went to the mosque, where he was given allegiance. Apart from a very small number, all the Anṣār gave him allegiance. At this Ṭalḥah remarked, "A dog just licking its nose is all we'll get from this!"[34]

---

31. Following the text's and Ibrāhīm's emendations, *fa-talakkā, fa-talakka'*. Caetani, VIII, 323, "sought an excuse to evade doing it." Pointing the ms. *fa-talakkaz*, see Hava (Syrian dialect), would mean "scoffed."

32. Reading either the ms. *fa-ṭamarā*, or Prym's and Ibrāhīm's emendation *faẓaharā* (Lane, 1879b–c, 1926b–c). Caetani, VIII, 323, "they went to Mecca." For the four months, see p. 43, below (a continuation of this report), and *EI²*, 414.

33. The famous historian.

34. I.e., no position in the rule. The ms. has *ka-nakhsah* "A dog poking its nose [in the earth] is all we'll get from this!" I.e., "we are only going to get hurt" for the text's *ka-ḥissah*. For the latter, de Goeje suggests "As much as a dog's nose smells, i.e., a very small thing" (*Glossarium*, CLXCII), but to judge by today's sniffer dogs this is not an apt simile.

[3070] According to ʿUmar [b. Shabbah]—Abū al-Ḥasan [al-Madāʾinī]—an elder from Banū Hāshim—ʿAbdallāh b. al-Ḥasan: When ʿUthmān was killed the Anṣār gave allegiance to ʿAlī, apart from a very small number of them, among whom were Ḥassān b. Thābit,[35] Kaʿb b. Mālik,[36] Maslamah b. Mukhallad,[37] Abū Saʿīd al-Khudrī,[38] Muḥammad b. Maslamah,[39] al-Nuʿmān b. Bashīr,[40] Zayd b. Thābit,[41] Rāfiʿ b. Khadīj,[42] Faḍālah b. ʿUbayd,[43] and Kaʿb b. ʿUjrah.[44] They were all of the ʿUthmāniyyah.[45]

According to ʿAbdallāh b. Ḥasan: Someone then asked him, "How come these men of the ʿUthmāniyyah refused to give allegiance?" He replied, "As for Ḥassān, he was a poet who didn't care what he did. As for Zayd b. Thābit, ʿUthmān put him in charge of the *dīwān*[46] and the treasury,[47] and, when ʿUthmān was besieged, he twice called out, 'Anṣār! Be helpers[48] of Allāh!' to which Abū Ayyūb[49] replied, 'You're only supporting him because he gave you many date palms.'[50] And, as for Kaʿb b. Mālik, ʿUthmān had put him in charge of alms from Muzaynah and let him keep what he took from them."[51]

[Again according to ʿAbdallāh b. Ḥasan]—anonymous—al-

---

35. A Khazrajī poet from Medina (*EI²*, s.v.), to whom poetry is ascribed in the *Sīrah* of Ibn Hishām. Cf. the slightly different list, p. 9, below.

36. Another Khazrajī poet to whom poetry is ascribed in the *Sīrah* of Ibn Hishām. After ʿUthmān's death he went to Muʿāwiyah (*EI²*, s.v.).

37. Al-Khazrajī (Caskel and Strenziok, I, 187, II, 401). Ibn Makhlad, according to Ibn Khaldūn, I, 439, and Caetani, VIII, 325.

38. Saʿd b. Mālik al-Khazrajī (Caskel and Strenziok, I, 188, II, 500).

39. Fought at Badr (Caskel and Strenziok, I, 180, II, 424). Al-Dīnawarī, 152.

40. A Khazrajī poet (Caskel and Strenziok, II, 451). After ʿUthmān's death he went to Muʿāwiyah, who later gave him the governorship of Kūfah (*EI¹*, s.v.).

41. Khazrajī secretary to the Prophet (*EI¹*, s.v.). The most prominent figure in the traditions about the collection of the Qurʾān; see Burton, index, s.v.

42. Companion of the Prophet and kinsman of Muḥammad b. Maslamah (Caskel and Strenziok, I, 180, II, 483), or perhaps al-Balī (329), kinsman of Kaʿb b. ʿUjrah.

43. Died as *qāḍī* of Damascus (Caskel and Strenziok, I, 177, II, 243).

44. Al-Balī, Companion of the Prophet (Caskel and Strenziok, I, 329, II, 366).

45. I.e., partisans of ʿUthmān.

46. The central register, said to have been instituted by ʿUmar (*EI²*, s.v.).

47. *Bayt al-māl* (*EI²*, s.v.).

48. *Anṣār*.

49. Khālid b. Zayd al-Najjārī al-Anṣārī; fought at Badr and was a close ally of ʿAlī. D. c. 49/669 (*EI²*, s.v. Abū Ayyūb; Caskel and Strenziok, I, 186, II, 343).

50. *ʿIddān*. IA, 191, has *ʿibdān* "slaves."

51. They should have been for the poor.

Zuhrī: A group of people fled from Medina to Syria without giving allegiance to ʿAlī, and Qudāmah b. Maẓʿūn,[52] ʿAbdallāh b. Sallām,[53] and al-Mughīrah b. Shuʿbah[54] did not give allegiance either.

According to others, Ṭalḥah and al-Zubayr only gave allegiance to ʿAlī unwillingly, and some said al-Zubayr did not give it at all.

Those who said this

According to ʿAbdallāh b. Aḥmad al-Marwazī—his father— Sulaymān—ʿAbdallah—Jarīr b. Ḥāzim—Hishām b. Abī Hishām, *mawlā* of[55] ʿUthmān b. ʿAffān—a Kūfan elder—another elder: ʿUthmān was besieged while ʿAlī was in Khaybar,[56] and, when he came back, ʿUthmān sent a message for him to come, so he set off quickly. So I said, "I'll set off with him and overhear their conversation." When ʿAlī came to him, ʿUthmān spoke with him, praised Allāh, and continued: "I have certain legal claims on you, the claim of Islam, the claim of brotherhood—as you know, the Messenger of Allāh made you and me brothers at the time he made the Companions brothers—and claims of blood and marriage, and the pacts and agreements you swore with me individually. By Allāh! Let's suppose none of these claims had any force and we behaved as if we were back in a *jāhiliyyah*. Then it would be thanks to the neglect of Banū ʿAbd Manāf[57] if the Taymī[58] usurped their power." ʿAlī praised Allāh and said, "All that you

[3071]

---

52. Al-Qurashī; fought at Badr and was governor of Baḥrayn under ʿUthmān (Caskel and Strenziok, I, 24, II, 470).

53. Is this the Medinan Jewish convert? (*EI*², s.v.; Watt, 197). Ibn Khaldūn I, 439. The ms. has ʿAbdallāh b. Salāmah (al-Aslamī(?) the companion of the Prophet; Caskel, table 201, no. 118; Ibn Hishām, 837, 842), but Prym suggests that the ms. originally may have read ʿAbdallāh b. Sallām wa-Salamah b. Salāmah, presumably following IA, 191, who has ʿAbdallāh b. Sallām wa-Ṣuhayb b. Sinān wa-Salamah b. Salāmah b. Waqsh. Cf. p. 9, below.

54. A Thaqafī from Ṭāʾif and governor of al-Baṣrah under ʿUmar (who was killed by his slave) and of al-Kūfah under Muʿāwiyah. During the caliphates of ʿUthmān and ʿAlī he retired from prominence (*EI*¹, s.v.).

55. Prym (followed by Caetani, VIII, 326) suggests inserting "the family of," but it was customary to refer to people in this way long after the original client and patron were dead.

56. An oasis, said to have been largely Jewish at the time of the Prophet, c. 150 km/95 miles to the north of Medina (*EI*², s.v.).

57. The clan of ʿUthmān (ʿAbd Shams) and ʿAlī (Hāshim).

58. Banū Taym was Ṭalḥah's clan; i.e., "Ṭalḥah will become caliph."

have mentioned about your claims on me is quite right, and your remark that, were we in such a *jāhiliyyah*, then it would be thanks to the neglect of Banū ʿAbd Manāf if the Taymī usurped their power is also true. I'll show you."[59] So ʿAlī then left and went to the mosque, where he saw Usāmah[60] sitting, so he called him and took hold of his arm and then set off for Ṭalḥah. I followed him, and we went into Ṭalḥah b. ʿUbaydallāh's house, which was crowded[61] with people. ʿAlī went up to Ṭalḥah and said, "What's this awful situation you've fallen into?" He replied, "Abū Ḥasan, you blame me after things have gotten so far out of control?"[62] ʿAlī said nothing in reply and came to the treasury and said, "Open this door!" When he could not get the keys he said, "Break it down!" So the door of the treasury was forced open, and he said, "Bring out the money!" He then began distributing the money to all the people.[63] When those who were in Ṭalḥah's house heard what ʿAlī was doing, they began secretly slipping away to him until Ṭalḥah was left on his own. When ʿUthmān heard of this, he was pleased. Ṭalḥah then walked back to ʿUthmān's house. I said to myself, "By Allāh! I'll see what he says." So I followed him. He asked ʿUthmān's permission to enter, and when he went in he said, "Commander of the Faithful, Allāh have mercy on me, I repent to him. I wanted something, but Allāh prevented me from attaining it." ʿUthmān replied, "By Allāh! You haven't come repentant but defeated. Allāh will punish you, Ṭalḥah."

According to al-Ḥārith—Ibn Saʿd—Muḥammad b. ʿUmar [al-Wāqidī][64]—Abū Bakr b. Ismāʿīl b. Muḥammad b. Saʿd b. Abī

[3072]

---

59. I.e., "I won't let Ṭalḥah take over."

60. Ibn Zayd b. Ḥārithah. Zayd was the Prophet's adopted son and former slave (*EI*[1], s.v.). Usāmah was a protégé of the Prophet and later of ʿUthmān and is said not to have given ʿAlī allegiance; see p. 9, below, and *EI*[1], s.v.

61. Reading *diḥās* as in Ibrāhīm, *Addenda*, DCXXXI, and *Glossarium*, CCXXXVI. Ibn Manẓūr (VII, 379 l. 14) cites the report about Ṭalḥah, in which his house was *diḥās, ay dhāt diḥās, wa-huwa al-imtilāʾ wa-al-ziḥām*. See also Hava, 198: *daḥḥas* "to fill (a house): crowd)."

62. Lit., "after the girth has touched the two teats"; it should be much farther forward; see Freytag, I, 293.

63. To wrong-foot Ṭalḥah.

64. D. 207/823 (*EI*[1]). See also Petersen, 84 n. 5.

Waqqāṣ[65]—his father [Ismāʿīl]—Saʿd [b. Abī Waqqāṣ].[66] Ṭalḥah said, "I gave allegiance with a sword over my head." I do not know whether the sword was over his head or not, but I do know he gave allegiance unwillingly. The people gave allegiance to ʿAlī in Medina, but seven men were cautious and did not give it. They were Saʿd b. Abī Waqqāṣ, Ibn ʿUmar, Ṣuhayb,[67] Zayd b. Thābit, Muḥammad b. Maslamah, Salamah[68] b. Waqsh, and Usāmah b. Zayd. As far as we know, not one of the Anṣār refrained from giving allegiance.

According to al-Zubayr b. Bakkār—his father's brother Muṣʿab b. ʿAbdallāh—his father, ʿAbdallāh b. Muṣʿab—Mūsā b. ʿUqbah[69] —Abū Ḥabībah,[70] *mawlā* of al-Zubayr: When the people killed ʿUthmān and gave allegiance to ʿAlī, the latter went to al-Zubayr and asked if he could come in. I informed al-Zubayr so he unsheathed his sword and put it under his bed and said, "Let him in!" So I let him in, and he greeted al-Zubayr, who was standing opposite him.[71] He then left, and al-Zubayr said, "Something occurred to the man that made him leave quickly. Stand where he was, and see whether any part of the sword would have been visible." I did so and could see the point of the sword, so I told him, and he said, "That's what hurried the man up." As he left, the people questioned ʿAlī, and he answered, "I found the most dutiful and friendly nephew,"[72] so they thought it had gone well. ʿAlī said that al-Zubayr had given him allegiance.

[3073]

---

65. The ms. (according to Prym, by dittography) has Abū Bakr b. Ismāʿīl b. Muḥammad b. ʿUmar.

66. Al-Qurashī, leader at Qādisiyyah; d. Kūfah 50 or 55 (Caskel and Strenziok, I, 20, II, 495; *EI¹*).

67. Ibn Sinān of Taghlib b. Wāʾil (Caskel and Strenziok, I, 163, II, 540; cf. IA, 191, and p. 66, below).

68. As in the text and Ibrāhīm. The ms. has Maslamah, apparently by dittography. IA has "Salamah b. Salāmah b. Waqsh [al-Anṣārī]"; cf. p. 7, above; Caskel and Strenziok, I, 179, II, 505.

69. Ibn Abī ʿAyyāsh al-Asadī, an important early historical writer; d. 141/758 (F. Sezgin, 286).

70. See Ṭabarī, I, 2981.

71. Reading either *bi-naḥwihi*, as in the text, or *bi-naḥrihi*, as in Ibrāhīm; *Addenda*, DCXXXI; *Glossarium*, DIII.

72. *Awṣal* refers to *ṣilat al-raḥim*. Al-Zubayr was the son of Ṣafiyyah, sister of Abū Ṭālib. He was also the son of the Prophet's wife Khadījah's brother and married Asmāʾ, daughter of Abū Bakr and sister of ʿĀʾishah.

According to al-Sarī (in writing)[73]—Shuʿayb—Sayf b. ʿUmar—Muḥammad b. ʿAbdallāh b. Sawād b. Nuwayrah, Ṭalḥah b. al-Aʿlam,[74] Abū Ḥārithah, and Abū ʿUthmān: Medina remained under the [interim] governorship of al-Ghāfiqi b. Ḥarb[75] for five days after the murder of ʿUthmān. During this time all the parties searched unsuccessfully for someone who would agree to take command. The Egyptians approached ʿAlī, but he hid from them and took refuge in the walled gardens of Medina. When they found him, he withdrew from them and repeatedly disowned them and their plan. The Kūfans searched unsuccessfully for al-Zubayr, so they sent messengers to wherever he was. He also withdrew from them and disowned their plan. The Baṣrans searched for Ṭalḥah, and when he encountered them he, too, withdrew from them and repeatedly disowned their plan. They were thus agreed about murdering ʿUthmān, but at odds over whom they wanted next. On finding no one to assist or respond, they adopted the evil course of accepting the first person to respond and said, "We'll appoint none of these three." So they sent a message to Saʿd b. Abī Waqqāṣ: "You were a member of the electoral council,[76] and we are unanimous [that you should lead]. So come forward for us to give you allegiance." He sent a message back: "Ibn ʿUmar[77] and I are not candidates, so I do not want to be involved in any way," and he quoted:

Never mix bad things with something good!
    Disrobe yourself of them, and escape naked!

Then they came to Ibn ʿUmar ʿAbdallāh and said, "You are the son of ʿUmar, so take this leadership up!" "It involves vengeance," he replied, "so I am not going to interfere with it. Look for someone else." This left them at a loss, not knowing what to do, even though they were in control of the city.

[3074]

---

73. Ibn Yaḥyā (Wellhausen, 5). See F. Sezgin's discussion of *kitābah* (241).

74. Al-Ḥanafī (see p. 52, below). A frequent authority of Sayf's but about whom little is known; see Hinds, "Sayf b. ʿUmar's Sources," 8.

75. Al-ʿAkkī, participant in the Egyptian opposition to ʿUthmān in Medina; see Hinds, "Murder," 456.

76. *Al-shūrā*, which elected ʿUthmān; see Smith, 142–63; Humphreys, 1990, 3 n. 5.

77. ʿAbdallāh; see note 24, above.

According to al-Sarī (in writing)—Shuʿayb—Sayf—Sahl b. Yūsuf
—al-Qāsim b. Muḥammad: When they[78] found Ṭalḥah he refused
and said,

"One of the surprises of fate and time is that I have
    remained alone, able neither to make bitter nor sweet."[79]

When they heard this they said, "You are threatening us!"[80] So
they stood up and left him. When they found al-Zubayr and said
they wanted him, he also refused and said,

"When you saddle up to leave a house in Fayḥān[81]
    and its courtyard,[82] the soldiers swear at you."

When they heard this they said, "You are threatening us." When
they found ʿAlī and said they wanted him, he also refused and
said,

"If the leaders of my people complied with me,
    I would give them a command that would subdue[83] the
    enemies."

When they heard this they said, "You are threatening us," and
they stood up and left him.

According to ʿUmar b. Shabbah—Abū al-Ḥasan al-Madāʾinī—
Maslamah b. Muḥārib—Dāwūd b. Abī Hind—al-Shaʿbī: After
ʿUthmān was killed the people came to ʿAlī in the market in
Medina and said to him, "Stretch out your hand so we can give
you allegiance!" "Don't be precipitate!" he replied. "ʿUmar was a
gifted man, yet he entrusted the matter to an electoral council, so   [3075]
wait until the people get together and consult." At this the people

---

78. The regicides again.
79. I.e., without any control at all. Ṭalḥah had expected to rule.
80. The frustrated ambitions expressed in the verse made them feel they would
not fare well if he were caliph.
81. A name with a pleasant sound in Arabic, in this case, Medina. Yāqūt,
Muʿjam, IV, 282, has a Fayḥān in Muzaynah territory. Al-Zubayr is referring to
himself and implying that the Medinans have treated him badly.
82. Reading wa-bāḥatihā with Ibrāhīm for the text's wa-bāʿatihā "and its mer-
chants."
83. The editor of IA (196 n. 3) suggests bi-dhabḥi for yudīkhu, i.e., "a command
to slaughter," but the latter reading is the famous one. This verse comes in two
other Sayf reports in the text, pp. 19 (again from the mouth of ʿAlī) and 40, below
(from the mouth of ʿĀʾishah and with a different second hemistich).

turned away from 'Alī. Some of them then said, "If the men return to their garrisons with the news of the murder of 'Uthmān, and no one taking on the command after him, we won't be safe from schism and the disintegration of the community." So they went back to 'Alī, and al-Ashtar took hold of 'Alī's hand, but 'Alī took his hand away and closed it. Al-Ashtar then said, "Yet again! After three times?![84] By Allāh! If you reject the rule again, you will look at it with pain for a long time."[85] The crowd then gave him allegiance. The Kūfans say that the first to give allegiance was al-Ashtar.

According to al-Sarī (in writing)—Shuʿayb—Sayf—Abū Ḥāri-thah and Abū 'Uthmān: Early on the Thursday, the fifth day[86] after 'Uthmān's assassination, [the besiegers][87] gathered the Medinese together. They then realized that Saʿd and al-Zubayr had left town, and they found that Ṭalḥah had gone off to a walled garden of his. They also found that the Umayyads had fled, all but those who were unable to do so. Al-Walīd and Saʿīd had fled to Mecca among the first who had left, and Marwān had followed them. Others followed successively. When the Medinese assembled before the [besiegers], the Egyptians said to the Medinese, "You are the people of the electoral council. You decide on the imamate and your decision holds good for the community as a whole. So, look for a man to appoint to office, and we will go along with you." At this most of them said, "'Alī b. Abī Ṭālib! He is our choice."

According to 'Alī b. Muslim—Ḥabbān[88] b. Hilāl—Jaʿfar b. Sulaymān—'Awf: As for me, I swear that I heard Muḥammad b. Sīrīn[89] say that 'Alī came and said to Ṭalḥah, "Put out your hand, Ṭalḥah, so that I can give you allegiance." Ṭalḥah had replied, "You have more right. You are Commander of the Faithful, so put

---

84. I.e., before allegiance was given to Abu Bakr, 'Umar, and 'Uthmān; see p. 51, below; *Addenda*, DCXXXI.

85. For the text's *'aynayka* de Goeje suggests *'anyataka*; see *Glossarium*, CDXXV; *Addenda*, DCXXXI. The latter is obscure and might mean "you will certainly confine your trouble to it for a time," i.e., "you will have trouble this time" (Lane, 2181a), but the text's reading is the famous one. IA conveniently omits this report.

86. See note 13, above.

87. The Kūfans, Baṣrans, and Egyptians.

88. Ḥibbān, according to Caetani, VIII, 333.

89. The famous traditionist (*EI²* s.v.).

out your hand." ʿAlī put out his hand, and he gave him allegiance.

According to al-Sarī (in writing)—Shuʿayb—Sayf—Muḥammad [3076] and Ṭalḥah: The Egyptians then said, "It's up to you,[90] people of Medina! We've given you two days and, by Allāh! if you don't sort it out,[91] tomorrow we'll kill ʿAlī and Ṭalḥah and al-Zubayr and many others beside." The people then came to ʿAlī and said, "We give you allegiance, for you see what has happened to Islam and how much we have suffered at the hands of relatives."[92] "Leave me alone and look for someone else," ʿAlī replied. "We are confronted with a problem that has so many different aspects that no agreement can be reached on it."[93] "We beg you by Allāh," they said. "Don't you see what we see? Don't you see Islam? Don't you see civil war? Don't you fear Allāh?" "I agree to your request on the basis of what I see," he replied, "but you must realize that I do so, provided that I may lead you the way I know. Should you leave me, then I am no different from any of you, except for the fact that I am the most ready of you to hear and obey the one you place in authority over you." On that understanding they dispersed to meet again the next day. The people then discussed it among themselves and said, "If Ṭalḥah and al-Zubayr join in,[94] then things will come right." So the Baṣrans sent one of their number, Ḥakīm b. Jabalah al-ʿAbdī,[95] with a group of men to al-Zubayr and said, "Be careful! Be straight with him!"[96] They brought him at sword point. To Ṭalḥah they sent a Kūfan, al-Ashtar, with a group

---

90. *Dūnakum,* or "Beware!"

91. Pointing the ms. *tufrikhū,* see Lane, 2362c. The text and Ibrāhīm adopt IA's *tafraġū,* meaning the same.

92. *Min dhawī al-qurba,* a reference to ʿUthmān's nepotism. IA has *min bayn al-qurā,* "the villages."

93. Lit., "many aspects, which hearts will not stand up to and minds will be puzzled by."

94. The allegiance.

95. Supporter of ʿAlī and leader of the Baṣran opposition to ʿUthmān. He was killed with seventy of his fellow ʿAbdīs defending al-Baṣrah before the Battle of the Camel; see p. 78, below. He was an outsider (Hinds, "Murder," 460–62). For the vocalization Ḥakīm, see Caskel and Strenziok, II, 295; Petersen, 81; Hinds, "Murder," 460. The text, IA (e.g., 214), Wellhausen (139), and Caetani, IX, 45–46, 65–66, have Ḥukaym.

96. *Ḥābā* here means to show false respect in order to make someone approve of you, to say things you want people to hear (Lane, 507c, gives meanings like "treat gently"). Ibrāhīm and Wellhausen (159) emend the text's and IA's *lā tuḥābihi* (here and with Ṭalḥah below) to *lā tuḥāddihi* "Don't stand up against him!" (cf. p. 58), but this does not fit. De Goeje also dismisses this emendation (*Addenda,* DCXXXI; *Glossarium,* CLXXIX).

of men and said, "Be careful! Be straight with him!" They brought him at sword point. The Kūfans and the Baṣrans were each well pleased at their captive's ignominy, and the Egyptians were delighted at what the Medinese had agreed to,[97] the Kūfans and the Baṣrans having been humiliated by being made subordinate to the Egyptians and a dependent group among them, and thus become even more enraged against Ṭalḥah and al-Zubayr. When Friday came and the people gathered in the mosque, ʿAlī arrived to ascend the *minbar* and said, "Men! By common consent and permission the matter is in your hands. Nobody has a right to it but him whom you appoint. We dispersed yesterday in agreement on a decision, so if you wish, I will take control. But if not, I will bear no anger against anyone." "We hold to our opinion that we had when we left you yesterday," they replied, and they brought Ṭalḥah and said, "Give allegiance!" He said, "I only do this unwillingly." So it was a man with a withered hand who was the first to give allegiance. There was a man who was looking on disapprovingly[98] from the back of the crowd, and when he saw that Ṭalḥah was the first to give allegiance he said, "We belong to Allāh and to him we return.[99] The first hand to give allegiance to the Commander of the Faithful is a withered hand. No good will come of this!"[100] Al-Zubayr was then brought, and he said similar words to Ṭalḥah and gave allegiance. However, there are different accounts about him. Then a group of men were brought who had held back, and they said, "We give allegiance on the understanding that the Book of Allāh is upheld toward both relative and stranger, rich man and poor." He accepted this and then everyone else proceeded to give allegiance.

According to al-Sarī (in writing)—Shuʿayb—Sayf—Abū Zuhayr al-Azdī—ʿAbd al-Raḥmān b. Jundab—his father: When ʿUthmān was killed and the people agreed on ʿAlī, al-Ashtar went and brought Ṭalḥah [to the mosque], who said to him, "Let me see what the people will do." But he did not let him and brought him,

---

97. I.e., ʿAlī. The Egyptian insurgents had always been pro-ʿAlī, whereas those from al-Kūfah were pro-al-Zubayr and those from al-Baṣrah pro-Ṭalḥah.

98. *Glossarium*, CCCLXXXIV.

99. Said on hearing of someone's death (Qurʾān 2:156). On p. 3, above, the man was named as Ḥabīb b. Dhuʾayb.

100. See p. 4, above.

pushing him violently. So he ascended the *minbar* and gave allegiance.

According to al-Sarī (in writing)—Shuʿayb—Sayf—Muḥammad b. Qays—al-Ḥārith al-Wālibī: Ḥakīm b. Jabalah brought al-Zubayr [to the mosque] to give allegiance, and al-Zubayr said, "One of the thieves of ʿAbd al-Qays[101] brought me, and I gave allegiance with a sword[102] at my neck."   [3078]

According to al-Sarī (in writing)—Shuʿayb—Sayf—Muḥammad and Ṭalḥah: Everyone then gave allegiance.

According to Abū Jaʿfar [al-Ṭabarī]: After these who had made stipulations,[103] those who had been brought[104] then complied as well. The authority of the Medinese was thus acknowledged as it had been in the past—except that the outsiders and riffraff came to have a say in it[105]—and they returned to their homes.

The Settlement of the Affair by Giving of Allegiance to ʿAlī b. Abī Ṭālib

According to Abū Jaʿfar [al-Ṭabarī]: ʿAlī was given allegiance on Friday, 25 Dhūʾl-Ḥijjah (June 24), but people reckon it from the day that ʿUthmān was killed.[106]

According to al-Sarī (in writing)—Shuʿayb—Sayf—Sulaymān b.

---

101. I.e., Ḥakīm; see p. 13, above.

102. *Al-lujj.* This was allegedly the name of al-Ashtar's sword (al-Zabīdī, II, 93) rather than that of Ḥakīm.

103. The Medinans, specifically those who had held back.

104. Forcibly like Ṭalḥah and al-Zubayr. Ṭabarī's Arabic is not clear.

105. *Law lā makānu al-nuzzāʿ wa-al-ǧawǧāʾ fīhim.* Generally *al-nuzzāʿ/nuzzāʿ al-qabāʾil/al-nuzzāʿ min al-qabāʾil* are strangers from certain tribes who live as neighbors to tribes other than theirs (Ibn Manẓūr, s.v.; Hinds, "Murder," 462), but in this section of al-Ṭabarī's history the words always apply to some of ʿUthmān's killers, e.g., p. 55, below. In the text here there has been some misunderstanding of the phrase *law lā makānu al-nuzzāʿ wa-al-ǧawǧāʾ fīhim.* Following Caetani (VIII, 335, 404), Petersen (152) takes this to be a thinly veiled reference to the Sabaʾiyyah and translates here "[the discontent of as-Sabaʾiyyah] already (then) was instrumental in fostering discords and tumults among them." However, this is to vocalize the ms. *makānu al-nizāʿ,* to take *ǧawǧāʾ* to mean "clamor, confusion of noise," and not to translate *law lā.* The Sabaʾiyyah were the alleged followers of ʿAbdallāh b. Sabaʾ, accused by anti-Shīʿī factions of being a Jew who introduced extreme ʿAlid doctrine (*EI²*, s.v.; al-ʿAskarī, passim; Ḥusayn, I, 43, 98–100, 131; Petersen, 78 ff.; Wellhausen, 6). He was probably not a Jew (Levi della Vida, 495).

106. The Saturday before, the 18th.

Abī[107] al-Mughīrah—ʿAlī b. al-Ḥusayn: ʿAlī, in his first *khuṭbah* (sermon) as caliph,[108] praised and extolled Allāh and then said:

> Almighty and Glorious Allāh has sent down a Book that guides. In it He has made clear what is good and what is evil, so take hold of the good and leave the evil. Perform the religious duties to Allāh, and He will lead you to Paradise. Allāh has made a number of inviolable ordinances, which are well known, and He has favored the inviolability of the Muslim over all others, strengthening the Muslims with the declaration and belief in one God. A Muslim is someone from whom[109] people are safe, except when there is just cause; and it is not allowed to harm a Muslim, except when it is obligatory. Hasten to the common cause, because the particular cause of each individual is death. The people are in front of you and behind you, urging you on, remember,[110] it is the Hour! Keep your load [of sins] light, and you will reach [Paradise quickly]. People are simply awaiting their Hereafter. Servants of Allāh! Fear Him in your dealings with His other servants and His places.[111] You are responsible even for land and animals, so obey Almighty and Glorious Allāh! Don't go against Him! So when you see good, follow it; when you see bad, leave it alone. "Remember when you were few in the land and considered weak."[112]

[3079]

When ʿAlī had finished his sermon and was still on the *minbar*, the Egyptians recited:

Take it, but beware, Abū Ḥasan!
We are settling the leadership the way we fix a nose rein.[113]

---

107. Prym suggests deleting "Abī"; Caetani, VIII, 335, does not.

108. Al-Jāḥiẓ II, 50 ff., citing Abū ʿUbaydah, and Ibn Abī al-Ḥadīd (I, 272 ff.) have quite different versions of his first *khuṭbah*. Cf. also al-Shaykh al-Mufīd, 46.

109. Lit., "from whose tongue and hand."

110. Reading *wa-innamā*, as in the ms. This gives more emphasis than Prym's *wa-inna mā*, in which the *mā* is presumably *zāʾidah* for the sake of rhetoric.

111. Rhetoric: *Ittaqū Allāha ʿibādahu fī ʿibādihi wa-bilādihi.*

112. Qurʾān 8:26. the implied remainder of the verse tells of Allāh's support.

113. This line also comes on p. 139, below.

The line should read:[114]

Take it to you, but beware, Abū Ḥasan!

'Alī recited in reply:

I was unable to do something and have no excuse.
  I will be shrewd after this and carry on.

According to al-Sarī (in writing)—Shuʿayb—Sayf—Muḥammad and Ṭalḥah: As 'Alī was about to leave for his house, the Sabaʾiyyah[115] recited:

Take it to you, but beware, Abū Ḥasan!
  We are settling the leadership the way we fix a nose-rein,
With an army's assault like barriers[116] against ships,
  with Mashrafiyyah swords like rivers of milk.[117]

And we stab the kingship with a flexible sword like a rope,
  until it is trained not to resist.[118]

'Alī then recited some verses, mentioning how they had left the camp, expecting[119] the fulfillment of a promise they had been given, at a time when some people criticized them, so they had returned to them, unable to desist until:[120]

I was unable to do something and have no excuse.   [3080]
  I will be shrewd after this and carry on.
I will lift from behind me what I have been dragging
  and will join up what has been separated and scattered.

---

114. To make the meter more correct.

115. Al-Sabāʾiyyah in the text, here as always.

116. *Asdād*, "mounds (cataracts) that obstruct sailing," with the strength of which the strength of a military marching column is being compared (*Glossarium*, CCLXXXVIII).

117. I.e., very many of them.

118. I.e., until it has been completely subdued (*Glossarium*, CDLXXXIV).

119. Or "insisting on": *wa-al-kaynūnah ʿalā*.

120. The ms. is corrupt; a line has been repeated by dittography but deleted, leaving a space. De Goeje translates this passage "and that they were holding the Medinans by promises that they had agreed with them, and motivated by which they had returned to them; whereas the Medinans were not able to resist" (*Glossarium*, CCCXCI).

If the speedy conqueror Death does not oppose me
    or they desert me when weapons are hastily taken up.

Then, when 'Alī had gone inside [his house], Ṭalḥah and al-Zubayr,
along with a number of Companions, came to him in a group and
said: "'Alī! We stipulated that Allāh's punishments should be
applied.[121] These people participated in the death of this man and
have thereby forfeited their lives." "My friends," he replied, "I am
not unaware of what you know, but how can I deal with people
who rule us, not we them? Your own slaves have rebelled with
them, and your bedouin have joined them. They live with you,
imposing on you what they want. So can you see a way of achieving any of what you want?" "No," they said. "No indeed," replied
'Alī. "I think there is only one thing to be said, and I expect you
will agree. This is something that does not belong to Islam,[122] and
so these people will find that they have a persistent problem. This
is that Satan has never made a religious law,[123] and those who
follow his decree will disappear from the earth forever. If it is
stirred up, Muslims will take up different positions with regard to
this matter. One group will share your views, another will have
views you do not share, and a third will disagree with both, until
the people calm down and return to their senses and claims can
be settled. So stop complaining to me, and see what will happen
to you. Then return to me." 'Alī was extremely restrictive with
Quraysh and prevented them from leaving town under any circumstances. This reaction in him had been stirred up by the
flight of the Umayyads. Then the people [who had assembled at
his house] dispersed, some of them saying: "If this upheaval goes
on, we won't be able to overcome these corrupt men.[124] Leaving

[3081]

---

121. *Iqāmat al-ḥudūd* (sing. *ḥadd*). This phrase, translated as "Allāh's punishments" or "restrictive ordinances," occurs several times in the text (see index),
e.g., on p. 39, below, where 'Ā'ishah claims Qur'ānic justification for setting up a
ḥadd over 'Uthmān's murder by stating that it was unjust (*maẓlūm*); she is referring to Qur'ān 17:33, which allows blood revenge in such cases: *wa-lā taqtulū
al-nafsa allatī ḥarrama Allāh illā bi-al-ḥaqqi waman qutila maẓlūman fa-qad
jaʿalnā li-wālihi sulṭānan fa-lā yusrif fī-al-qaṭli innahu kāna manṣūran.* Cf. *EI²*,
s.v. al-Djamal.
122. Lit., "This is an affair of a *jāhiliyyah.*"
123. *Sharīʿah.*
124. The killers of 'Uthmān.

this to what 'Alī said[125] is better." Others were saying: "We will fulfill our duty[126] and won't delay the matter.[127] By Allāh! In his opinions and orders 'Alī pays no attention to us, and we definitely see him being more harsh than anyone against Quraysh."

When 'Alī was told this, he stood up, praised Allāh, and magnified Him. He then mentioned their excellence, his need for them, and his regard for them and that he was working for their defense. He pointed out that he wanted no more power over them than that and that his reward was with Almighty and Glorious Allāh. He then proclaimed, "The religious obligation to protect a slave who fails to return to his masters is null and void."[128] The Saba'iyyah then conspired with the bedouin to fight.[129] "We'll get the same treatment tomorrow," they said, "and we won't have any argument against them."

According to al-Sarī (in writing)—Shu'ayb—Sayf—Muḥammad and Ṭalḥah: 'Alī went out to the people on the third day and said: "All you citizens, expel the bedouin from among you! And all you bedouin, go back to your own wells!" But the Saba'iyyah refused, and the bedouin followed their lead. So 'Alī went into his house, followed by Ṭalḥah and al-Zubayr and a number of the Companions of the Prophet. And 'Alī said: "Your revenge is right in front of you! So kill!"[130] They replied, "They[131] won't understand that!"[132] But 'Alī replied: "By Allāh! Tomorrow they'll be yet more dim-witted and rebellious," and he recited:

If the majority of my people complied with me,   [3082]
    I would give them a command that would subdue the
      enemies.[133]

---

125. I.e., temporizing.

126. I.e., kill the killers.

127. 'Alī's position.

128. An attempt to split off the slave elements of the opposition. See also *EI²*, s.v. 'Abd; Dhimma; cf. Ayoub.

129. *Fa-tadhāmarat.* The fifth stem, "then angrily blamed each other over their loss," might be preferable; it is a bit early for talk of fighting.

130. 'Alī is mocking Ṭalḥah and al-Zubayr. They had advocated immediate revenge, but here they were retreating from the (alleged) regicides.

131. The Saba'iyyah and the bedouin.

132. I.e., "It's no use trying to convince them that retaliation is right"; they are making excuses.

133. 'Alī is criticizing Ṭalḥah and al-Zubayr and their followers for not listening to his advice. Cf. p. 11, above, and p. 40, below.

Ṭalḥah then said, "Allow me to go to al-Baṣrah, and you'll be shocked by how quickly I can rally a force."[134] "Let me think about it," 'Alī replied. Al-Zubayr said, "Allow me to go to al-Kūfah, and you'll be shocked by how quickly I can rally a force." 'Alī replied, "Let me think about it."

Al-Mughīrah [b. Shu'bah] heard about this meeting. He came to see 'Alī and said: "You have the right of obedience and sincere advice. What will happen tomorrow is protected by a good decision today and destroyed by failing to make one today. Confirm Mu'āwiyah in his governorship; confirm Ibn 'Āmir[135] in his and the other governors over their provinces. Then, when you receive their obedience and the armies' allegiance, you can replace or leave them." "I will see," he said. Al-Mughīrah then left 'Alī, but he returned the following day and said: "I advised you to make a decision yesterday, but now a better one is that you dismiss them from office with haste. Then it will be known who obeys you and who does not, and your authority will be accepted." As al-Mughīrah was leaving, 'Abdallah b. 'Abbās met him on his way in. When he got to 'Alī he said: "I've just seen al-Mughīrah leaving you. What did he come to you about?" "He came to me yesterday about such and such, and he came to me today about such and such." "As for yesterday," Ibn 'Abbās replied, "he advised you well, but, as for today, he misled you." "What should be done then?" asked 'Alī. Ibn 'Abbās said:

> What you should have done was to have left when the man was killed or even before that and gone to Mecca, entered your house, and locked the door behind you. Then, if the Arabs[136] should have amassed and become stirred up after your withdrawal, they would only have had you [to turn to]. But today there are among the Umay-

---

134. Lit. "horses," i.e., against the regicides, but there is an element of threat against 'Alī.

135. 'Abdallāh b. 'Āmir b. Kurayz of 'Abd Shams Quraysh, first maternal cousin of 'Uthmān, who made him governor of al-Baṣrah in 29 (649/50); see I, 2828 ff.; Caskel and Strenziok, I, 13, II, 106. He joined forces with 'Ā'ishah in Mecca (Abbot, 'Ā'ishah, 133).

136. Al-'Arab, especially the settled ones, as opposed to al-A'rāb, the bedouin. Here they are assembling without a leader; cf. pp. 22, 41, below.

yads some[137] who approve the search for revenge [for
'Uthmān], saying that you had a share in the affair. They
will mislead the people and make demands similar to   [3083]
what the Medinese have made. You cannot fulfill what
they[138] want, but neither can they[139]—even if matters
should turn out in their favor[140]—so they would be even
more unable [than you] to fulfill their[141] claims and more
ineffective, except for the suspicions they have already
managed to stir up [against you].

Al-Mughīrah confessed, "I gave him good advice, by Allāh! but
when he didn't accept it, I misled him." And he left to go to
Mecca.

According to al-Ḥārith—Ibn Saʿd—al-Wāqidī—Ibn Abī Sabrah
—ʿAbd al-Majīd[142] b. Suhayl—ʿUbaydallāh b. ʿAbdallāh b. ʿUtbah
—Ibn ʿAbbās: ʿUthmān called for me and appointed me over the
Ḥajj. So I left for Mecca, organized the Ḥajj for the people, and
read ʿUthmān's letter to them. I then came to Medina. ʿAlī had
already been given allegiance there, and when I came to him in
his house I found al-Mughīrah b. Shuʿbah having a private inter-
view with him. So he detained me until al-Mugīrah had left him.
Then I asked, "What did this man say to you?" ʿAlī replied, "He
said to me on a previous occasion: 'Send ʿAbdallāh b. ʿĀmir and
Muʿāwiyah and ʿUthmān's governors their contracts, confirming
them in office and that they should get the people's allegiance to
you, for they will bring peace to the land and will calm the
people.' But I[143] rejected his suggestion that day and said: 'By
Allāh! Even if I had had only one hour of one day, I would have
made the decision not to appoint any one of these. Nor should
any of their ilk be appointed!' As he left me I realized he thought I
was mistaken. So he came back to me again today and said: 'I
made that first suggestion to you, but you disagreed with me. So

---

137. Nöldeke suggests reading *qawm* or *rijāl* "a group" (*Addenda*, DCXXXI).
138. The Medinese.
139. The Umayyads.
140. I.e., "Should you let them stay in office," as al-Mughīrah advised.
141. The Medinese.
142. As in Ibrāhīm; *Addenda*, DCXXXI. The text has al-Ḥamīd.
143. I.e., ʿAlī.

I had another idea. That is that you do as you thought and dismiss them and look for assistance from those you trust. Allāh's help will suffice; their[144] fighting power is less than it was.'"

[3084]

So I said to ʿAlī, "The first time he gave you good advice, but the last time he deceived you." "Why do you say he gave me good advice?" asked ʿAlī. "Because you know that Muʿāwiyah and his allies are men of the world," replied Ibn ʿAbbās, "and, should you confirm their posts, they wouldn't care who had the overall command. But should you remove them they would say, 'He has assumed overall command without an electoral assembly, and he killed our companion,' and they would stir up the Syrians and Iraqis to rebel against you. I'm also not at all sure that Ṭalḥah and al-Zubayr won't turn against you." "Regarding what you said about confirming them, replied ʿAlī, "then, by Allāh I've no doubt that it would be best for *islāh*[145] in *this* life. But I have obligations to the truth, and I know ʿUthmān's governors, so by Allāh! I'll never appoint a single one of them! If they come[146] it'll be best for them, for if they stay back I'll be generous to them with the sword." "Then do as I say," Ibn ʿAbbās replied. "Enter your house and stay on your estate in Yanbūʿ.[147] Lock the gate after you, for the Arabs are stirred up[148] and milling around en masse, and they won't find anyone apart from you [to turn to]. But, by Allāh! If you rise up with these men[149] today, the people will make you responsible for the blood of ʿUthmān tomorrow."

But ʿAlī ignored this advice and said to Ibn ʿAbbās: "Go to Syria! I've appointed you its governor." "This isn't the right decision," replied Ibn ʿAbbās. "Muʿāwiyah is a man[150] of Banū Umayyah. He is the son of ʿUthmān's father's brother and governor of Syria. I won't be safe from his breaking my neck for ʿUthmān. Or else the

[3085]

least he will do is throw me in jail and pass sentence on me." "Why?" ʿAlī asked him. "Because you and I are related," he said, "and because everything imputed to you is imputed to me also.

---

144. The Umayyads.
145. (Re)conciliation, setting things right (*EI*[1], s.v.).
146. I.e., and give allegiance.
147. As in Ibrāhīm; IA. It is the port of Medina on the Red Sea (*EI*[1], s.v.).
148. After ʿAlī's withdrawal (cf. p. 20, above).
149. The regicides.
150. I.e., he has a responsibility to retaliate.

No, you should write to Mu'āwiyah, raise his hopes, and make him promises!" But 'Alī refused and said, "By Allāh! This will never be."

According to Muḥammad—Hishām b. Sa'd—Abū Hilāl—Ibn 'Abbās: Five days after the murder of 'Uthmān, I arrived in Medina from Mecca. I went to go and visit 'Alī but was told that al-Mughīrah b. Shu'bah was with him. So I sat at the entrance for an hour. When al-Mughīrah came out, he greeted me and said, "How long ago did you get here?" "This past hour," I replied. I then went into 'Alī, and greeted him. He asked me, "Did you meet al-Zubayr and Ṭalḥah?" "I met them in al-Nawāṣif."[151] "Who was with them?" he asked. "Abu Sa'īd b. al-Ḥārith b. Hishām with a Qurashī force," I replied. 'Alī then said: "I'm sure they'll never refrain from coming out and saying, 'We seek repayment for 'Uthmān's blood.' By Allāh! We know that they are the ones who killed 'Uthmān."

"Commander of the Faithful!" said Ibn 'Abbās. "Tell me about the business with al-Mughīrah and why he had a private audience with you." He said: "He came to me two days after the murder of 'Uthmān and said to me, 'May I have a private word with you?' I agreed, and he said: 'Good advice costs nothing. You are the most excellent in the community, and I have some sincere advice for you. I advise you to return 'Uthmān's governors to office this year, so write to them confirming their governorships. When they have given you allegiance and things have settled down under your command, then you may remove or confirm whomever you wish.' So I replied, 'By Allāh! I don't compromise my religion by cheating, nor do I give contemptible men [a say] in my command.'[152] 'If you insist on rejecting this suggestion,' he replied, 'then remove whomever you will, but leave Mu'āwiyah. Mu'āwiyah is daring, [3086] and the Syrians listen to him. Moreover, you have good reason to keep him in office, for 'Umar b. al-Khaṭṭāb made him governor of the whole of Syria.' 'By Allāh! no,' I replied. 'I would never appoint Mu'āwiyah as governor, even for two days!' Al-Mughīrah then left me without further suggestion. However, he came back again and said to me: 'I gave you some advice, but you didn't agree with me.

---

151. Yāqūt has a place of this name only in what he thinks is 'Umān (V, 306).
152. Cf. I, 1545 l. 18, 1546 l. 3, where 'Umar says something similar.

So I thought about it and realized that you were right. You should not assume your authority deceitfully. There should be no fraud in your rule'"

"So I said to ʿAlī," said Ibn ʿAbbās, "his first suggestion advised you well; his last deceived you. I advise you to confirm Muʿāwiyah. If he gives you allegiance, then I will undertake to topple him from his position." ʿAlī replied, "By Allāh! no. I will give him nothing but the sword." And he quoted the following verse:

Death, if I die without weakness, is no
    disgrace when the soul meets its destruction.[153]

"Commander of the Faithful!" I replied, "you're a courageous man, but you aren't a warmonger. Didn't you hear the Messenger of Allāh say, 'War is deceit'?"[154] "Indeed I did," said ʿAlī. "By Allāh! If you do as I say," replied Ibn ʿAbbās, "I'll take them back to the desert after a watering,[155] and I'll leave them staring at the backside of things whose front side they have no idea of, and you will incur neither loss nor guilt." "Ibn ʿAbbās," said ʿAlī, "I don't want anything to do with these mean schemes of yours or of Muʿāwiyah's. You give me advice, and I consider it. If I go against you, then you do as I say." "I will," I replied. "Obedience is my first and foremost obligation to you."

The Expedition of Qusṭanṭīn, King of Rūm, against the Muslims

Abū Jaʿfar al-Ṭabarī said: According to Muḥammad b. ʿUmar al-Wāqidī—Hishām b. al-Ghāz—ʿUbādah b. Nusayy: In this year, that is, 35, Qusṭanṭīn b. Hirqal[156] set sail with a thousand ships for the territory of the Muslims. But Allāh caused a windstorm[157]

[3087]

---

153. Ibn Manẓūr, XIV, 20.

154. *Al-ḥarb khudʿah;* Wensinck, I, 443b. For slight variations in meaning, see Lane, 710a.

155. I.e., as above, "I'll topple them."

156. Rather than Constantine, son of Heraclius, who died in 641 (Bury, et al., 391), this was Constantine (popularly called Constans), the nephew of Heraclius, who became sole emperor in 641. See also Humphreys, 74 n. 128.

157. Cf. Qurʾān 17:69.

to overpower and drown them. Quṣṭanṭīn b. Hirkal, however, survived and got to Sicily.[158] But they prepared a bath for him there, and when he got in they killed him, saying, "You killed our leaders."

---

158. These events have been telescoped. Constantine went to Sicily in 663, some seven years later, and it was not until 668 that he was blinded by soap in the bath and killed by being hit on the head with a silver ewer (Bury et al., 394–95).

The
Events of the Year

36

(JUNE 30, 656–JUNE 18, 657)

Alī Sends Out His Governors to the Garrison Cities[159]

At the beginning of the year 36 ʿAlī despatched his governors.

According to al-Sarī (in writing)—Shuʿayb—Sayf—Muḥammad and Ṭalḥah: ʿAlī sent his governors to the garrison cities: ʿUthmān b. Ḥunayf[160] to al-Baṣrah; ʿUmārah b. Shihāb, who had the merit of a *hijrah*,[161] to al-Kūfah, ʿUbaydallāh b. ʿAbbās[162] to Yemen; Qays b. Saʿd[163] to Egypt; and Sahl b. Ḥunayf[164] to Syria.

As for Sahl, he set off until he came to Tabūk,[165] where some

---

159. IA, 201–5; Caetani, IX, 8–12.

160. Al-Anṣārī (Caskel and Strenziok, I, 177, II, 579).

161. *Wa-kānat lahu hijrah*, i.e., with the Prophet, "one of the Muhājirūn" (Caetani, IX, 8). Al-Dīnawarī (149) calls him ʿUmārah b. Ḥassān, who was a Kalbī (Caskel and Strenziok, I, 289, II, 571).

162. Brother of ʿAbdallāh. Later he was joint leader of al-Ḥasan's army but deserted to Muʿāwiyah.

163. Ibn ʿUbādah al-Anṣārī (Caskel and Strenziok, I, 187, II, 462). See p. 175, below. Later he was joint leader of al-Ḥasan's army.

164. Al-Anṣārī, brother of ʿUthmān, who fought at Badr (Caskel and Strenziok, I, 177, II, 498).

165. About 350 miles northwest of Medina.

horsemen met him and said, "Who are you?" He replied, "A commander." "Over what?" they asked. "Over Syria." "If 'Uthmān has sent you, you are more than welcome, but, if someone else has, go back to where you came from," they said. "Have you not heard what has happened?" he asked. "Indeed we have," they replied. So he went back to 'Alī.

As for Qays b. Sa'd, when he reached Aylah[166] some horsemen met him and said, "Who are you?" "I am one of 'Uthmān's defeated fugitives,[167] and I am looking for someone to take refuge with who will give me military support," he replied. "But who *are* you?" they asked. "Qays b. Sa'd." "You may pass," they said. So he continued on his way until he reached Egypt.

Now the Egyptians split into factions. One faction gave allegiance to 'Alī[168] and so were with Qays b. Sa'd. Another faction refused to give allegiance and withdrew to Kharbitā,[169] saying: "We will join you if 'Uthmān's murderers are executed. Otherwise we will stay in this area[170] to keep up our opposition[171] unless we achieve what we want." A third faction said, "We are with 'Alī so long as he does not retaliate against our brothers,"[172] and thus they did give allegiance. Qays wrote to the Commander of the Faithful about all this.

As for 'Uthmān b. Ḥunayf, he set off, and no one resisted his entry into Baṣrah. Ibn 'Āmir[173] showed no decisiveness, determination, or independent initiative to fight him. The people there

[3088]

---

166. Modern Eilat, at the top of the Gulf of 'Aqabah.

167. *Fāllah;* Ibn Manẓūr, XIV, 46 ll. 12 ff.; Caetani, IX, 9. Qays was shrewder than Sahl. He mentioned 'Uthmān, rather than 'Alī. That he had to go to Egypt alone and disguised suggested to Caetani (IX, 11 n. 1) that Mu'āwiyah had taken every precaution to prevent 'Alī's representatives from reaching Egypt.

168. *Dakhalat fī al-jamā'ah.*

169. Following Ibrāhīm. The text has both Khiribtā and Kharibtā, the latter noted as corresponding more closely to the Coptic form. Hence it was preferred by Caetani (IX, 11 n. 2), who inferred that because it was west of Alexandria (*al-ḥawf al-gharbī*), this opposition to 'Alī was not instigated by Mu'āwiyah. See also p. 179, below. IA, 201, 205, has Kharanbā, which is an error; see Yāqūt, II, 355, 362.

170. *Fa-naḥnu 'ala jadīlatinā;* see Lane, 392c; p. 105, below. Or perhaps "we will continue this course of action."

171. *Ḥattā nuḥarrik* "and keep alive the agitation" (Caetani, IX, 8), "create trouble" (De Goeje's *turbas movit, Glossarium,* CLXC).

172. I.e., those who killed 'Uthmān.

173. 'Abdallah b. 'Āmir b. Kurayz.

also were divided. One faction followed the opposition, another faction gave allegiance to 'Alī, and a third said, "We shall see what the Medinans do, and we will do likewise."

As for 'Umārah, he advanced as far as Zubālah,[174] where Ṭulay-ḥah b. Khuwaylid[175] met him. Now this man, when he had heard of what had happened to 'Uthmān, had gone out calling for revenge for his blood, saying: "How I regret what has happened! It has not escaped me, nor have I caught up with it.[176]

If only I had been a youth when it happened,
    I would have turned and attacked in the fray and set to."[177]

Ṭulayḥah went out with those who had responded to al-Qa'qā'[178] and accompanied him until he got to al-Kūfah, whereupon he was met by 'Umārah, who was approaching al-Kūfah. "Go back!" Ṭulay-ḥah said. "The people aren't interested in anyone replacing their commander.[179] If you refuse, I will cut off your head." So 'Umā-rah went back, saying: "Beware of danger when it comes near you![180]

---

174. On the Mecca-Kūfah road between Wāqiṣah and al-Tha'labiyyah (Yāqūt, III, 129).

175. Al-Asadī, a *riddah* leader who was defeated by Khālid b. al-Walīd at Buzākha in A.H. 11 yet distinguished himself at the battles of Qādisiyyah and Nihāwand (Caskel and Strenziok, I, 50, II, 559; cf. Hinds, "Kūfan Political Align-ments," 353). Caetani (IX, 11 n. 3) thought it probable that the names of bedouin warriors like Ṭulayḥah and al-Qa'qā' were simply added to the narration by Sayf to give it body.

176. I.e., "I was still living when it happened and have yet to fulfill my duty to retaliate."

177. The last word, *wa-'aḍa'*, might mean "and put in [my feet]," i.e. "I would fight mounted and on foot." The religious poet Waraqah b. Nawfal al-Qurashī (Caskel and Strenziok, I, 19, II, 587) is said to have spoken the first hemistich regarding the Prophet (Ibn Manẓūr, IX, 395 l. 1).

178. Ibn 'Amr b. Mālik al-Tamīmī (*EI*², s.v.). He was a leader at Qādisiyyah, sent in 35 by 'Uthmān's governor in Kūfah to help 'Uthmān during the insurrection; nevertheless, he was an ally of 'Alī and later one of 'Alī's leaders in the Battle of the Camel. See also Donner, 390–91; Landau-Tasseron.

179. Abū Mūsā al-Ash'arī, 'Uthmān's governor in Kūfah; see p. 29, below.

180. *Iḥdhar al-khaṭar mā yumāssuk* (*mā ẓarfiyyah*). It is omitted in IA, 202. Caetani interprets it as "Guard against the next danger. Bad. . . ." (IX, 9). Nöldeke suggests inserting *lam*, to read *mā lam yumāssuk*, but de Goeje sees a conative element to the verb, providing the meaning *quando te tangere conatur* "when it tries to touch you" (*Addenda*, DCXXXI). *Iḥdhar* could be *aḥdhar*, an elative: "The danger most to be guarded against is. . . ."

Bad is better than worse."[181] So he returned to 'Alī with the news.   [3089]
This saying dogged 'Umārah from the time[182] of this difficult
situation until he died.

'Ubaydallāh b. 'Abbās set off for Yemen, so Ya'lā b. Umayyah[183]
gathered up all the tax revenue and left Yemen with it. He went
his way[184] to Mecca, where he arrived carrying the money.

When Sahl b. Ḥunayf turned back from his journey to Syria and
heard the news and when the others had returned, 'Alī called
Ṭalḥah and al-Zubayr and said: "What I was warning all you
people about has happened, and it can only be contained by sup-
pressing it. It is a fiery rebellion;[185] the more it is fueled, the more
it increases and flares out."[186] "Then let us leave Medina," the
two replied, "for either you let us go, or we will treat you with
scornful disobedience."[187] "I will keep control by political means
as long as that is possible," 'Alī replied, "but if there is no choice
the final cure[188] will be cautery." So he wrote to Mu'āwiyah[189]
and Abū Mūsā.[190] The latter wrote back that the Kūfans had
obeyed and given allegiance, clarifying in the letter who was unwilling to do so, who was willing, and who was in between in
such a way that it was as though[191] 'Alī were actually there in the
presence of the Kūfans. 'Alī's messenger to Abū Mūsā was

---

181. This justifies his return, which was obviously a bad thing but not as bad as
getting killed.

182. Wright, II, 165D.

183. Al-Tamīmī, on 'Ā'ishah's side at the Battle of the Camel, was killed at Ṣiffīn
on 'Alī's side. He was usually called Ya'lā b. Munyah after his mother (Caskel and
Strenziok, I, 67, II, 590; Abbott, *Aishah*, 134 n. 139).

184. Lane, 652c.

185. *Fitnah*.

186. *Istanārat*, i.e., "it must be stopped now." IA, 202: *istathārat* "provokes,
rouses, is seditious."

187. *Nukābir*. IA, 202: *nukāthir* "vie in number."

188. Reading *dawā'* as in Ibrāhīm and Caetani, IX, 10, rather than *dā'*, as in the
text and IA, 202.

189. The first Umayyad caliph.

190. 'Abdallāh b. Qays b. Sulaym al-Ash'arī, Companion of the Prophet, replaced
al-Mughīrah b. Shu'bah as 'Umar's governor of al-Baṣrah in 17/638; he was one of
the two arbitrators appointed at Ṣiffīn and probably died 42/662–63 (Caskel and
Strenziok, I, 273, II, 116; *EI²*, s.v. al-Ash'arī).

191. Reading *ka-an 'Alī* or *ka-anna 'Aliyyan*, as in Ibrāhīm and *Glossarium*, DL 6
ll. 5–6, for *kān 'Alī* in the text.

Maʿbad[192] al-Aslamī, and his messenger to Muʿāwiyah was Sabrah al-Juhanī.[193] When Sabrah came to him, Muʿāwiyah neither wrote anything nor replied to him but sent him away. Each time ʿAlī tried to get[194] a reply from Muʿāwiyah, he said no more than

Be firm and steadfast as a fortress, or you will find[195]
    a devouring war from me, setting wood and coal ablaze,
Over your neighbor and your son, for his[196] murder
    was a hideous act, turning the hair on temples and the
    sides of the neck white,
Ruled and rulers alike becoming incapacitated by it, and no
    master or arbiter for it will be found but I.

Each time al-Juhanī tried to get him to write a reply, Muʿāwiyah said no more than these verses. When Ṣafar came, the third month after ʿUthmān's murder,[197] Muʿāwiyah called a man from the Banū Rawāḥah of the Banū ʿAbs called Qabīṣah[198] and handed him a sealed scroll with the address "From Muʿāwiyah to ʿAlī." He said, "When you enter Medina, hold the scroll from the bottom."[199] He then advised him what to say and dismissed ʿAlī's messenger. So they both set off, arriving at Medina on the first day of Rabīʿ al-Awwal. When they entered Medina, al-ʿAbsī held up the scroll as ordered, and the people came out to see it. They then returned to their houses, aware that Muʿāwiyah was rebelling. He then went to visit ʿAlī and handed him the scroll. He broke its seal but found nothing written inside it. So he asked the messenger, "What is going on?" "Am I safe?" he replied. "Yes," replied ʿAlī. "Messengers are safeguarded and may not be killed." "What

---

192. Following IA, 202. The text seems to have Saʿīd.

193. Al-Ḥajjāj b. Ghāziyah al-Anṣārī, according to al-Dīnawarī, 150 l. 11. Caetani puts little store in the accuracy of either (IX, 15 n. 1). Caskel and Strenziok have al-Ḥajjāj b. Ghuzayy, with a brother Ghāziyah of al-Qayn (I, 313).

194. *Tanajjaz*, as in the text and IA, 202. ʿAlī appears to have sent more than one messenger.

195. As in Caetani IX, 10. Ibrāhīm has *aw khudan* and IA, 202 *aw khudhā* "or take!" for *aw jidan* (energetic imperative) in the text.

196. ʿUthmān.

197. Ṣafar was in fact only the second month after ʿUthmān's murder (Caetani, IX, 12 n. 5).

198. Caetani (IX, 10). Rawāḥah was a clan of ʿAbs (Caskel and Strenziok, I, 132).

199. So that the lack of the title "caliph" for ʿAlī was for all to see (Caetani, IX, 10).

is going on is that I have come from a people who will be satisfied
only by retaliation." "Against whom?" asked ʿAlī. "Against you
yourself.[200] I left sixty thousand elders of the community crying   [3091]
at the sight of the shirt of ʿUthmān as it was raised up for them
and draped over the *minbar* in Damascus." "They are seeking
revenge for ʿUthmān's blood against *me*?" exclaimed ʿAlī. "This is
making me as badly wronged as ʿUthmān was![201] By Allāh! You
know I am innocent of any involvement in ʿUthmān's murder. By
Allāh! We will stab his murderers,[202] unless Allāh should will
otherwise.[203] If He wants a thing, He attains it. Leave now!" "Am
I still safe?" asked Muʿāwiyah's messenger. "You are still safe." So
al-ʿAbsī left, whereupon al-Sabaʾiyyah shouted out, "This dog,
this emissary of dogs, kill him!" So al-ʿAbsī called out: "Men of
Muḍar! Men of Qays![204] To your horses and your arrows! I swear
by Allāh! may His name be exalted, if you kill me[205] four thousand eunuchs will retaliate against you. Look at you! Where are
your real men and your mounts!" There was much shouting
against him,[206] but Muḍar protected[207] him, telling him, "Keep
quiet!" But he replied: "No, by Allāh! These men will never succeed. What they have been threatened with is coming to
them."[208] They repeated, "Keep quiet!" But he carried on: "What
they feared is upon them. There is no more for them to do. Their
time is up![209] By Allāh! This evening will not pass without their
humiliation becoming evident.

---

200. *Min khayṭ nafsik*, lit., "against your spinal cord" or "the cord of your
neck" (IA, 203: *min khayṭ raqabatik*). See also Abbot, *Aishah*, 135–36.

201. *Alastu mawtūran katirat ʿUthmān*, following IA, 203. See Ibn Manẓūr, VII,
135 l. 22.

202. Reading *najaʾu* (root *wjʾ*) in the text. Ibrāhīm and IA, 203, have *najā*, which
would mean "His real murderers, by Allāh! are going free."

203. A Qurʾānic phrase; see, e.g., Qurʾān 6:111, 7:89, 12:76.

204. ʿAbs was part of Ghaṭafān, a northern Qays tribe, and Qays was part of
Muḍar (*EI*², s.v. Ḳays ʿAylān; Hawting, 54).

205. Understood. This is cryptic Arabic, but it seems that al-ʿAbsī is insulting
and ridiculing them—first, implying that so many of them are attacking a single
man and, second, that they are not real men because retaliation, like for like, will
be by eunuchs.

206. *Wa-taʿāwaw ʿalayhi*; Lane, 2186a. IA, 203, has *wa-taʿāwanū ʿalayhi* "So
they ganged up on him."

207. Reading *manaʿathu*.

208. Here and in his next words he is using Qurʾānic words and phrases.

209. Lane, 1181b.

Ṭalḥah and al-Zubayr Ask ʿAlī If They Can Leave

According to al-Sarī—Shuʿayb—Sayf—Muḥammad and Ṭalḥah: Ṭalḥah and al-Zubayr asked ʿAlī if they could go on the *ʿumrah*[210] pilgrimage. He allowed them to go, and they entered Mecca.

Now the men of Medina wished to learn ʿAlī's opinion about Muʿāwiyah and his rebellion so they could find out what he thought about fighting fellow Muslims.[211] Would he venture against him or abstain? They had heard that ʿAlī's son al-Ḥasan[212] had gone to see him and counseled him to stay put and not get involved with them. So they secretly made Ziyād b. Ḥanẓalah al-Tamīmī, who was devoted to ʿAlī, go to him to find out. He did so and sat with him for an hour. ʿAlī then said to him, "Get ready, Ziyād!" "For what?" "You are going to attack Syria!" "Patience and conciliation would be better," replied Ziyād, and he quoted:

He who does not take many matters gently
    gets bitten fiercely by eyeteeth and stamped underfoot.[213]

ʿAlī then quoted the following verse, implying that he did not want to [accept his advice to take it easy]:

When you combine the clever mind, the strong sword,
    and self-confidence, oppressive situations will avoid you.[214]

Ziyād then went back out to the people. They were waiting for him and asked, "What have you discovered?" "Listen, men! It's the sword!" They now realized what ʿAlī was going to do. ʿAlī then called Muḥammad b. al-Ḥanafiyyah and handed him the banner. He put ʿAbdallāh b. ʿAbbās in charge of the right flank and ʿUmar b. Abī Salimah[215] or ʿAmr b. Sufyān b. ʿAbd al-Asad[216] in charge of the left. He called Abū Laylā b. ʿUmar b. al-Jarrāḥ,[217] the son of

---

210. The shorter pilgrimage, performed at any time of year.

211. *Ahl al-qiblah*, i.e., the Syrians (Caetani, IX, 23).

212. *EI*[2], s.v.

213. By camels, i.e., if one does not relax in life, difficulties come; from the *muʿallaqah* of Zuhayr; see al-Zawzanī, 87.

214. A verse of Ibn Barāqah al-Hamadhānī; see Ibrāhīm, 445 n. 2; IA, 204.

215. For the same configuration later, see p. 84, below.

216. Al-Qurashī. For his father and brother, ʿAbdallāh and Ḥabbār, see Caskel and Strenziok, I, 22.

217. Al-Qurashī. For Abū ʿUbaydah and al-Jarrāḥ, see Caskel and Strenziok, I, 35; *EI*[2], s.v. Abu ʿUbaydah.

Abū 'Ubaydah b. al-Jarrāḥ's brother, and set him over the vanguard. He appointed Qutham b. 'Abbās[218] deputy for Medina but did not give positions to anyone who had opposed 'Uthmān. He wrote to Qays b. Sa'd,[219] 'Uthmān b. Ḥunayf,[220] and Abū Mūsā[221] with orders to send their men toward Syria. He then dedicated himself to getting ready and equipping himself.

He made a speech to the Medinan people, calling them to rise up against the schismatics:

> Almighty and Glorious Allāh sent a guiding, guided Messenger with an eloquent Book and a clear, upright message.[222] If someone dies without following it, they are the real losers.[223] Innovations and deceptions, these are what cause the loss of the Hereafter, except for those whom [3093] Allāh protects. In the rule of Allāh is total protection for you. Give Him therefore your obedience, without deviousness or compulsion. By Allāh! You must do it, or He will take the rule of Islam away from you and never bring it back to you until rule is fixed back[224] in Medina.[225] Rise up against these men, whose aim is to make divisions in your community! Hopefully Allāh will restore through you what the provincials have ruined, and you will accomplish[226] your duty.

As they were thus engaged, news suddenly arrived that the Meccans were going in a completely different direction. So 'Alī stood up among them to address them on the subject and said:

> Almighty and Glorious Allāh has appointed pardon and forgiveness to those who oppress this community and success and salvation to those who are loyal to the rule and straightforward. Those for whom truth is restrictive

---

218. Brother of 'Abdallāh (Caskel and Strenziok, I, 6, II, 473).
219. In Egypt.
220. In al-Baṣrah.
221. In al-Kūfah.
222. *Amr*, lit., "order."
223. I.e., of the hereafter.
224. Reading *ya'riza* with the text and IA, 204.
225. See Ibrāhīm, 445 n. 3, and *Addenda*, DCXXXI.
226. Reading *wa-taqḍūn*, as in IA, 205.

adopt falsehood. Ṭalḥah and al-Zubayr and the Mother of the Faithful have certainly joined together in discontent with my rule and have called on the people to set things right,[227] but I will be patient as long as I have no fear about your unity. I will hold back if they do the same, and I will not take much action over the reports I hear about them.

But news then came to him that they were heading for Baṣrah to see the people there and to set things right,[228] so he made preparations to go out against them. "If they have done this," he said, "then the structure of the community will have been badly damaged. Had they stayed with us they would have been neither molested nor compelled [to do what they objected to]."

[3094] The Medinans were stunned by the severity of the problem, so ʿAlī sent Kumayl al-Nakhaʿī[229] to get ʿAbdallāh b. ʿUmar.[230] When he brought him ʿAlī said, "Join up with me!" "I am a member of the Medinan community," he replied. "I am simply one man among them. They have taken up this position, and I am in it with them. I am not going to go my own way. If they come out to fight [against you], so will I. If they hold back, so will I." "Then give me a surety that you won't come out," said ʿAlī. "No, I'm not giving you surety," ʿAbdallāh replied. "But for my experience of your brusque nature as a child and as a man," said ʿAlī, "you would see another reaction from me.[231] Let him be! I will be surety for him."[232]

So ʿAbdallāh b. ʿUmar returned to Medina, where they were saying: "No, by Allāh! We don't know what to do. We are dubious about this whole matter. We will stay here until light is thrown upon it and it becomes clear." He left the same night and told ʿAlī's daughter Umm Kulthūm[233] what he had heard from the

---

227. *Iṣlāḥ.*
228. *Iṣlāḥ.*
229. Kumayl b. Ziyād, kinsman of al-Ashtar (Caskel and Strenziok, I, 264, II, 373).
230. Probably in Medina.
231. Reading *la-ankartanī* as in Ibrāhīm and *Addenda*, DCXXXI, lit., "you would not know me." See also p. 4, above.
232. Cf. Qurʾān 12:72.
233. Not the daughter of the Prophet (*EI*[1], s.v.).

men of Medina. He said that he was leaving on the *'umrah* pilgrimage but maintaining obedience to 'Alī, except with respect to mobilizing forces. He was completely honest. He then stayed with her. The next morning someone said to 'Alī, "Something far worse for you than Ṭalḥah and al-Zubayr and the Mother of the Faithful and Mu'āwiyah put together happened yesterday." "What was that?" "Ibn 'Umar has left for Syria."

So 'Alī went to the marketplace, called for riding beasts, made the men mount, and arranged scouts for each road. Medina was in commotion. When Umm Kulthūm heard what 'Alī was doing, she called for her mule and mounted it on a saddle.[234] She found 'Alī standing in the marketplace, dividing the men into groups to look for 'Abdallāh. She asked: "What's wrong with you? Don't get worked up about this man! The rumors and tales that have reached you are completely contrary to what has happened. I guarantee him." 'Alī was delighted. "You can go," he said to them. "She didn't lie, nor did he. He has my trust." So they left.

According to al-Sarī—Shu'ayb—Sayf—Muḥammad and Ṭalḥah: When 'Alī saw these things[235] from the Medinans he was not satisfied with their obedience unless they also supported him. He stood up in their midst and got the Medinan leaders to gather round [3095] him and said: "The end of this affair will be made good only by what made good its beginning.[236] You have seen the results of Almighty Allāh's judgment on those of you who died.[237] Assist Allāh, and He will give you victory[238] and set your situation right." Two prominent Anṣāris then joined 'Alī: Abū al-Haytham al-Tayyihān,[239] a veteran of the Battle of Badr, and Khuzaymah b. Thābit[240] (not the

---

234. *Fī raḥl. Addenda,* DCXXXI suggests *rajl* "with a group of men."

235. Reading *wa lammā ra'ā . . . ma ra'ā,* as in Ibrāhīm; cf. *Addenda,* DCXXXI.

236. I.e., the way of the Prophet.

237. During 'Uthmān's killing.

238. Cf. Qu'ān 47:7.

239. Of 'Abd al-Ashhal through his mother (Watt, 159, 180; cf. Caskel and Strenziok, I, 179).

240. Caskel and Strenziok (I, 182, II, 351) have only one Khuzaymah b. Thābit "Dhū Shahādatayn" and say he took part with 'Alī at the Battles of the Camel and Ṣiffīn.

Khuzaymah called Dhū Shahādatayn, who died during ʿUthmān's time[241]).

According to al-Sarī—Shuʿayb—Sayf—Muḥammad—ʿUbaydallāh—al-Ḥakam: He was asked, "Was Khuzaymah b. Thābit Dhū al-Shahādatayn present at the Battle of the Camel?" "No, that wasn't he but some other Anṣārī. Dhū al-Shahādatayn died during the time of ʿUthmān b. ʿAffān."

According to al-Sarī—Shuʿayb—Sayf—Mujālid—al-Shaʿbī: By Allāh, alongside whom no other deity exists! No more than six, or seven at the most, of those present at Badr[242] fought in this *fitnah*.

According to al-Sarī—Shuʿayb—Sayf—ʿAmr b. Muḥammad—al-Shaʿbī: By Allāh, alongside whom no other deity exists! Only six of those present at Badr fought in this affair; there was no seventh. "You contradict each other,"[243] I remarked.[244] "No we don't. It's just that al-Shaʿbī wasn't sure whether or not Abū Ayyūb had already joined up when Umm Salimah[245] sent him to ʿAlī after Ṣiffīn. He was sure that he had joined ʿAlī, however, at the time of al-Nahrawān."[246]

[3096]

According to al-Sarī—Shuʿayb—Sayf—ʿAbdallāh b. Saʿīd b. Thābit—a man—Saʿīd b. Zayd: Four Companions of the Prophet never got together and surpassed others in achieving something good without ʿAlī b. Abī Ṭālib's being one of them.

Later, when Ziyād b. Ḥanẓalah saw the men's lack of action on behalf of ʿAlī, he hurried up to ʿAlī and said, "There may be those who hold back from you, but we are active for you and will fight for your sake."

ʿAlī was walking in Medina one day when he heard Zaynab bint Abī Sufyān[247] saying, "The causes of our complaint about injustice[248] are two: a man with eye shadow and an eye-shadow

---

241. Year 37 (Caetani, IX, 627–28).

242. A force of about 300, who became special men in Muslim history, fought at this first battle of the Prophet's career in 2/624 (*EI²*, s.v.).

243. ʿAmr and Mujālid (see previous tradition).

244. Sayf.

245. Hind bt. al-Mughīrah, one of the Prophet's wives (Watt, 396), often called Umm Salamah.

246. Year 38/658.

247. Sister of the first Umayyad caliph, Muʿāwiyah.

248. Presumably the killing of ʿUthmān.

case."[249] "She should be well aware that I[250] am not a target of retaliation for her!" said 'Alī.

According to al-Sarī—Shu'ayb—Sayf—Muḥammad and Ṭalḥah: 'Uthmān was killed on 18 Dhū al-Ḥijjah (June 17, 35). The governor of Mecca was 'Abdallāh b. 'Āmir al-Ḥaḍramī,[251] and 'Abdallāh b. 'Abbās was in charge of the pilgrimage at the time. 'Uthmān had sent him while under siege. Some of them traveled back to Medina hastily with Ibn 'Abbās in two days. They arrived after 'Uthmān had been killed but before 'Alī had received allegiance. Banū Umayyah fled and reached Mecca. On Friday, 25 Dhū al-Ḥijjah (June 24), 'Alī was given allegiance. The fugitives rushed to Mecca, where 'Ā'ishah was staying to perform the Muḥarram[252] 'umrah pilgrimage. As they hastened in she asked them for news.[253] "'Uthmān has been killed," they told her, "but no one has agreed to take command." "But how shrewd they are!"[254] 'Ā'ishah responded. "For they do this after all the frus-

---

249. *Mudammam wa-mukhulah* makes a parallelism and can mean "a man with eyeshadow and an eyeshadow case," perhaps implying two dissimulators. These could be Ṭalḥah and al-Zubayr; oppression against 'Uthmān, head of the Umayyads, had come from them. So Prym (text n. c), but this does not make much sense of the following *humā*. According to *Addenda*, DCXXXI and Ibrāhīm (448 n.), Muḥammad b. Abī Bakr (brother of 'Ā'ishah) and Muḥammad b. Ja'far b. Abī Ṭālib ('Alī's nephew), who are often paired (they had the same mother), are probably meant, but in this case *anā* (the emendation for *humā*) is difficult. If the reference is taken to be to the two Muḥammads, Ibrāhīm's *hammā* ("She is well aware that those two didn't hasten to retaliate against her") provides a little more sense. Nöldeke (*Addenda*, DCXXXI) considers the first to refer to Muḥammad b. Abī Bakr but reads *mudhammam* "much blamed, most blameworthy," possibly a distortion of *muḥammad* "much praised" (Wellhausen, 159). This is possible, as Muḥammad b. Abī Bakr was said to have been one of the first to enter 'Uthmān's presence and humiliate him, but the parallelism is lost. In the text 3217, l. 16, Muḥammad b. Abī Bakr is indeed called "Mudhammam," the opposite of "Muḥammad," by 'Ā'ishah, and the similar alliterative opposite—*akhūk al-birr . . . 'aqūq*—on p. 157, below (3217 l. 2) disallows a pointing *mudammam*. Nöldeke further considers *mukhulah* to refer to 'Alī, which fits *anā* (Wellhausen, 159), i.e.: "Why is the woman saying this? I didn't kill 'Uthmān." See also Ibn 'Abd Rabbihi (II, 278 ll. 5–16, esp. l. 15), where *mudhammam* could even refer to 'Alī, although, according to Caetani, IX, 70, it refers to Muḥammad b. Abī Bakr (cf. p. 100, below).

250. Reading *anā* (Wellhausen, 159); see note 249.

251. Abbott, *Aishah*, 130 ff.

252. A special *'umrah* for the first month of the year.

253. Abbott, *Aishah*, 129 ff.

254. *Wa-lākin akyās*. De Goeje, referring to the marginal gloss, suggests insert-

trated attempts that went on between you to improve the situation."[255] Then she completed the *ʿumrah*, left, and arrived at Sarif,[256] where she was met by a maternal relative called ʿUbayd b. Abī Salimah, called after his mother Umm Kilāb.[257] He was from Banū Layth,[258] with whom she had friendly connections. "What news?" she asked. He kept silent and then muttered something. "Confound you! Is it bad for us or good?" "You don't know! ʿUthmān was killed, and they waited eight nights." "Then what did they do?" she asked. "They made the men of Medina agree to elect ʿAlī, and the city is under the control of the rebels." At this she returned to Mecca and said not a word. Indeed she said nothing until she had dismounted at the door of the mosque, gone to the Ḥijr,[259] and curtained herself off, and the people had gathered round.

[3097]

"People of Mecca!" she said. "The mob of men from the garrison cities and the watering places and the slaves of the people of Medina have[260] conspired together. They charged this man who was killed yesterday with deceit, with putting young men in high positions where older ones had been before, and with reserving certain specially protected places[261] for them, although they[262] had been arranged before him and could not properly be changed. Nevertheless he went along with these people, and in an attempt to pacify them he withdrew from these policies. When they could then find neither real argument nor excuse, they became irrational. They showed their hostility openly, and their deeds didn't fit their words. They spilled forbidden blood, they violated the sacred city, they appropriated sacred money, and they profaned the sacred month. By Allāh! One of ʿUthmān's fingers is better than a whole world of their type. Save yourselves from being associated with

---

ing *hiya* after *wa-lākin*, which would take the phrase out of ʿĀʾishah's response (*Addenda*, DCXXXII).

255. I.e., with ʿUthmān before his death, because the attempts failed.

256. Six to twelve miles from Mecca (Yāqūt, III, 212).

257. I.e., ʿUbayd b. Umm Kilāb. Correctly emended by Prym; see p. 52, below.

258. Part of Bakr b. ʿAbd Manāt of Kinānah (Caskel and Strenziok, I, 36; Watt, 81).

259. The semicircular wall by the Kaʿbah. See also p. 53, below.

260. Prym suggests *qad* "already" was to have been added here.

261. Which should have been the right of all Muslims. Cf. *EI*², s.v. ḥimā.

262. Following Prym's emendation.

them, and let others punish them and their followers be scared
off. By Allāh! Even if what they reckon against him were a crime
he would have been cleared of it, as gold is cleaned of its impuri-   [3098]
ties or a garment of its dirt, for they have rinsed[263] him as a
garment is rinsed with water." "I'm here with her, the first to
seek revenge," called out 'Abdallāh b. 'Āmir al-Ḥaḍramī. He was
indeed the first to respond and to get others to do so.

According to 'Umar b. Shabbah—Abū al-Ḥasan al-Madā'inī—
Suhaym, the *mawlā* of Wabrah al-Tamīmī—'Ubayd b. 'Amr al-
Qurashī: 'Ā'ishah had left [Medina] while 'Uthmān was being besieged. A man [just in from Medina] called Akhḍar came up to her
in Mecca, so she asked, "What are the people doing?" "'Uthmān
has killed the Egyptians,"[264] he replied. "We belong to Allāh and
to Him we return!"[265] exclaimed 'Ā'ishah. "Does he kill people
who come seeking justice and denouncing injustice? By Allāh!
We don't approve of such a thing." Presently another man came.
"What are the people doing?" she asked. "'Uthmān has been
killed by the Egyptians," he replied. "Akhḍar amazes," she said.
"He alleged that the killed was the killer." It was about him that
the saying "More lying than Akhḍar"[266] was coined.

According to al-Sarī—Shu'ayb—Sayf—'Amr b. Muḥammad—
al-Sha'bī: After 'Uthmān had been killed 'Ā'ishah left Mecca on
her way to Medina. She met a maternal relative and asked, "What
news?" "'Uthmān has been killed, and the people have agreed on
'Alī. The mob rules." "I don't think this is over yet," she said [to
those with her]. "Take me back!" So she set off back to Mecca.

When she had entered, 'Abdallāh b. 'Āmir al-Ḥaḍramī, 'Uthmān's governor there, came to her and asked, "What made you
return, Mother of the Faithful?" "The fact that 'Uthmān has been
killed unjustly[267] and that as long as the mob rules order will not
be established. Seek revenge for the blood of 'Uthmān, and you
will strengthen Islam!" So 'Abdallāh b. 'Āmir al-Ḥaḍrami became
the first to respond to her call, and this was the first response by

---

263. With blood.
264. *Al-miṣriyyīn*, perhaps "the men from the garrison cities," but the leaders
of the insurgents were Egyptians (Hinds, "Murder").
265. Qur'ān 2:157, said on hearing of someone's death.
266. *Akdhab min Akhḍar.*
267. Qur'ān 17:33; *EI¹*, 414a.; p. 18 and n. 121, above.

[3099] Banū Umayyah[268] in the Ḥijāz. After this their morale returned,[269] and they were joined by Saʿīd b. al-ʿĀṣ, al-Walīd b. ʿUqbah, and the rest of Banū Umayyah. ʿAbdallāh b. ʿĀmir [b. Kurayz] from Baṣrah, Yaʿlā b. Umayyah from Yemen, and Ṭalḥah and al-Zubayr from Medina had joined them. After lengthy deliberations they all agreed on al-Baṣrah. "Listen, you people!" ʿĀʾishah addressed them. "This is a heinous crime, a forbidden thing. March therefore to your brothers in al-Baṣrah and denounce it! The Syrians have already done this on your behalf.[270] We hope Almighty and Glorious Allāh will help ʿUthmān and the Muslims[271] get their blood revenge speedily."

According to al-Sarī—Shuʿayb—Sayf—Muḥammad and Ṭalḥah: The first to respond were ʿAbdallāh b. ʿĀmir and Banū Umayyah, who had hastened toward Mecca after ʿUthmān's murder. ʿAbdallāh b. ʿĀmir [b. Kurayz] then came to Mecca, as did Yaʿlā b. Umayyah, and they met there. Yaʿlā had brought 600 camels and 600,000 dirhams. He stopped the camels and encamped at al-Abṭaḥ. Ṭalḥah and al-Zubayr joined them, and, when they met ʿĀʾishah, she asked, "What news?" "The news is that we loaded up lock, stock, and barrel, fleeing Medina and its rabble and bedouin, and left behind us a confused populace, neither acknowledging right nor rejecting wrong and not defending themselves." "Agree on a plan of action; then mobilize yourselves against this mob!" replied ʿĀʾishah and quoted the verse:

If the leaders of my people complied with me,
    I would save them from ropes[272] or dismemberment.

After consultation the men said, "To Syria!" "Those stationed[273] in the province of Syria have already done the job for you up there," replied ʿAbdallāh b. ʿĀmir. "Then where to?" [3100] Ṭalḥah and al-Zubayr asked him. "To al-Baṣrah," he answered. "I

---

268. The narrator is confusing the two ʿAbdallāhs here. ʿAbdallāh b. ʿĀmir b. Kurayz was of Umayyah.

269. After being dashed at ʿUthmān's murder.

270. By rebelling against ʿAlī and calling for blood revenge, so there is no need to go there to get support.

271. As though ʿAlī were not one.

272. I.e., imprisonment. This verse is usually quoted by ʿAlī with a different second hemistich; see p. 19, above. Abbott, *Aishah*, 137.

273. Covering both Prym's emendations *yastamirr* and *yastaḥriz*.

have influence there, and they like Ṭalḥah." "May Allāh damn you!" they exclaimed. "You make neither peace nor war. Why didn't you stay there, as Muʿāwiyah did, and do the job for us? We could have gone to al-Kūfah and blocked all the roads against these people."[274] Thus they did not find his response acceptable. But when their minds had been made up to go to al-Baṣrah they said, "Mother of the Faithful, leave Medina alone! Those with us aren't sufficient for that mob there. Accompany us to al-Baṣrah. We will arrive at a city now lost to us. They will produce their allegiance to ʿAlī b. Abī Ṭālib as an argument against us, but you will mobilize them, just as you did with the Meccans. Then you will be able to sit back, and, if Allāh puts things right, it will be as you want. If not, we will leave things to Him and do our best to push the case forward until Allāh executes His will." "Agreed!" she said on hearing this—for the matter could be resolved only by her.

Now the wives of the Prophet were with ʿĀʾishah in wanting to go to Medina, but when she changed her mind for al-Baṣrah, they also gave up the idea. The men then went to consult Ḥafṣah,[275] who said, "My opinion is subordinate to ʿĀʾishah's." When nothing therefore was left but to set off they asked, "How can we depart when we don't have the wherewithal to equip the army?" "I have 600,000 dirhams and 600 camels, so mount them!" said Yaʿlā b. Umayyah. "And I have such and such," added Ibn ʿĀmir. This set them up, and the crier called out: "The Mother of the Faithful and Ṭalḥah and al-Zubayr are proceeding to al-Baṣrah. Whoever desires to fortify Islam, to fight the sacrilegious, and to seek revenge for the blood of ʿUthmān but who does not have a mount or equipment, then here is equipment, and here are funds." They then mounted 600 men—beside those who already had mounts—on 600 she-camels,[276] making a total of 1,000, and they supplied themselves with money. They called out that they were ready to leave, and they set off walking.

Ḥafṣah wanted to go with them, but ʿAbdallāh b. ʿUmar[277] came and asked her to stay. She stayed but sent a message to ʿĀʾishah:

[3101]

---

274. ʿUthmān's killers.
275. Bint ʿUmar b. al-Khaṭṭāb, wife of the Prophet (Watt, 396).
276. They were he-camels a minute ago!
277. Her brother.

"'Abdallāh has prevented me from coming out." "May Allāh forgive him!" said 'Ā'ishah.[278] Umm al-Faḍl bint al-Ḥārith[279] sent a man from Juhaynah[280] called Ẓafr and paid him to go secretly to 'Alī with her letter. So he came to 'Alī with Umm Faḍl's letter and news.

According to 'Umar b. Shabbah—'Alī—Abū Mikhnaf—'Abdallāh b. 'Abd al-Raḥmān b. Abī 'Amrah[281]—his father:[282] Abū Qatādah said to 'Alī: "Commander of the Faithful! The Messenger of Allāh invested me with this sword, and I put it in its sheath. It has been there too long, and the time for unsheathing it has now come—against this company of criminals who constantly deceive the community. So, if you wish, put me in the front line." Umm Salimah then got up and said: "Commander of the Faithful! But for the fact that I would be disobeying Allāh[283] and that you wouldn't accept it from me, I would come out with you. But here is my son 'Umar[284]—dearer to me than my very self, by Allāh! He will come out with you and will be there with you at your battles." At that 'Umar came out and stayed with 'Alī, who made him governor of Baḥrayn until he replaced him with al-Nu'mān b. 'Ajlān al-Zuraqī.[285]

[3102]

According to 'Umar—Abū al-Ḥasan—Maslamah—'Awf: Ya'lā b. Umayyah assisted al-Zubayr with 400,000 dirhams and provided mounts for seventy men from Quraysh. He also had 'Ā'ishah mounted on a camel called 'Askar, which he had obtained for 80 dinars. As they set off [from Mecca] 'Abdallāh b. al-Zubayr looked toward the mosque and said, "Never have I seen anything more of a blessing to the seeker of good or the shunner of evil than you."

---

278. I.e., she would not.

279. The wife of 'Abbās, 'Alī's uncle, and full sister of Maymūnah, one of the Prophet's wives (Watt, 380, 397; see Abbott, *Aishah*, 139, n. 153 for other references).

280. Watt, 81–87, 409.

281. *Addenda*, DCXXXII. Born before 10/622 (U. Sezgin, 190). The text has Abū 'Umrah.

282. Abū 'Amrah al-Anṣārī al-Najjārī, a Companion of the Prophet (U. Sezgin, 190).

283. Qur'ān 33:33.

284. Before she married the Prophet she was married to Abū Salimah (Salamah, according to Watt, 396), who died at Uḥud.

285. Caskel and Strenziok, I, 192, II, 451.

According to al-Sarī—Shuʿayb—Sayf—Muḥammad and Ṭalḥah: When al-Mughīrah[286] and Saʿīd b. al-ʿĀṣ[287] had traveled a
day's journey from Mecca with the army, Saʿīd asked al-Mughīrah,
"What's the best course of action?" "I'm sure the best course is to
stand aside. They[288] won't succeed. But, should Allāh give him
victory, then we can come to him and say, 'Our emotions and our
inclinations were with you.'" So they stood aside and stopped
traveling. Saʿīd then returned to Mecca and stayed there. ʿAbdallāh b. Khālid b. Asīd[289] returned with them.

According to Aḥmad b. Zuhayr—his father—Wahb b. Jarīr b.
Ḥāzim—his father—Yūnus b. Yazīd al-Aylī—al-Zuhrī: They
went down[290]—Ṭalḥah and al-Zubayr—to Mecca four months after the killing of ʿUthmān. Ibn ʿĀmir, a very rich man, was
there,[291] and Yaʿlā b. Umayyah had arrived with him with a large
sum of money and more than 400 camels. They gathered together
in ʿĀʾishah's house and exchanged opinions.[292] "Let's go to ʿAlī and
fight him," they said. "We don't have the strength to fight the
people of Medina," one of them replied. "Let us rather go and enter
al-Baṣrah and al-Kūfah. Ṭalḥah has a following and popularity in al-
Kūfah, and al-Zubayr has popularity and support in al-Baṣrah."[293]
So they agreed to go to al-Baṣrah and al-Kūfah, and ʿAbdallāh b.   [3103]
ʿĀmir gave them much money and camels. Seven hundred men
from Medina and Mecca set off, and others joined, until their
number reached 3,000. News of their departure reached ʿAlī,[294]
who put Sahl b. Ḥunayf al-Anṣārī in charge of Medina, set off
himself, and traveled to Dhū Qār,[295] where he pitched camp. It
took him eight nights to get there with a company of Medinans.

---

286. Ibn Shuʿbah al-Thaqafī (Caskel and Strenziok, I, 118, II, 419).
287. Al-Qurashī, governor of Kūfah (30–34) and of Medina (49–56) (Caskel and
Strenziok, I, 9, II, 500).
288. I.e., ʿĀʾishah's army.
289. Al-Qurashī, third cousin of Saʿīd b. al-ʿĀṣ (Caskel and Strenziok, I, 9, II,
112).
290. Reading *ṭamarā* for *ẓaharā*; cf. p. 5, above, of which this is a continuation.
For the four months, see p. 5, above; *EI²*, 414.
291. *Bihā yajurr al-dunyā* or perhaps "where Ibn ʿĀmir had great influence."
292. *Fa-adārū al-raʾy*. Ibrāhīm has *fa-arādū*.
293. With the insurgents in Medina, the Kūfans were backing al-Zubayr and the
Baṣrans were backing Ṭalḥah; see p. 10, above.
294. *Addenda*, DCXXXII.
295. A watering place near al-Kūfah in the direction of Wāsiṭ (*EI²*, s.v.).

According to Aḥmad b. Manṣūr—Yaḥyā b. Maʿīn—Hishām b. Yūsuf, *qāḍī* of Ṣanʿāʾ—ʿAbdallāh b. Muṣʿab b. Thābit b. ʿAbdallāh b. al-Zubayr[296]—Mūsā b. ʿUqbah—ʿAlqamah b. Waqqāṣ al-Laythī: At Dhāt ʿIrq[297] on their way Ṭalḥah and al-Zubayr and ʿĀʾishah inspected the army. ʿUrwah b. al-Zubayr[298] and Abū Bakr b. ʿAbd al-Raḥmān b. al-Ḥārith b. Hishām[299] they found too young, so they sent them back.

According to ʿUmar b. Shabbah—Abū al-Ḥasan—Abū ʿAmr—ʿUtbah b. al-Mughīrah b. al-Akhnas: At Dhāt ʿIrq Saʿīd b. al-ʿĀṣ met Marwān b. al-Ḥakam[300] and his men and asked: "Where are you heading for? Those from whom you seek revenge are on the rumps of camels.[301] Kill them, and then go back to your houses! Don't kill yourselves!" "No, we will press on," replied Marwān. "Hopefully we will kill every one of the killers of ʿUthmān." Saʿīd then spoke in private with Ṭalḥah and al-Zubayr: "If you are victorious, to whom will you give the caliphate? Tell me the truth." "To one of us, whichever the men choose." "No," he replied. "Give it to ʿUthmān's son. You've come out in revenge for his blood, haven't you?" "You want us to pass over the elders of the Muhājirūn and appoint their sons over them?" replied Ṭalḥah and al-Zubayr. "But you seem to want me to work to remove it from Banū ʿAbd Manāf!"[302] answered Saʿīd and left. ʿAbdallāh b. Khālid b. Asīd left also.

[3104] "Saʿīd's opinion is the right one," said al-Mughīrah b. Shuʿbah. "Let all those here from Thaqīf go back!"[303] So he went back, but the main company continued, among them Abān b. ʿUthmān[304] and al-Walīd b. ʿUthmān. Then they disagreed about the route to

---

296. Governor of Medina and then Yemen under Rashīd (Caskel and Strenziok, I, 19, II, 115).

297. On the borders of Najd and Tihāma on the Mecca-Iraq road (Yāqūt, IV, 107–8).

298. The well-known traditionist (Caskel and Strenziok, I, 19, II, 575).

299. Al-Qurashī. For his brothers, see Caskel and Strenziok, I, 19.

300. The future caliph Marwān I, 64–65/683–85.

301. I.e., here with you.

302. I.e., from ʿAlī. Saʿīd is curtly reminding Ṭalḥah and al-Zubayr that not only is ʿAlī one of the Muhājirūn, but he also belongs to their best group.

303. Three hundred went back at this point, according to some accounts, leaving 700.

304. Ibn ʿAffān, governor of Medina, 75–83/694–701 (Caskel and Strenziok, II, 101). Al-Walīd was also governor of Medina (Caskel and Strenziok, I, 11).

take, saying. "Whom shall we summon to our cause?"[305] When al-Zubayr was alone with his son 'Abdallāh and Ṭalḥah was alone with 'Alqamah b. Waqqāṣ al-Laythī (whom he preferred to his son), one said, "Go to Syria!" and the other, "Go to Iraq!" So the two then discussed the matter between themselves and agreed to go to al-Baṣrah.

According to al-Sarī—Shu'ayb—Sayf—Makhlad[306] b. Qays—al-Agharr: When Banū Umayyah, Ya'lā b. Munyah, Ṭalḥah, and al-Zubayr had gathered in Mecca, they consulted together. They all agreed to seek revenge for the blood of 'Uthmān and to fight the Saba'iyyah until they were avenged and requited. 'Ā'ishah then ordered them to go to Medina, but the men all decided on al-Baṣrah and made her change her opinion. Ṭalḥah and al-Zubayr said to her: "Unless you go out and give the command you gave in Mecca and then return, we shall be going to a lost place, one that will have gone over to 'Alī.[307] He forced us to give him allegiance, so they will use that against us and leave our cause." So it was announced, "'Ā'ishah is going to al-Baṣrah, but 600 camels are not enough for you to satisfy[308] the rabble and hordes[309] of bedouin and slaves spread out [along the way] who are ready with out-stretched arms to assist the first caller." 'Ā'ishah then sent a message to Ḥafṣah. She wanted to come out, but Ibn 'Umar advised her strongly against it, so she stayed. Accompanied by Ṭalḥah and al-Zubayr, 'Ā'ishah set off and appointed 'Abd al-Raḥmān b. 'Attāb b. Asīd al-Qurashī leader of the prayer. He led them in the prayer as they traveled and in al-Baṣrah until he was killed.[310] Marwān set off with her along with most of the rest of Banū Umayyah, apart from those who were too scared. At Awṭās[311] she turned to the right, 600 horseriders with her, not counting those with other

[3105]

---

305. I.e., the Iraqis or the Syrians?

306. Ibrāhīm has Muḥammad.

307. I.e., Ibn 'Āmir's influence in al-Baṣrah would be lost if they did not go there then.

308. I.e., as gifts, reading *tughnūn* with Ibrāhīm and Wellhausen, 159. The text's *tu'nūn* might mean "to subdue." Cf. Lane, 2178b–c, and *Glossarium*, CCCLXXXI.

309. Reading *wa-jalabah* with Ibrāhīm and Nöldeke (*Addenda*, DCXXXII) for the text's *wa-jāliyah*. Wellhausen, 159 suggests *wajā'ilah*, which would mean very much the same, comparing p. 51, below, and points out the unusual syntax.

310. At the Battle of the Camel (Caskel and Strenziok, I, 8, II, 128).

311. A *wādī* in Hawāzin territory, where the Battle of Ḥunayn was fought.

beasts. Then she turned right again one night, leaving the road as though they were a caravan seeking pasture near the seashore, not one of them going close to al-Munkadir,[312] Wāsiṭ,[313] or Falj.[314] That year was a fruitful one, and as they came to al-Baṣrah 'Ā'ishah quoted the following verses.[315]

Leave the lands of mass oppression when their waters[316] are
    pure
    there, and proceed with fear!
Choose those plants[317] outside the settled areas, and graze
    there,
    and [choose] a place down in a valley, deep and well
    watered.

According to 'Umar—Abū al-Ḥasan—'Umar b. Rāshid al-Yamāmī—Abū Kathīr al-Suḥaymī—Ibn 'Abbās: The followers of the camel set out, numbering 600, among them 'Abd al-Raḥmān b. Abī Bakrah and 'Abdallāh b. Ṣafwān al-Jumaḥī.[318] As they were passing Bi'r Maymūn,[319] they came upon a she-camel that had just been slaughtered, and blood was flowing from her neck. They saw this as a bad omen.

When Marwān had left Mecca he had called to prayer, so now as he arrived he went up to Ṭalḥah and al-Zubayr and asked, "Which
[3106]   one of you should I hail as caliph when I call to prayer?" "Abū 'Abdallāh!" replied 'Abdallāh b. al-Zubayr. "Abū Muḥammad!" replied Muḥammad b. Ṭalḥah. 'Ā'ishah then sent to Marwān, asking: "What are you up to? Are you wanting to make divisions in our leadership? Let my sister's son[320] lead the prayer." So 'Abdallāh b. al-Zubayr did so until they came to al-Baṣrah. Mu'ādh b. 'Ubaydallāh remarked [later], "If victory had been ours we would

---

312. A road between Yamāmah and Syria or al-Kūfah (Yāqūt, V, 216).
313. Wāsiṭ al-Yamāmah, not the famous Wāsiṭ, built only forty years later.
314. On the road between al-Baṣrah and Yamāmah or between al-Baṣrah and Mecca (Yāqūt, IV, 272).
315. As though to the whole company and in optimistic mood.
316. I.e., people.
317. I.e., allies.
318. Al-Qurashī (Caskel and Strenziok, I, 24, II, 118).
319. An ancient well in the environs of Mecca; EI², s.v.
320. 'Abdallāh b. al-Zubayr's mother was 'Ā'ishah's sister Ṣafiyyah.

have been caught up in civil war: Al-Zubayr wouldn't have let
Ṭalḥah rule, nor would Ṭalḥah have let al-Zubayr."

ʿAlī Leaves for al-Rabadhah[321] on His Way to al-Baṣrah

According to al-Sarī—Shuʿayb—Sayf—Sahl b. Yūsuf—al-Qāsim
b. Muḥammad: News about Ṭalḥah and al-Zubayr and the Mother
of the Believers reached ʿAlī, so he appointed Tammām b. al-ʿAbbās[322] over Medina and sent Qutham b. al-ʿAbbās to Mecca. He
then set out, hoping to intercept them on the road and intending
to block their path. At al-Rabadhah, however, it became clear to
him from news brought by ʿAṭāʾ b. Riʾāb, *mawlā* of al-Ḥārith b.
Ḥazn,[323] that they had passed by ahead of him.

According to al-Sarī—Shuʿayb—Sayf—Muḥammad and Ṭalḥah: ʿAlī was in Medina when he heard the news of their decision
to leave [Mecca] for al-Baṣrah and of what Ṭalḥah, al-Zubayr,
ʿĀʾishah, and their followers had all decided upon. On hearing
about ʿĀʾishah's speech,[324] ʿAlī set out against them in haste with
the troops he had been mustering to go to Syria.[325] He was also
joined by those Kūfans and Baṣrans who were active and quickly
equipped, totaling 700. ʿAlī's plan was to catch up with them and
stop them leaving. Just then ʿAbdallāh b. Salām[326] met him and
took hold of his reins, warning: "Don't leave Medina,[327] Commander of the Faithful! By Allah! If you do, neither you nor rule
over the Muslims will ever return here again." Those there began
swearing at him, but ʿAlī said: "Leave him alone! He's a good man
and a Companion of Muḥammad." ʿAlī nevertheless set off, but
on reaching al-Rabadhah he heard that they had passed through
ahead of him, so he ordered a halt at al-Rabadhah to confer.

[3107]

---

321. Within three days of Medina on the road to Mecca (Yāqūt, III, 24); it was
the burial place of Abū Dharr al-Ghifārī.
322. Caskel and Strenziok, I, 6, II, 544.
323. Ibn Bujayr al-ʿĀmirī (Caskel and Strenziok, I, 110, II, 307).
324. To the pilgrims in Mecca.
325. To confront Muʿāwiyah.
326. Following Ibrāhīm and *Addenda*, DCXXXII. He was the famous Jewish convert to Islam. The text has Sallām.
327. See *Addenda*, DCXXXI on p. 33, above.

According to al-Sarī—Shuʿayb—Sayf—Khālid b. Mihrān al-Bajalī—Marwān b. ʿAbd al-Raḥmān al-Ḥumaysī[328]—Ṭāriq b. Shihāb:[329] We had left al-Kūfah on the *ʿumrah* pilgrimage when we heard of the killing of ʿUthmān. When we got to al-Rabadhah in the early dawn we encountered troops, some of them urging[330] each other on. "What's going on?" I asked. "It's the Commander of the Faithful," they replied. "What's happened to him?" "Ṭalḥah and al-Zubayr have got the better of him, so he has come out to block their way and force them back. But he now hears that they have gone on ahead of him, so he wants to pursue them farther." "We belong to Allāh, and to Him we return,"[331] I replied. "Either I join ʿAlī and fight these two men and the Mother of the Faithful, or else I disobey him. What a sorry state of affairs!" So I went and joined him. The prayer was performed before dawn, with ʿAlī praying out front. Then, when he had completed it, his son al-Ḥasan came up to him, sat down, and said, "I gave you orders, but you disobeyed me, so tomorrow you will be killed in a place of destruction[332] with no one to help you." So ʿAlī said to him: "You do go on whimpering like a little girl![333] What orders did you give me that I disobeyed?" "When ʿUthmān was besieged," he replied, "I commanded you to leave Medina so that when he was killed you wouldn't be present. Then the day he got killed I commanded you not to take on the allegiance until the delegations from the garrison cities and the Arab tribesmen and every area's allegiance had come to you. Then, when these two men[334] did what they did, I commanded you to stay at home until they had got their settlement.[335] If things then went badly wrong, it would clearly

[3108]

---

328. Ibrāhīm has al-Khumaysī.

329. Ibn ʿAbd Shams of Bajīlah (Caskel and Strenziok, I, 223, II, 557).

330. Following Ibrāhīm's *yaḥdū* for the text's *yadū*.

331. Qurʾān 2:151. Said when faced with a catastrophe, like the choice here.

332. I.e., in battle. Reading *bi-maḍīʿa* with Ibrāhīm, Addenda DCXXXIII, and Wellhausen, 159. This could also mean "a desolate place," which might fit the following phrase better. The text has *bi-maṣbaʿah* "in arrogance." IA, 222 n. 1, has *bi-maʿṣiya* "in disobedience/sin," which is extremely derogatory, but it fits al-Ḥasan's *amartuk fa-aṣaytanī*. Cf. note 349, below; for other instances of these words used of subordinates to their superiors, see p. 194, below.

333. *Taḥinn ḥanīn al-jāriyah*. Ibrāhīm follows IA and has *takhinn khanīn* . . . "sniveling." The same applies to p. 51, below.

334. Ṭalḥah and al-Zubayr.

335. *Ḥattā yaṣṭaliḥu*. They had been calling for *iṣlāḥ*.

have been others' doing. But you disobeyed me in all this." 'Alī
replied, "All right, dear boy, as for your words, 'If only you had left
Medina when 'Uthmān was besieged,' by Allāh! we were under
siege no less than he! Then, as for your words 'Do not take on
the allegiance until allegiance from the garrison cities comes,' the
choice of ruler belonged to the people of Medina, and we didn't
want to destroy that tradition. Then, as for your words 'when
Ṭalḥah and al-Zubayr left,' the whole Muslim community was
facing weakness. By Allāh! Since I became caliph things have
continually gone against me and diminished me, and I never attain anything I should. Then, as for your words 'Sit at home,' how
then could I fulfill my responsibilities? What do you want me to
be? Do you want me to be like the hyena that gets surrounded and
calls *dabābi dabābi*[336] until its hocks are untied[337] and it is
forced to come out? This is no situation for me to be in. If I don't
look after my responsibilities and concerns in this question, then
who will? So that's enough, dear boy."

The Buying of the Camel for 'Ā'ishah and the Report about the Dogs of al-Ḥaw'ab[338]

According to Ismā'īl b. Mūsā al-Fazārī—'Alī b. 'Ābis al-Azraq—
Abū al-Khaṭṭāb al-Hajarī—Ṣafwān b. Qabīṣah al-Aḥmasī—al-
'Uranī, the owner of the Camel:[339] I was traveling on my camel
one day when a rider appeared in front of me. "Owner of the
camel," he asked, "will you sell your camel?" "Yes," I replied.   [3109]
"For how much?" "A thousand dirhams."[340] "You must be mad,"
he said. "Can a camel cost a thousand dirhams?" "Yes, this Camel of mine." "How so?" "I've never gone after anyone on him," I
replied, "without catching up with him, and no one has ever[341]

---

336. Said to be the sound by which a hyena is enticed from its lair; see *Glossarium*, CCLXXV, as also for a dismissal of the view that it should rather be *zabābi
zabābi*, as in *Addenda*, DCXXXII. See also lane, 1208b.

337. After capture.

338. A watering place of Abū Bakr b. Kilāb on the Ḥijāz-Baṣrah road (Yāqūt, II,
314).

339. IA, 210, 222.

340. In 20/641 the top annual stipends for various grades of Muhājirūn and
Anṣār were only 3,000 to 5,000 dirhams (Hinds, "Kūfan Alignments," 349).

341. Ibrāhīm omits *qaṭṭ*.

come after me when I was on him without my escaping them."
"If you knew whom we wanted him for," he replied, "you'd give
us a better deal." "So whom do you need him for?" I asked. "For
your mother." "But I left my mother sitting in her tent, not wanting to go anywhere." "I want it for the Mother of the Faithful,
ʿĀʾishah, that's who." "He's yours, then. Take him for nothing!"
"No, no! Come back with us to where we're camped," he replied,
"and we'll give you a Mahriyyah she-camel[342] and some dirhams
as well."

So I went back, and they gave me a Mahriyyah she-camel of hers
and 400—or was it 600?—dirhams as well. He then asked me,
"Brother of ʿUraynah, can you guide the way?"[343] "Certainly! Better than most," I replied. "Come with us then!" So I went with
them. Every time I passed by a valley or a watering place they
questioned me about it, until we came late one evening to the
water of al-Ḥawʾab and the dogs there barked at us. "What water
is this?" they asked. "The water of al-Ḥawʾab," I replied. At this
ʿĀʾishah shrieked at the top of her voice and hit the upper foreleg
of her camel to make it kneel down. "By Allāh!" she said. "I'm
the one the dogs of al-Ḥawʾab have barked at night at![344] Take me
back!" She said this three times. She then made her camel kneel,
and so did everyone else around her; they remained like this with
her, refusing to move for a full twenty-four hours. Ibn al-Zubayr
then came up to her and said: "Escape! Escape! ʿAlī b. Abī Ṭālib is
upon you, by Allāh!" So they saddled up and insulted me.[345] So I
went a different way.

I had not gone far before I came upon ʿAlī and about 300 riders
with him. "Rider!" ʿAlī called out to me, so I went up to him.
"Where did you come upon the howdah?" he asked. "In such and
such a place," I replied, "and this is her she-camel. I sold them my
male." "She rode him then, did she?"[346] "She did," I replied, "and
I accompanied them until we got to the water of al-Ḥawʾab,

[3110]

---

342. I.e., from Mahra in ʿUmān. Mahriyyah camels were famous for their speed
and intelligence (Lane, 2740b).

343. *Dalālah* is not just knowledge of a route but also of its tribal agreements.

344. See p. 68, below; Abbott, *Aishah*, 143–44.

345. Implying that al-ʿUranī had told them a lie; see p. 68, below, where Ibn al-
Zubayr makes it explicit.

346. Indicating that she was on the warpath (Abbott, "Women").

whereupon the dogs there barked at her and she said these words. So when I saw their confusion, I turned and left, and they moved off." "Can you guide us to Dhū Qār?" asked 'Alī. "I could be the best guide around." "Come with us then!" said 'Alī. So we traveled until we stopped at Dhū Qār. 'Alī b. Abī Ṭālib asked for two saddlebags; they were joined together, and a camel saddle was brought and put on top of them. He then walked up, got up on it, and let both his legs down on one side. He then praised and magnified Allāh and prayed for blessings upon Muḥammad and said to those present, "You have seen what these people and this woman have done!" Just then al-Ḥasan[347] came up in front of him, crying. "Here you come whimpering[348] like a little girl!" 'Alī said to him. "Yes indeed!" replied al-Ḥasan. "I gave you orders, but you disobeyed me, so today you will be killed in a place of destruction[349] with no one to help you." "Tell the men what you commanded me to do!" said 'Alī. "When the people went to 'Uthmān I commanded you not to receive allegiance until the Arabs had amassed,[350] for they would never make a major decision without you. But you didn't obey me. Then, when this woman set off and her followers did what they did, I commanded you to stay in Medina and to send for those of your followers who would comply with you." "By Allāh! Yes, he did say all that! But my little son! I'm not one to be like the hyena listening for the sound of a falling stone.[351] The Prophet died, and I saw no one more fit for the command than I, but the people gave allegiance to Abū Bakr, so I followed suit. Then Abū Bakr passed away, and I saw no one more fit for the command than I. But the people gave allegiance to 'Umar b. al-Khaṭṭāb, so I followed suit. Then 'Umar passed away, and I saw no one more fit for the command than I. But they made me just one of six votes, and the people gave allegiance to 'Uthmān. Again, I followed suit. The people then came to 'Uthmān and killed him. Then they came to me and gave

[3111]

---

347. His son.
348. See p. 48, above.
349. I.e., in battle. Reading *bi-maḍī'a* with Ibrāhīm for the text's *bi-maṣba'ah*, "in arrogance," see note 332, above.
350. Cf. p. 45, above.
351. "I'm not going to be duped"; see Ibn Manẓūr, XVI, 12 l. 17; Ibn Abī al-Ḥadīd, I, 223–25; Guillaume, 732, n. 301; p. 49, above.

me allegiance obediently and voluntarily. I will therefore fight whoever opposes me with those who follow me "until Allāh judges between me and them. He is the best judge."[352]

ʿĀʾishah's Remark "By Allāh! I Will Seek Vengeance for the Blood of ʿUthmān!" and Her Departure for al-Baṣrah with Ṭalḥah and al-Zubayr and Their Followers[353]

According to ʿAlī b. Aḥmad b. al-Ḥasan al-ʿIjlī (in writing)—al-Ḥusayn b. Naṣr al-ʿAṭṭār—his father, Naṣr b. Muzāḥim al-ʿAṭṭār[354]—Sayf b. ʿUmar—Muḥammad b. Nuwayrah and Ṭalḥah b. al-Aʿlam al-Ḥanafī.[355] Also[356] ʿUmar b. Saʿd[357]—Asad b. ʿAbdallāh—a scholar contemporary with the events: As ʿĀʾishah arrived at Sarif on her way back from visiting Mecca, ʿUbayd[358] b. Umm Kilāb met her. He was ʿUbayd[359] b. Abī Salāmah but named after his mother. "What is the matter?" ʿĀʾishah asked him. "They killed ʿUthmān and then did nothing for eight nights." "What did they do then?" she asked. "The people of Medina handled the affair by consensus, and matters proceeded very well for them. They agreed upon ʿAlī b. Abī Ṭālib." "By Allāh!" she replied. "Would that the sky were overturned if the command is decided in favor of your leader! Take me back! Take me back!"[360] So she departed for Mecca, saying: "By Allāh! ʿUthmān has been killed unjustly,[361] and I will seek revenge for his blood!" Ibn Umm Kilāb said to her: "How is that? By Allāh! You were the first to incline the blade against ʿUthmān and were saying 'Kill

[3112]

---

352. Qurʾān 7:87 (where it has *baynanā*, rather than *baynī wa-baynahum*). Shuʿayb is addressing the people of Madyan.

353. IA, 206.

354. Author of *Waqʿat Ṣiffīn*.

355. Are these names fuller than usual because they come at the start of a new volume?

356. Al-Ḥusayn heard it from; cf. Caetani, IX, 33.

357. Or Saʿīd; cf. the text, 3111 n. *d*.

358. For the text's ʿAbd. He was from Banū Layth and related to ʿĀʾishah on her mother's side (see p. 38, above; IA, 206).

359. For the text's ʿAbd. For Abū Salāmah, see Watt, 378, 396.

360. To Mecca to get support. Mecca would still have been crowded from the *ḥājj*.

361. Cf. Qurʾān 17:33.

Na'thal,[362] for he has become a disbeliever!'" "They asked him to repent," she replied, "and then they killed him. I said things, and they said things, but my latter statement was better than my former one." Ibn Umm Kilāb then recited:[363]

From you come new opinions, from you comes change,
     from you are the winds, and from you the rain!
You ordered the killing of the imām
     and told us that he was an unbeliever.
Suppose we did obey you and kill him;
     nevertheless his killer, to our mind, was the one who
     issued the order.
The roof did not fall down from over us;
     our sun and moon were not eclipsed.
The people have given allegiance to one with power,
     who will remove the sting and establish pride.
He will put on the clothes for war.
     He who fulfills is not like he who has broken contract.

She then set off for Mecca. She dismounted by the entrance of the mosque and made for the Ḥijr, where she curtained herself off. The people gathered around her, and she said to them, "'Uthmān has been killed unjustly, and, by Allāh, I will seek vengeance for his blood!"

According to al-Sarī (in writing)—Shuʿayb—Sayf—Muḥammad and Ṭalḥah:[364] ʿAlī was worried which direction[365] ʿĀʾishah's party might take, and he did not know their destination. He preferred them to go to al-Baṣrah, so when he learned that they had taken[366] the Baṣrah road he was pleased and remarked, "The Arab leaders and the families with pedigree are in al-Kūfah." Ibn ʿAbbās, however, replied, "What pleases you about that displeases me. Al-Kūfah is a garrison town. There are indeed Arab tribal leaders there, but they do not have the support of many of the people.[367]

[3113]

---

362. An insulting nickname for ʿUthmān; it means "hyena."
363. Caetani, IX, 34.
364. Muir, 242. IA glosses part of and omits the whole last third of this (terse) report. Caetani, IX, 35, omits all of it. See also p. 80, below.
365. Reading *min*, rather than Ibrāhīm's *man*.
366. *Yuʿāriḍūn*; see Lane, 2004b, 2005a; IA, 205.
367. Cf. Hinds, "Kûfan Political Alignments," 351.

What is more, some of them are ambitious for authority that they cannot attain. This being so, they stir up trouble against[368] the one who has attained it until they break his power[369] and corrupt one another." "You appear to be right," replied ʿAlī, "but I will select the people of obedience in preference[370] to anyone else, and I will rely on[371] those of them who have the greatest priority and seniority[372] in Islam. If they settle down, we shall forgive them and set them right. If that satisfies them, it will be best for them; if it does not, we shall be forced to set them right, which will be bad for those already in a bad situation."[373] "Satisfaction is the only way,"[374] replied Ibn ʿAbbās.

According to al-Sarī (in writing)—Shuʿayb—Sayf—Muḥammad and Ṭalḥah: When Ṭalḥah and al-Zubayr, the Mother of the Faithful, and the Muslims of Mecca had decided to leave for al-Baṣrah and to take revenge on ʿUthmān's killers, al-Zubayr and Ṭalḥah went out to meet Ibn ʿUmar, and they invited him to hasten and help[375] them. He said, "I am from Medina, and, if the people of Medina agree to rise up, so will I. But, if they agree to remain quiescent, I will too." So the two left him and returned.

According to al-Sarī (in writing)—Shuʿayb—Sayf—Saʿīd b. ʿAbdallāh—Ibn Abī Mulaykah: When he was about to depart, al-Zubayr gathered his sons.[376] He said farewell to some but ordered others to come out with him, including both sons of Asmāʾ.[377]

---

368. Reading ʿalā, rather than ʿalayya "he who has attained [what he wanted] will stir up trouble against me," as in Ibrāhīm; IA, 205 l. 13.

369. Ḥattā yaftha'ahu; see *Glossarium*, CCCXCVII. IA has ḥattā tuksar ḥiddatuhu "until their vehemence is broken."

370. Taking al-uthrah li- to mean wa-innī astaʾthir ʿalā; cf. note 539, below. It could also be translated as "preference will be given to the people of obedience."

371. Wa-alḥaqu bi- or "and the truth is to be found among" if wa-laḥaqqu bi- is read.

372. Sābiqah wa-qudmah or "veterans of the early campaigns"; see Hinds, "Kūfan Political Alignments," 348, 352; Humphreys, 57, 58 n. 95.

373. Or "bad for those it is bad to."

374. I.e., you won't be able to do it by force.

375. Al-khufūf; see Hava, s.v., and Ibrāhīm, n. 1.

376. Ḥamzah, ʿUrwah, ʿAmr, Jaʿfar, ʿAbdallāh, ʿUbaydah, Muṣʿab, and al-Mundhir (Caskel and Strenziok, I, 19). For others, see al-Zubayrī, 236.

377. Bint Abī Bakr. She was the mother of ʿAbdallāh, ʿUrwah, and al-Mundhir (*EI*[1], s.v. Zubayr). The two referred to here are the latter two, ʿAbdallāh not being in question, as the eldest and the only one full grown.

"So and so, stay!" he said. "'Amr,[378] stay!" When 'Abdallāh b. al-Zubayr saw this, he said, "'Urwah, stay! Mundhir, stay!"[379] "Certainly not!" replied al-Zubayr. "I will take my two sons [from Asmā'] as companions and enjoy their company." He said: "If you are taking all your sons, then go! But, if you are leaving any behind, you must leave those two. Don't expose Asmā' only from among your wives to childlessness." At this he wept and left the two of them behind. They departed and came to the mountains of Awṭās, where they turned right and followed a road going toward al-Baṣrah, leaving the main road to al-Baṣrah on the left. When they neared al-Baṣrah, they entered it and rode up al-Munkadir.

According to al-Sarī (in writing)—Shuʿayb—Sayf—Ibn al-Shahīd—Ibn Abī Mulaykah: Al-Zubayr and Ṭalḥah departed and went separate ways. 'Ā'ishah then departed for Dhāt 'Irq, followed by the Mothers of the Faithful.[380] There has never been a day more full of tears for or against Islam than that day, called the Day of Wailing. She put 'Abd al-Raḥmān b. 'Attāb in charge. He led the prayer and acted as arbiter[381] among the people.

According to al-Sarī (in writing)—Shuʿayb—Sayf—Muḥammad b. 'Abdallāh—Yazīd b. Ma'n al-Sulamī: When her army turned right at Awṭās, they came upon Malīḥ b. 'Awf al-Sulamī, who was supervising his property. He greeted al-Zubayr. "Abū 'Abdallāh," he said, "What's going on?" "The Commander of the Faithful has been attacked and killed with neither blood revenge nor excuse." "By whom?" "By the riffraff from the garrison towns and outsiders from the tribes assisted by bedouin and slaves." "So what do you want to do?" asked Malīḥ. "To rally the people and let this blood be revenged," said al-Zubayr, "lest it be spilled in vain, because, if it is, the power of Allāh will be forever weakened among us. If the people aren't separated from acts like this, then no imām will survive without being killed by this sort [of scoundrel]."[382] "By Allāh!" he said. "To neglect this would be ex-

[3114]

[3115]

---

378. A later opponent of his brother 'Abdallāh (Caskel and Strenziok, II, 187).

379. 'Urwah, later a prominent traditionist, was born 23–29 (so he would have only been thirteen years old at the most at the time) and died 91–99 (EI¹, s.v.). Al-Mundhir died 73/692 with 'Abdallāh in Mecca (Caskel and Strenziok, II, 430).

380. Other wives of the Prophet.

381. *Glossarium*, CCCLIII.

382. *Glossarium*, CCCXXXIII.

tremely serious, and who knows what it might lead to?" They
then both said farewell to each other and departed, and the army
traveled on.

Their Entry into al-Baṣrah and the Battle between Them and ʿUthmān b. Ḥunayf

According to al-Sarī (in writing)—Shuʿayb—Sayf—Muḥammad
and Ṭalḥah: The army traveled on until, after turning off the road
at the esplanade of al-Baṣrah, they were met by ʿUmayr b. ʿAbdallāh al-Tamīmī. "Mother of the Faithful!" he said. "I implore you
in Allāh's name to contact those men today to whom you haven't[383] yet sent any message, and He will then protect you from
them." "You have given me sound advice," she said. "You are[384] a
good man." "Then send Ibn ʿĀmir [b. Kurayz] immediately," he
replied. "Let him enter. He has contacts. Let him go to them, and
then let them meet the rest of the Baṣran people. You may then go
yourself, and they will listen to the reasons why you have all
come." So she sent him, and he stole into al-Baṣrah and went to
his contacts. ʿĀʾishah then wrote to a number of Baṣran leaders, to
al-Aḥnaf b. Qays,[385] to Ṣabrah b. Shaymān,[386] and to other similar
prominent men. She then moved across to al-Ḥufayr and awaited
information in response. When the men of al-Baṣrah heard of this,
ʿUthmān b. Ḥunayf called ʿImrān b. Ḥuṣayn,[387] a newcomer,[388]
and teamed him up with Abū al-Aswad al-Duʾalī,[389] a veteran.[390]
"Go to this woman," he said, "and find out what's in her mind
and in the minds of those with her." They set off and reached her
and the people there while they were at al-Ḥufayr. Their request

---

383. Ibrāhīm omits *lam*.

384. Ibrāhīm omits *wa-anta*.

385. Called al-Aḥnaf (*EI²*, s.v.), although his name was al-Ḍaḥḥāk, leader of
Tamīm in Baṣrah; died 67/686–86 (Caskel and Strenziok, I, 76, II, 146, 240).

386. Leader of the Azd al-Sarāt in al-Baṣrah and on ʿĀʾishah's side in the Battle of
the Camel (Caskel and Strenziok, I, 216, II, 534).

387. Al-Kindī (Caskel and Strenziok, I, 236, II, 357).

388. *Rajul ʿāmmah* (Hinds, "Kûfan Political Alignments," 354).

389. Ẓālim b. ʿAmr b. Sufyān of Kinānah, died either 69 or 99–101 (Caskel and
Strenziok, I, 43, II, 199, 614; Brockelmann, I, 42, 98, S, I, 72). He was an early
grammarian.

390. *Rajul khāṣṣah* (Hinds, "Kûfan Political Alignments," 354).

for permission to enter was granted, and after greetings they said:
"Our commander has sent us to you to ask where you are heading. Are you going to tell us?"   [3116]

"By Allāh!" she replied. "I am not one to conduct things in
secret or to cover up information for her sons. The riffraff of
provincials and outsiders from the tribes committed aggression in
the Messenger of Allāh's sacred enclave, perpetrated crimes there,
and gave refuge to the criminals. They therefore deserve the curse
of Allāh and His Messenger along with what they have been debited for killing the imām of the Muslims without blood debt or
excuse. They desecrated sacred blood and shed it; they plundered
sacred property and profaned the sacred city and the sacred
month. They ruined people's honor and persons and stayed in the
houses of people who hated their staying there—harming and
intimidating, useless and fearless of Allāh, incapable of restraint
and insecure. I have therefore come out among the Muslims to let
them know what this group has perpetrated, how those left behind me are faring, and what they have to do to set things right."
She then recited: " 'There is no good in most secret talks, unless
someone be arranging charity or good works or setting things
right[391] between people.'[392] To set things right[393] we are raising
support from those whom Almighty and Glorious Allāh and His
Messenger have commanded[394]—the young and the old, the male
and the female. So this is our concern: [There is] a right we are
enjoining on you and encouraging you toward, and [there is] a
wrong we are prohibiting you from and urging you to alter."

According to al-Sarī (in writing)—Shuʿayb—Sayf—Muḥammad
and Ṭalḥah: Abū al-Aswad and ʿImrān then left her. They came to
Ṭalḥah and asked him, "What brings you here?" "The search for
revenge for the blood of ʿUthmān." "But didn't you give allegiance
to ʿAlī?" they asked. "I did—but with the sword against my neck.
However, I don't demand the abrogation[395] of my allegiance to
ʿAlī—provided he doesn't obstruct our way to ʿUthmān's killers."

---

391. Iṣlāḥ.
392. Qurʾān 4:114.
393. Iṣlāḥ.
394. I.e., who are able-bodied.
395. Lane, 2997c; *Glossarium*, CDXLIII, suggests, "I don't forgive ʿAlī or
forget."

[3117] They then came to al-Zubayr and asked him, "What brings you here?" "To seek revenge for the blood of ʿUthmān." "But didn't you give allegiance to ʿAlī?" they asked. "I did—but with the sword against my neck. However, I don't demand the abrogation of my allegiance to ʿAlī—provided he doesn't obstruct our way to ʿUthmān's killers." Then they returned to the Mother of the Faithful to bid farewell to her. She said goodbye to ʿImrān and said: "Abū al-Aswad! Watch out that whim doesn't steer you into the Fire!" She then sent them on their way, quoting the Qurʾānic verse "Be upright toward Allāh, witnesses of justice! [. . . and do not follow caprice]."[396] Her public announcer then called out that she was setting off, so the two of them went to ʿUthmān b. Ḥunayf. Abū al-Aswad hastened to speak before ʿImrān and said:

"Ibn Ḥunayf! They have advanced against you, so hurry [toward them]!
  Stab at the enemy, struggle, and endure!
Go out to them with breastplate and robe rolled up for action!"

"We belong to Allāh and to Him we return!"[397] said ʿUthmān. "By the Lord of the Kaʿbah! The millstone of Islam is turning out of balance, and look at the way it will swagger on round!"[398] "It's true, by Allāh!" added ʿImrān. "It will grind you long and hard, and those of you left won't add up to much." "So what do you advise me to do, ʿImrān?" "I'm not getting involved, so don't you either!" he replied. "No," said ʿUthmān. "I will stop them until ʿAlī the Commander of the Faithful comes." "But Allāh will judge as He wishes,"[399] said ʿImrān and left for his house, and ʿUthmān carried out his plan. Hishām b. ʿĀmir then came to him and said, "ʿUthmān, this plan you are intent on will lead to worse than what you hate most. It's a tear that won't get mended, a fracture that won't be repaired. So comply with their wishes until ʿAlī's command comes. Don't oppose them."

[3118] But ʿUthmān refused and announced to the people that they

---

396. 4:135, where the text is in a different order: "Be strict observers of justice, witnesses to Allāh."
397. Qurʾan 2:157, said on hearing of a calamity.
398. I.e., "look at the deception that will go on!" Cf. *Glossarium*, CCLXXXIII.
399. Cf. Qurʾan 5:1.

should make preparations. So they put on their weapons and gathered together at the main Friday mosque. Now 'Uthmān devised a stratagem to trick the people and see how they were thinking. So he ordered them to make preparations and also ordered a man to go and infiltrate among them, pretending to be a Qaysī from al-Kūfah. He did so and stood up and said: "Listen, you men! I am Qays b. al-'Aqadiyyah al-Ḥumaysī. This army that has come to you, if they have come out of fear, then they have come from the place where even birds are safe![400] But, if they have come seeking revenge for 'Uthmān's blood, then we aren't 'Uthmān's killers.[401] So do what I say with this army. Send them back where they came from!" Then al-Aswad b. Sarī' al-Sa'dī[402] stood up and replied: "Are they in fact claiming that we are the killers of 'Uthmān? They have fled to us only to get our assistance[403] against those killers of 'Uthmān among us and others. If the army has been forced out of its quarters as you suggested,[404] then who will protect it from this expulsion—men or cities?"[405] But they pelted him[406] with stones, so 'Uthmān realized that they had allies in al-Baṣrah who would support them, and it demoralized him.

'Ā'ishah and her men then advanced as far as al-Mirbad.[407] They entered it at the top, where they stayed. They halted there until 'Uthmān and his army had come out. Those Baṣrans who wanted to join 'Ā'ishah did so. They gathered in al-Mirbad and collected together until it was choked with men. Ṭalḥah, on the right side of al-Mirbad with al-Zubayr, then spoke up. 'Uthmān was on its left, and they all listened to what he was about to say. He praised Allāh and magnified Him. Then he mentioned the caliph 'Uthmān and his good qualities and the city and how it had been

---

400. I.e., so why did they ever leave Mecca? Hunting is forbidden in the Meccan sacred enclave.

401. I.e., they've come to the wrong place.

402. Pro-'Ā'ishah.

403. Ibrāhīm follows Nöldeke in correcting *yasta'īnū* to *yasta'īnūn* (*Addenda*, DCXXXII).

404. Out of fear.

405. He is calling for help. Alternatively, "then who can prevent them [in their turn] from expelling men or even cities?" if *al-rijāla aw al-buldāna* is read.

406. Qays; Prym, n. f.

407. The market and camel camp southwest of the city (al-'Alī, 282; Massignon, 157; Le Strange, 45).

[3119]

profaned. Then he emphasized what a terrible thing it was that had happened and called upon them to seek revenge for his blood. "To do so will glorify Allāh's religion and dominion," he said, "and to seek revenge for the blood of the unjustly killed[408] caliph is [to carry out] one of the divine punishments.[409] If you do it, you will have done right, and authority will return to you. If you neglect it, neither power nor order will be yours." Al-Zubayr then spoke similarly. Those on the right side of al-Mirbad said: "They are both correct and have spoken the truth. They have spoken justly and have ordered aright." But those on the left side said: "They have lied and acted treacherously. They have spoken falsely and have ordered so. Both gave allegiance, yet here they come saying these things." The people then threw dirt at one another and pelted one another with stones, raising an uproar.[410]

Then ʿĀʾishah spoke up. She had a strong voice—it could be extremely loud, like the voice of a woman of high rank.[411] She praised Glorious and Almighty Allāh and magnified Him. "The people used to accuse ʿUthmān of crimes he never did," she said.

> They would belittle his governors and then come to us in Medina to ask our advice over tales they told us about them, expecting good words from us to solve things.[412] But, whenever we looked into the matter, we would find him innocent, God-fearing, and faithful and would find them lying, treacherous,[413] and deceitful, attempting to do the opposite of what they were showing. Then, when they became strong enough to rely on greater numbers, they did so. They attacked his house and desecrated sacred blood, sacred property, and the sacred city without blood debt or excuse. Therefore what is now imperative—

---

408. *Maẓlūm*. See p. 39, above.
409. *Ḥadd min ḥudūd Allāh*, or prescriptive ordinances or statutes (*EI²*, s.v.).
410. *Wa-arhajū*, or "dust."
411. A *jalīlah* was a woman who used to urge on fighters with her high voice.
412. Reading *wa-yarawn ḥusnan min kalāminā* (with Ibrāhīm), which is not all that different from the text's *wa-yurawn ḥusnan min killāminā* "and were shown a good thing in our speaking (i.e., were spoken to well and rightly) about reconciliation between them."
413. Ibrāhīm omits *ghadarah*.

and you have no alternative—is to arrest the killers of 'Uthmān and establish the authority of the Book of Almighty Allāh, which says "Have you not seen those who were given a part of the Book being called to the Book of Allāh for it to judge between them?"[414]   [3120]

Then the followers of 'Uthmān b. Ḥunayf split into two. One group said: "By Allāh! She is correct and has spoken the truth. By Allāh! Her advice is acceptable." But the others said: "By Allāh! You all lie. We don't accept what you say." Then they threw dirt at one another and pelted one another with stones, raising an uproar.

When 'Ā'ishah saw this, she went down, as did the people on the right flank. They went away from 'Uthmān to take up a position in al-Mirbad at the tanners' location. The followers of 'Uthmān remained where they were, pushing and shoving each other until they separated. Some went down to 'Ā'ishah; others stayed with 'Uthmān at the entrance to the road. 'Uthmān b. Ḥunayf and his followers then took up a position at the entrance to the road— the road leading to the mosque—on the right of the tanners' location, where they confronted their opponents and barred them from its entrance.

According to Naṣr b. Muzāḥim—Sayf—Sahl b. Yūsuf—al-Qāsim b. Muḥammad: Jāriyah b. Qudāmah al-Saʿdī[415] came up and said: "Mother of the Faithful! By Allāh! The killing of 'Uthmān b. ʿAffān is a lesser matter than your coming out from your house on this accursed camel, exposing yourself to armed combat! Allāh curtained you off and gave you sanctity. You have torn down the curtain and profaned your sanctity.[416] Anyone who thinks you should be fought also thinks you should be killed. If you have come to us obedient, then return home! If you have been forced by someone to come to us, then seek help from the people [against him]!"

---

414. "But a party of them then turn away in opposition" (Qur'ān 3:23)—the implication being that anyone who opposes "us in Medina" has departed from Islam.

415. Al-Tamīmī, faithful ally of ʿAlī (Caskel and Strenziok, I, 75, II, 259).

416. The Prophet's wives stayed screened off behind a special curtain and had a special status. Cf. Qur'ān 33:33. By coming out, 'Ā'ishah exposed and disgraced herself.

A young *ghulām*[417] from Banū Saʿd[418] then went out to Ṭalḥah and al-Zubayr and said: "As for you, Zubayr, you are the disciple of the Messenger of Allāh, and as for you, Ṭalḥah, you preserved the Messenger of Allāh with your own hand.[419] I see your Mother is with you. Have you brought your wives too?"[420] "No," they both replied. "I have nothing to do with you then," the Saʿdī said and withdrew. He said the following verses about this:

[3121]

You preserved the honor of your wives yet led out[421] your
        mother.
    By Allāh! There is little justice in this!
She was commanded to trail her hems at home,
    but she had a whim to cross the deserts at the gallop,
[Making herself] a target that her sons must defend by fighting
    with arrows and Khaṭṭī spears[422] and swords.
Her curtains have been ripped down by Ṭalḥah and al-
        Zubayr.[423]
    No further tale needs to be told about them!

A *ghulām* from Banū Juhaynah then came up to Muḥammad b. Ṭalḥah,[424] who was a pious man, and said, "Tell me about the killers of ʿUthmān." "I will," he replied. "ʿUthmān's blood divides into three: A third is debited against the woman of the howdah, that is, ʿĀʾishah; a third is against the rider of the red camel, that is, Ṭalḥah;[425] and a third is against ʿAlī b. Abī Ṭālib." The *ghulām* laughed and said, "Well, well! I see that I'm wrong!" and left him for ʿAlī. He composed a poem about this:[426]

I asked Ibn Ṭalḥah about someone who perished
    in the heart of Medina and was not buried.[427]

---

417. A slave boy (*EI²*, s.v.).
418. I.e., Jāriyah's clan.
419. At the Battle of Uḥud.
420. Cf. pp. 101, 126, below. Caetani, IX, 41, n. 1.
421. *Wa-qudtum*, perhaps with an implication of "were a pimp with" (Lane, 2572c).
422. After al-Khaṭṭ, a strip of coast on the Persian Gulf (*EI²*, s.v.; Lane, 760c).
423. By talking to them face to face.
424. Killed in the Battle of the Camel (Caskel and Strenziok, II, 424).
425. His own father!
426. Caetani (IX, 41 n. 3) considers this preceding story made up to provide a framework for the poem. IA omits it all.
427. ʿUthmān was not buried until after the allegiance to ʿAlī.

"There were three of them," he replied. "They
        murdered Ibn 'Affān, so weep![428]
That woman in her howdah, she owes a third,
        and the rider of the red camel owes another.
'Alī b. Abī Ṭālib owes the last third.
        We are in a flat, unhealthy land!"[429]
So I said, "You are right about the first two
        but wrong about the resplendent third."

Return to Sayf's account from Muḥammad and Ṭalḥah   [3122]

Abū al-Aswad and 'Imrān left;[430] Ḥakīm b. Jabalah approached,
having come out with horsemen. He initiated battle, so 'Ā'ishah's
men aimed their spears but held back so that they[431] would do so
too. But he did not desist and was not to be turned back and began
fighting them. 'Ā'ishah's[432] followers held back, except from defending themselves. Ḥakīm urged on his horsemen and attacked
with them,[433] calling out: "She belongs to Quraysh.[434] Her cowar-
dice and indecision[435] will certainly destroy her!" So they fought at
the entrance to the road. Those in the houses round about who
liked one or other of the parties looked down [from their roofs] and
threw stones at the other side. Then 'Ā'ishah ordered her men to go to
the right to the graveyard of Banū Māzin, where they waited a while.
The opposing forces hastened toward them, but night intervened.
So 'Uthmān returned to the castle and the men to their tribes.

Then Abū al-Jarbā',[436] a member of Banū 'Uthmān[437] b. Mālik b.
'Amr b. Tamīm, came to 'Ā'ishah, Ṭalḥah, and al-Zubayr and
advised them to take up a better position. They thought his

---

428. Or "and he wept."
429. I.e., this is a very bad situation, but the text is uncertain. Prym's emendation fits the meter.
430. They were 'Uthmān's messengers to 'Ā'ishah, Ṭalḥah, and al-Zubayr; see
p. 56, above.
431. Ḥakīm and his men (IA, 214).
432. IA, 214.
433. IA, 214.
434. Disliked by other tribes because of their superiority.
435. Reading *ṭaysh* with the text and taking the next letter as a line filler (Prym,
n. e).
436. 'Āṣim b. Dulaf (Caskel and Strenziok, II, 203).
437. More correctly, Ghaylān (Caskel and Strenziok, I, 82; Prym, who leaves it
as 'Uthmān, as a feature of Sayf's tradition. Ibrāhīm does also).

advice was good. They followed his suggestion and left the grave-yard of Banū Māzin and went toward al-Baṣrah's dam, opposite al-Jabbānah,[438] as far as al-Zābūqah.[439] They then moved on to the graveyard of Banū Ḥiṣn, backing on to the Dār al-Rizq,[440] and spent the night preparing themselves. All night the men kept coming to them, and when morning came they were ready to fight in the open area in front of Dār al-Rizq.

[3123]

In the morning ʿUthmān b. Ḥunayf went to them just before sunrise, as did Ḥakīm b. Jabalah, talking excitedly and clutching a spear. "At whom are you swearing and saying what I hear?" asked a man from ʿAbd al-Qays. "ʿĀ'ishah," he replied. "Son of a slut!" he said. "Do you say such things to the Mother of the Faithful?" Ḥakīm thrust the head of his spear through the center of his chest and killed him. He then went past a woman as he was swearing at her, that is, at ʿĀ'ishah, and she said, "Who could have driven you to such abuse?" "ʿĀ'ishah," he replied. "Son of a slut!" she said. "Do you say such things to the Mother of the Faithful?" Ḥakīm stabbed her through the center of her chest, killed her, and went off.[441]

Once they had gathered, they stood over against them. There was an intense battle at Dār al-Rizq that day, from sunrise until afternoon. There were a great many fatalities among ʿUthmān b. Ḥunayf's men, and the wounds were heavy on both sides. ʿĀ'ishah's crier kept calling out, asking them to hold back, but they refused. It was only when evil had touched them hard and bitten into them that they called out to ʿĀ'ishah's followers to make peace and negotiate, and the latter acceded. So they made promises to each other[442] and drew up a document between them to the effect that they would send a messenger to Medina and that when he returned, if the two had given their allegiance under duress,[443] then ʿUthmān would leave them and yield al-Baṣrah to

---

438. The desert burial ground.

439. Al-ʿAlī, 292; lit., "angle of a house" (Lane).

440. Store for soldiers' pay; shown in the center of Massignon's map of old Baṣrah, 157.

441. This paragraph could be an interpolation. Caskel and Strenziok note that Sayf paints Ḥakīm very badly (II, 295).

442. *Wa-tawāʿadū.* IA, 214 has *wa-tawādaʿū* "they made peace."

443. Their allegiance to ʿAlī.

them both. But, if they had not been forced, then Ṭalḥah and al-Zubayr would leave.

The document ran:

> In the name of Allāh, the Merciful and Compassionate. This is the agreement reached between Ṭalḥah and al-Zubayr and their allies from the Muslims and the Believers, and ʿUthmān b. Ḥunayf and his allies from the Muslims and the Believers. That ʿUthmān will remain where he was and with what he had when the truce was drawn up, and that Ṭalḥah and al-Zubayr will remain where they were and with what they had when the truce was drawn up, until such time as the representative and messenger of the two parties, Kaʿb b. Sūr,[444] returns from Medina. Neither of the two parties will harm the other in mosque, market, street, or place of access. There shall be mutual abstention from fighting between them[445] until Kaʿb returns with the information. If he returns to report that the people forced Ṭalḥah and al-Zubayr, then the command belongs to them, and it is up to ʿUthmān whether he leaves and goes to his own chosen place or joins Ṭalḥah and al-Zubayr. If he returns to report that they were not forced, then the command belongs to ʿUthmān, and it is up to Ṭalḥah and al-Zubayr whether they stay and give their allegiance to ʿAlī or whether they go to their own chosen place. The Believers shall assist the party that is successful.

[3124]

So Kaʿb left for Medina. The people there gathered together for his arrival—it was a Friday. He stood up and said: "Men of Medina! I am the messenger to you from the people of al-Baṣrah. Did these people force these two men to give allegiance to ʿAlī, or did they give it voluntarily?" Not one of those assembled answered

---

444. An influential Azdī and Baṣran judge (Abbot, *Aishah*, 150; Caskel and Strenziok, I, 211, II, 366), who fell in the Battle of the Camel. This sentence could be a gloss.

445. See Lane, 2206c, where a similar phrase from the treaty of al-Ḥudaybiyyah is cited.

except Usāmah b. Zayd,[446] who stood up and said: "I swear by Allāh! They[447] were definitely coerced into giving allegiance." Tammām[448] gave the order, and Sahl b. Ḥunayf and others sprang upon him. Fearing that Usāmah would be killed, Ṣuhayb b. Sinān and Abu Ayyūb Zayd[449] leaped in with a number of Companions of the Messenger of God, including Muḥammad b. Maslamah.[450] "By Allāh!" swore Ṣuhayb. "Break off from the man!" They did so, and Ṣuhayb led him out by the hand and took him into his house. "You knew that the hyena is stupid,"[451] he said. "Wasn't the silence we were keeping good enough for you?" "No, by Allāh! But I had no idea that things would reach this pass. It has led us into disaster."

So Ka'b returned. Ṭalḥah and al-Zubayr had meanwhile kept a count of incidents, all of which were of the sort one would make note of—among them that Muḥammad b. Ṭalḥah, who was in the habit of performing prayers [in the mosque], happened to stand close to 'Uthmān b. Ḥunayf. Some of the Zuṭṭ and Sayābijah[452] then feared that he had come for some other reason,[453] so they pushed him away.[454] Ṭalḥah and al-Zubayr then sent 'Uthmān a message: "That's one thing you've done!"[455]

News of the events in Medina reached 'Alī, so he hastily sent a letter to 'Uthmān, accusing him of weakness and saying: "By Allāh! The two weren't forced except out of fear of schism and for the sake of unity and merit. If they want to depose me, they have

---

446. Al-Kalbī (Caskel and Strenziok, I, 291, II, 576), son of the Prophet's adopted son, Zayd, and leader of the successful raid against Mu'tah just before the Prophet's death (Watt, 323, 343).

447. Ibrāhīm has *innahumā* for the text's *innahum*, following *Addenda*, DCXXXII.

448. Ibn al-'Abbās (IA, 215).

449. Brother of Usāmah?

450. Al-Khazrajī (Caskel and Strenziok, I, 180, II, 424), leader of various successful expeditions for the Prophet (Watt, 340–41, 411).

451. I.e., "You knew that those people would get angry"; Freytag, I, 405.

452. The guards of 'Uthmān b. Ḥunayf. The Zuṭṭ were a gypsy type of people, probably originally from India (*EI*¹, s.v.). The Sayābijah were merceneries from Sind (*EI*¹, s.v.).

453. Quite rightly.

454. Emending the text's and Ibrāhīm's *fa-naḥḥayāh* to *fa-naḥḥūh*. Otherwise, either, as Prym notes, there must be a lacuna in the text, or there is a false dual from the Zuṭṭ and Sayābijah.

455. Many others will follow.

no excuse; but, if they want something else, then we'll look into the matter with them." The letter reached 'Uthmān b. Ḥunayf.

Ka'b then arrived, and they sent a message to 'Uthmān: "Go away from us!" But 'Uthmān argued [against withdrawing],[456] on the basis of 'Alī's letter, saying, "This is another question, distinct from the one we were negotiating." Ṭalḥah and al-Zubayr then assembled their army. It was a cold, dark night with wind and rain.[457] They headed for the mosque, arriving there at the time of the evening prayer. But the Baṣrans were in the habit of postponing it, and 'Uthmān b. Ḥunayf had not yet arrived, so Ṭalḥah and al-Zubayr put 'Abd al-Raḥmān b. 'Attāb as imām. At this the Zuṭṭ and Sayābijah unsheathed their weapons and thrust them among them. Ṭalḥah and al-Zubayr's men advanced against them, and they battled inside the mosque and kept on until they had killed all forty of them. They then sent their fighters in to 'Uthmān to bring him out to them. When he came to them, they debased[458] him, and not one hair was left on his face. Ṭalḥah and al-Zubayr considered this very serious and sent a report to 'Ā'ishah about what had happened, seeking her advice. She sent back, saying: "Set him free! Let him go where he wants. Don't imprison him!"[459] So they expelled the guards who were with 'Uthmān in the castle, and they entered it. They used to alternate guarding 'Uthmān, forty each day and forty each night.

[3126]

'Abd al-Raḥmān b. 'Attāb led the prayer in the evening and at dawn, and he was the messenger between 'Ā'ishah and Ṭalḥah and al-Zubayr. He would come to her with news and then take her response back to them. He was the messenger of their army.

According to 'Umar b. Shabbah—Abū al-Ḥasan—Abū Mikhnaf —Yūsuf b. Yazīd—Sahl b. Sa'd: When they had captured 'Uthmān b. Ḥunayf, they sent Abān b. 'Uthmān to 'Ā'ishah to find out what they should do with him. "Kill him!" she said. But a woman said: "I beg you by Allāh, Mother of the Faithful! Remember 'Uthmān and his Companionship with the Prophet!" "Send Abān back!" 'Ā'ishah said. So they did so, and she said to him, "Imprison him,

---

456. Despite the double evidence that they *had* been forced.
457. *Nadan.* IA has *maṭar.*
458. By plucking his beard, lit., "trampled on him."
459. Cf. the next report, where she first orders him to be killed.

but don't kill him!" "If I had known this was why you called for me," he replied, "I wouldn't have returned." Mujāshiʿ b. Masʿūd[460] then said to them, "Flog him and pluck the hair of his beard!" So they flogged him forty lashes, plucked the hair of his beard, his head, and his eyebrows and eyelashes and imprisoned him.

According to Aḥmad b. Zuhayr—his father—Wahb b. Jarīr b. Ḥāzim—Yūnus b. Yazīd al-Aylī—al-Zuhrī: I was told that, when Ṭalḥah and al-Zubayr heard that ʿAlī had encamped at Dhū Qār, they left for al-Baṣrah and took the road to al-Munkadir. ʿĀʾishah then heard the dogs barking and asked, "What water is this?"[461] "Al-Ḥawʾab," they replied. "We belong to Allāh, and to Him we return,"[462] she exclaimed. "I am she! I heard the Messenger of God say in the presence of his wives, 'I wish I knew at which of you the dogs of al-Ḥawʾab will bark!'"[463] and she wanted to turn back. ʿAbdallāh b. al-Zubayr came up to her, and it is said that he told her, "Whoever said that this was al-Ḥawʾab was lying,"[464] and then persisted with her until she set off. They came to al-Baṣrah, the governor of which was ʿUthmān b. Ḥunayf, and he asked them, "What makes you angry at your companion?"[465] "We don't consider him more eligible for leadership than we," they replied, "after what he has done." "The man[466] made me governor, so I will write to him and inform him why you have come," said ʿUthmān, "on the condition that I lead the prayer until his reply comes." So they held back from him, and he rode off.

[3127]

But they waited only two days and then attacked ʿUthmān and fought with him at al-Zābūqah near the supply center.[467] They gained the upper hand and captured ʿUthmān. They were about to kill him, but then they feared the wrath of Anṣār. So they attacked his hair and body instead.

Ṭalḥah and al-Zubayr then rose to make speeches and said:

---

460. Killed in the Battle of the Camel (Caskel and Strenziok, II, 419).
461. See p. 50, above.
462. Qurʾān 2:157.
463. See Wensinck, VI, 340, for Arabic sources.
464. Said to have been the first *shahādah bi-al-zūr* (false testimony) in Islam.
465. ʿAlī. IA, 216.
466. ʿAlī.
467. *Madīnat al-rizq*, often *dār al-rizq*.

"People of al-Baṣrah! Repentance should fit the crime. We wanted the Commander of the Faithful only to get ʿUthmān to satisfy [our complaints]. We didn't want him to be killed, but the fools prevailed over the wise men and killed him." "But Abū Muḥammad!" the people replied to Ṭalḥah. "The letters you sent us said otherwise." "Did you receive any letter from me about what he was doing?" asked al-Zubayr, going on to mention ʿUthmān's murder and what led to it and to emphasize ʿAlī's blame in it. At this a man from ʿAbd al-Qays stood up facing him and said: "Be silent, man! And listen so that we may speak." ʿAbdallāh b. al-Zubayr retorted, "What position are you in to speak?" "Company [3128] of Muhājirūn!" said the ʿAbdī. "You were the first to respond to the Messenger of God, and you gained favor through that, and then everyone else entered Islam following your example. Then when the Messenger of God died you gave allegiance to one of your number, but, by Allāh! you didn't consult us in any way about it. We gave our approval nevertheless and went along with you, and Almighty and Glorious Allāh blessed the Muslims through His caliphate. Then he died, having appointed a man caliph in his place over you. Again, you didn't discuss it with us, but we gave our approval and accepted. When this caliph died, he placed the decision in the hands of six men, and you chose ʿUthmān and gave him allegiance without consulting us. Then you found some fault with this man, so you killed him without consulting us. Then you gave allegiance to ʿAlī without consulting us. So what exactly are you angry with him about that we should join and fight him? Has he appropriated booty or carried out some injustice? Has he done something you object to such that we should join you against him? If not, then what's going on?" Ṭalḥah and al-Zubayr's men then tried to kill this ʿAbdī, but his clansmen stood in their way. But the next morning they leaped upon him[468] and his men and killed seventy men.[469]

Return to Sayf's account from Muḥammad and Ṭalḥah

By the following morning the treasury and the guards were under Ṭalḥah and al-Zubayr's control. The people were also with

---

468. In two mss. of IA "upon ʿUthmān."
469. Cf. Conrad.

them—those who were not were under cover trying to keep hidden. So first thing that morning they sent a message [to ʿĀʾishah] that Ḥakīm was still there among the opposing company. "Don't detain ʿUthmān! Let him go!" came her reply. So they let ʿUthmān go, and he left and went where he wanted. The morning found Ḥakīm b. Jabalah with his horsemen at the ready with his ʿAbdī followers and allies of theirs from the splinter groups[470] of Rabīʿah. They then headed for Dār al-Rizq, Ḥakīm saying, "I'm not his brother if I don't come to his[471] aid." He began insulting ʿĀʾishah, and a woman from his own tribe[472] heard him. "Son of a bitch!" she said. "It's you that deserves the insults." So he stabbed her and killed her. The ʿAbdīs, apart from those consumed by their hatred, were enraged at this. "Yesterday you did an evil deed,[473] and you've done the like again today," they said. "By Allāh! We will leave you, so that Allāh may retaliate against you." So they went back and left him. So Ḥakīm b. Jabalah[474] continued with those outsiders from all the tribes who had attacked and surrounded ʿUthmān b. ʿAffān with him. They had realized that they could no longer maintain any position in al-Baṣrah, so they gathered to him, and he took them to al-Zābūqah near Dār al-Rizq.

"Kill only those who fight you!" proclaimed ʿĀʾishah, "and call out to those who are not ʿUthmān's killers to withdraw from us! For the killers of ʿUthmān are the only ones we are after. We will not start against anyone else." Ḥakīm then began the fighting, unintimidated[475] by the herald.[476] "Praise Allāh!" said Ṭalḥah and al-Zubayr, "for He has assembled those we wish to retaliate against among the Baṣrans. O Allāh! Do not spare a single one of them! Take retaliation against them today,[477] and kill them!"

---

470. Hinds, "Murder," 462.

471. ʿUthmān b. Ḥunayf.

472. ʿAbd al-Qays.

473. He killed a man.

474. Following Ibrāhīm and Wellhausen, 159. The text and *Addenda*, DCXXXII, have ʿUthmān bin Ḥunayf.

475. Reading *wa-lam yuraʿ* (stem I passive, Lane, 1187c) with Ibrāhīm and Wellhausen, 159. *Wa-lam yarʿu* (the text and *Glossarium*, CCLXV) would mean "not refraining because of" (Lane, 1108a). De Goeje, following Nöldeke, unnecessarily suggests emending it to *wa-lam yanziʿ* "did not incline to" (*Addendum*, DCXXXII).

476. Reading *munādī* for the text's *munādā*.

477. *Wa-aqid minhum al-yawm*. The ms. has *wa-aqdimhum li-al-yawm* "and bring them all on to the Day!"

So they fought them with all their might, and the fight could
not have been more fierce. There were four leaders, including
Ḥakīm. Ḥakīm faced Ṭalḥah, Dharīḥ[478] faced al-Zubayr, Ibn al-
Muḥarrish[479] faced ʿAbd al-Raḥmān b. ʿAttāb, and Ḥurqūṣ b.   [3130]
Zuhayr[480] faced ʿAbd al-Raḥmān b.[481] al-Ḥārith b. Hishām.[482]
Ṭalḥah advanced his army toward Ḥakīm, who had 300 men and
who began brandishing his sword and reciting:

I strike them with a stiff [sword],[483]
    as a frowning young man strikes,
Despairing of life,
    hankering after [heavenly] rooms

A man then struck his foot and cut it off. He crawled until he got
hold of it and threw it at his opponent. It hit him in the body and
knocked him down. Ḥakīm then went and killed him, propped
himself up against him, and recited:

Thigh of mine! Fear not!
    My arm is still with me,
And with it I will protect my shank.[484]

He then went on, in *rajaz* meter:

It is not to my shame that I die.
    Shame among people is fleeing.
Perishing does not make glory into disgrace.

A man then came up to Ḥakīm, half dead with his head on the
other man,[485] and asked, "What has happened to you, Ḥakīm?"
"I've been killed." "By whom?" "By my cushion." He then carried him off to be among seventy of his men. While standing on

---

478. Ibn ʿAbbād al-ʿAbdī was one of the main leaders of the Baṣran opposition to
the caliph ʿUthmān (Hinds, "Murder," 461).

479. Ibn ʿAbd ʿAmr al-Ḥanafī was another main leader of the Baṣran opposition
to the caliph ʿUthmān (Hinds, "Murder," 461).

480. Al-Saʿdī was the overall leader of the Baṣran opposition to the caliph
ʿUthmān (Hinds, "Murder," 461). Later he became a Khārijī opponent of ʿAlī.

481. From ʿAttāb to this word is missing from the ms.

482. Caskel and Strenziok, I, 23, II, 129.

483. No use using wood that is not seasoned and mature. See Humphreys, 214
for the same poem, with a slight difference.

484. This third verse added to the text from IA.

485. Reading ʿalā al-ākhar with Ibrāhīm and Wellhausen, 159; see *Addenda*,
DCXXXII) for the text's ʿalā ākhar.

one foot that day with the swords overcoming them, Ḥakīm said, without faltering as he said it: "When we left these two men they had given 'Alī allegiance and obedience. Then they come rebelling, waging war and seeking revenge for the blood of 'Uthmān b. 'Affān. They made a split between us,[486] when we were fellow citizens together and good neighbors. O Allāh! They don't want [retaliation for] 'Uthmān!"[487] "You scum!" someone cried out. "Now that Allāh's punishment bites you, you hide your grief behind the words of the one who promoted you and your followers for what you committed against the unjustly wronged imām and for splitting the community and shedding blood and gaining worldly goods. So taste the penalty[488] of Allāh and His vengeance, and take up residence [in hell], you and those with you!"

Dharīḥ and those with him were killed, but Ḥurqūṣ b. Zuhayr and a group of his followers escaped and took refuge with their tribe. Then Ṭalḥah and al-Zubayr's public announcer in al-Baṣrah called out, "Those of you who have anyone among your tribes who attacked Medina, bring him to us!" They were brought to them as dogs are and killed. Out of all the Baṣrans, only Ḥurqūṣ b. Zuhayr escaped—his tribe, Banū Sa'd, protected him. For this it paid very dearly and was given a time limit to release him. All this alienated Banū Sa'd. It was formerly allied to 'Uthmān, but now its people said, "We're pulling out of this dispute."[489]

The 'Abdīs joined in rage with Banū Sa'd because of those [seventy] of them who were killed after the battle and those who fled to them because they wanted to maintain obedience to 'Alī. Then Ṭalḥah and al-Zubayr ordered the troops to be given their pay, provisions, and [other] dues; and they gave the obedient ones bonuses. But 'Abd al-Qays and many of Bakr b. Wā'il[490] defected when they disdained to give *them* bonuses and rushed to the treasury. But the people there attacked them and inflicted casu-

[3131]

---

486. Baṣrans.
487. They want something else.
488. Cf. Qur'ān 5:95.
489. *Na'tazil.*
490. This tribe belonged to the same people—later known as Rabī'ah—as 'Abd al-Qays (*EI*[2], s.v.).

alties among them. This group[491] then left and set off down the road to ʿAlī.

Ṭalḥah and al-Zubayr then settled down in al-Baṣrah, the only revenge outstanding there being on Ḥurqūṣ, and wrote to the Syrians about what they had done and achieved:

> We came out to wage war and to uphold the Book of Allāh by carrying out Allāh's punishments on the high and the low, on the many and the few. Only Allāh himself can turn us away from all this. The cream of the Baṣrans and their best-bred gave us allegiance, and their dregs and their strangers rebelled against us. They forced us back with arms, saying, among other things, "We will take the Mother of the Faithful hostage" because she commanded them[492] to do right and encouraged them toward it! And Allāh showed them the example of the Muslims[493] time after time. Then, when there remained neither proof nor excuse, the killers of the Commander of the Faithful rushed headlong into battle and came out to their graves. None of them escaped to tell the tale except Ḥurqūṣ b. Zuhayr, and Allāh Most High will wreak vengeance on him, if He wills! They were as described by Allāh,[494] and we implore you by Allāh for the safety of your very souls—you must rise up as we have done. We will meet Allāh, and so will you, but we have already exonerated ourselves and fulfilled our duty.

[3132]

They sent this [to Syria] by the hand of Sayyār al-ʿIjlī and wrote similarly to the Kūfans by a man from Banū ʿAmr b. Asad[495] called Muẓaffar b. Muʿarriḍ. They wrote to the people of Yamāmah,[496] whose governor at that time was Sabrah b. ʿAmr al-ʿAnbarī, by al-Ḥārith al-Sadūsī,[497] and they wrote to the people

---

491. ʿAbdīs and Bakrīs.

492. Ibrāhīm wrongly has *amartahum*.

493. *Fa-aʿṭāhum . . . sunnat al-Muslimīn*, i.e., to try to reason with the opponent before taking up arms (*Glossarium*, CCCLXVII).

494. In the Qurʾān, i.e., in hell.

495. Of Rabīʿah (Caskel and Strenziok, I, 141, II, 172).

496. Some seventy miles southeast of present-day al-Riyādh.

497. Ibn Shujāʿ b. al-Ḥārith b. Sadūs? (Caskel and Strenziok, I, 153).

of Medina by Ibn Qudāmah al-Qushayrī, who secretly infiltrated among them.

ʿĀʾishah then wrote to the Kūfans by their messenger:

> After greetings. I am reminding you of Allāh and of Islam. Uphold the Book of Allāh by carrying out what it says: "Fear Allāh and hold on tight to His rope!"[498] Follow His Book, for we came to Baṣrah, and we appealed to them to uphold the Book of Allāh by carrying out His punishments. The upright among them responded to us, but the good-for-nothings received us with weapons and said, "We will certainly make you follow ʿUthmān [b. ʿAffān]."[499] [They said this] in order to increase[500] the ineffectiveness of the punishments [of Allāh], and they rebelled and accused us of unbelief and spoke very badly to us. But we recited the Qurʾānic verse: "Have you not seen those who have been given part of the Book? They are called to the Book of Allāh, that it may judge between them, [but. . . .]."[501] Some of them then acknowledged me but disagreed among themselves, so we let them be. But this didn't prevent those with the earlier opinion from drawing swords against my followers. ʿUthmān b. Ḥunayf insisted that their only course of action[502] was to fight me. But Allāh protected me with devout men, and He threw their trickery back in their faces.[503] We then spent twenty-six days inviting them to the Book of Allāh and to carry out His punishments, in this case with respect to the prevention of the shedding of blood of anyone who had not deserved capital punishment.[504] But they refused and produced various arguments, which we accommo-

[3133]

---

498. Conflation and contraction of parts of two verses, 3:102–3.

499. I.e., to the grave.

500. Reading *li-yazīdū* with Ibrāhīm rather than the text's *li-yartaddū* "forsake the punishments unenforced."

501. Qurʾān 3:23; see note 414, above, for the implication.

502. Reading *illā* with the text and Ibrāhīm for *illā mā* in the ms. De Goeje's suggested *lammā* (*Addenda*, DCXXXII) "urged them on when they fought," is unnecessary.

503. Lit., "throats."

504. Homicide does not in fact occasion *ḥadd* in classical law (*EI*2, s.v. Ḥadd).

dated. But they became afraid and treacherous; they became deceitful and ganged together.[505] But Allāh collected the blood revenge for 'Uthmān from them[506] and retaliated, and only one of them escaped. Allāh helped us and protected us from them by means of 'Umayr b. Marthad and Marthad b. Qays[507] and men from Qays and men from al-Ribāb[508] and al-Azd.[509] So [people of al-Kūfah] do not withdraw your approval from anyone except the killers of 'Uthmān b. 'Affān, that Allāh might receive His rights. Do not argue on behalf of the traitors,[510] or protect them, and do not approve of the attenuation[511] of Allāh's punishments, lest you join the ranks of the unjust. I am writing [this] to specific men. Stop the people's protecting these killers or assisting them, and remain in your houses. These men were not satisfied with what they did to 'Uthmān b. 'Affān and with splitting the togetherness of the community and going against the Book and the *sunnah*: they [went farther and] even accused us of unbelief over our commands and our encouragement to them to uphold the Book of Allāh and carry out His punishments. They spoke to us in a very bad way. But the devout disagreed with all this and found their words very serious. "You aren't satisfied with killing the imām," they said, "but even come out against the wife of your Prophet. For commanding you the truth you would kill her, the Companions of the Messenger of God, and the leaders of the Muslims!" Then they, and 'Uthmān b. Ḥunayf with them, [3134] cajoled whoever would join up with them—ignoramuses, riffraff, Zuṭṭ, and Sayābijah. So we took shelter from them

---

505. *Fa-khāfū wa-ghadarū wa-khānū wa-ḥasharū*. Wellhausen, 159, emends *fa-khāfū* to *fa-khānū* to make, in his view, a better rhetorical parallelism. De Goeje thinks Wellhausen had not noticed that *khānū* would then come twice and suggests *fa-ḥāfū* "but they acted unjustly" for the second element (*Addenda*, DCXXXII). Ibrāhīm omits "*wa-ḥasharū*."
506. Reading *tha'rahum* with Ibrāhīm for the text's *tha'rahu*.
507. From Madhḥij? (Caskel and Strenziok, I, 269).
508. Of Tamīm (Watt, 138).
509. Southern Arabs (*EI*[2], s.v.; Hawting, 54).
510. Ibrāhīm omits *'an*: "Do not quarrel with the traitors."
511. Lane, 989b.

with a section of the garrison, and this was how it was for twenty-six days. We were calling them to the truth and not to intervene between us and the truth, but they practiced deception and treachery. We did not do the same. They used Ṭalḥah and al-Zubayr's allegiance [to ʿAlī] as evidence against them, and they dispatched a messenger [to Medina], who returned to them with evidence [they were not wanting]. But they did not accept the truth and would not put up with it, so they came at me before first light to kill me and those with me who were fighting them. They continued until they reached the threshold of the house where I was staying. A guide was with them, leading them to me, but they found some men at the door of my house, among them ʿUmayr b. Marthad, Marthad b. Qays, Yazīd b. ʿAbdallāh b. Marthad, and some men from Qays, and some men from al-Ribāb and al-Azd. So the millstone ground them round—the Muslims encircled them and killed them. Thus Allāh caused all the Baṣrans to agree with Ṭalḥah and al-Zubayr's aims. So if we killed seeking our revenge, our excuse is more than sufficient.

The battle took place on 25 Rabīʿ II 36/21 October 656. ʿUbayd b. Kaʿb[512] held that it was in Jumādā.[513]

According to ʿUmar b. Shabbah—Abū al-Ḥasan—ʿĀmir b. Ḥafṣ—his teachers: It was a man called Ḍukhaym[514] from al-Huddān[515] who beheaded Ḥakīm b. Jabalah. His head was dangling backward, hanging on only by its skin, and his face was turned against his back. Ibn al-Muthannā al-Ḥuddānī said: "the man who killed Ḥakīm was Yazīd b. al-Asham al-Ḥuddānī. Ḥakīm was found killed between the dead bodies of Yazīd b. al-Asham and Kaʿb b. al-Asham.

[3135]   According to ʿUmar—Abū al-Ḥasan—Abū Bakr al-Hudhalī—Abū al-Malīḥ: When Ḥakīm b. Jabalah had been killed, they tried to kill ʿUthmān b. Ḥunayf, but he said: "As you wish, but Sahl b.

---

512. Caskel and Strenziok, I, 245/ 301/ II, 560.
513. I.e., at least five days later; cf. pp. 81, 133, below.
514. Or perhaps Suhaym; cf. the following Yazīd and text n. e.
515. Of al-Azd (Caskel and Strenziok, I, 216).

Hunayf is governor of Medina. If you kill me, he will retaliate on my behalf."[516] So they let him go.

They were at variance over [who should lead] the prayer, so 'Ā'ishah appointed 'Abdallāh b. al-Zubayr, and he led the prayer. Now al-Zubayr wanted the army to be given its pay and what was in the treasury to be divided, but 'Abdallāh his son pointed out, "If the army is paid it will disperse." So they agreed to put 'Abd al-Raḥmān b. Abī Bakr[517] in charge of the treasury.

According to 'Umar—Abū al-Ḥasan 'Alī—Abū Bakr al-Hudhalī[518]—al-Jārūd b. Abī Sabrah: It was the night when 'Uthmān b. Ḥunayf had been captured. In the square in front of Madīnat al-Rizq sat provisions for supplying the army. Now 'Abdallāh was about to supply his men with them, but Ḥakīm b. Jabalah had heard what had been done to 'Uthmān, and he said, "I have no fear of Allāh if I don't come to his aid!" so he went along with a company of men, mostly from 'Abd al-Qays but some from Bakr b. Wā'il. Ibn al-Zubayr then approached Madīnat al-Rizq and asked, "What do you want, Ḥakīm?" "We want to get supplies from these provisions," he replied, "and we want you to release 'Uthmān so that he can stay in the governor's house until 'Alī comes, as you agreed in writing between you. By Allāh! If I could find supporters against you with whom to smash you, I wouldn't put up with this from you, but I would kill the same number from you as you killed [from us]! To spill your blood is now in fact lawful for us, to the extent of those of our brothers you've killed. Do you have no fear of Almighty and Glorious Allāh! On what grounds do you consider the shedding of blood lawful?" "It was to repay 'Uthmān b. 'Affān's blood," replied Ibn al-Zubayr. "But those you killed, did they kill 'Uthmān?![519] Do you not fear Allāh's hatred?" he replied. But 'Abdallāh b. al-Zubayr said to him: "We will not supply you with any of these provisions. Nor will we release 'Uthmān b. Ḥunayf until he withdraws his allegiance to 'Alī." "O Allāh! You are a just arbiter. Be my witness!" exclaimed Ḥakīm, and, turning to his men, he said: "I have no doubts about

[3136]

---

516. *Intaṣar*; cf. Qur'ān 54:10.
517. The son of the first caliph (Caskel and Strenziok, I, 21, II, 128).
518. Sulmī b. 'Abdallāh (Caskel and Strenziok, I, 58, II, 518).
519. Whether a question or a statement, this is heavy sarcasm, to which 'Abdallāh has no reply.

fighting these men! Anyone who does, let them leave!" So he fought them, and a fierce battle ensued. A man struck Ḥakīm in the foot and cut it off,[520] so Ḥakīm grabbed it, hurled it, and hit him in the neck, knocking him down senseless. Ḥakīm b. Jabalah then crawled over to him, killed him, and rested his head against him. "Who killed you?" asked a passer-by. "My pillow."

Seventy from ʿAbd al-Qays were killed there. Al-Hudhalī added: Ḥakīm said the following verses when his foot was cut off:

When my courage faltered, I said
    to the foot, "Foot of mine! don't be frightened!
I still have my forearm to assist me."

ʿĀmir and Maslamah added: Ḥakīm's son al-Ashraf and brother al-Riʿl b. Jabalah[521] were killed with him.

According to ʿUmar—Abū al-Ḥasan—al-Muthannā b. ʿAbdallāh —ʿAwf al-Aʿrābī:[522] A man came up to Ṭalḥah and al-Zubayr while they were in the mosque in al-Baṣrah. "I ask you in Allāh's name," he said, "did the Messenger of God ever give the two of you any authority to set out like this?" Ṭalḥah rose [to go] and gave no reply, so the man adjured al-Zubayr, who said, "No, but we heard you had dirhams so we've come to share them with you!"

According to ʿUmar—Abū al-Ḥasan—Sulaymān b. Arqam— Qatādah—Abū ʿUmrah, the *mawlā* of al-Zubayr: When the Baṣrans gave allegiance to al-Zubayr and Ṭalḥah, al-Zubayr said, [3137] "Are there not a thousand horsemen to ride with me to ʿAlī?! I will attack him, either by night or in the morning, and I should kill him before he reaches us!"[523] But no one responded. "This really is the *fitnah*[524] we were told about!" he continued. "Do you call it a *fitnah* when you are fighting in it?!" his *mawlā* said to him. "We see, damn you! But we do not understand.[525] There's never before been a situation when I didn't know my next step, but with this one—I don't know whether I'm coming or going."

---

520. Omitted in Ibrāhīm.
521. Khayyāṭ wrongly "al-Zaʿl."
522. Occurs in an *isnād* in Humphreys, *Crisis*, 33.
523. ʿAlī was on the way to al-Baṣrah.
524. Dissension, civil war (*EI*², s.v.).
525. *Glossarium*, cxxxiv.

According to Aḥmad b. Manṣūr—Yaḥyā[526] b. Maʿīn—Hishām
b. Yūsuf the *qāḍī* of Ṣanʿāʾ—ʿAbdallāh b. Muṣʿab b. Thābit b.
ʿAbdallāh b. al-Zubayr—Mūsā b. ʿUqbah—ʿAlqamah b. Waqqāṣ al-
Laythī:[527] When Ṭalḥah and al-Zubayr and ʿĀʾishah set out, I noticed that Ṭalḥah preferred to sit alone and would flick his beard
against his chest.[528] So I said to him: "Abū Muḥammad! I see that
you prefer to sit alone and keep flicking your beard against your
chest. If there's something you dislike [going on], sit [and talk
about it]!" "ʿAlqamah b. Waqqāṣ," he replied to me, "we were all
united against others. But now we've become two mountains of
iron,[529] each seeking [to finish] the other. There was indeed something I did against ʿUthmān, and my penance for it can be nothing
less than having my blood spilled in the course of seeking vengeance for his blood." "So send Muḥammad b. Ṭalḥah back," I
said, "for you have an estate and households, and if something
happens[530] he can take your place." "I don't wish to stop anyone I
see active in this affair."[531] he replied. So I went to Muḥammad b.
Ṭalḥah and said: "Why don't you stay home? Then if something
happens to your father you can take his place in his households
and estate." "I don't want to be asking this man and that man[532]
about what happened to him," he replied.

According to ʿUmar b. Shabbah—Abū al-Ḥasan—Abū [3138]
Mikhnaf—Mujālid b. Saʿīd:[533] When ʿĀʾishah arrived at al-Baṣrah,
she wrote to Zayd b. Ṣūḥān:[534] "From ʿĀʾishah bint Abī Bakr,
Mother of the Faithful, beloved of the Messenger of God, to her
devoted son Zayd b. Ṣūḥān. After greetings. When this letter of
mine reaches you, come and assist us in this undertaking! If you
don't, then at least make the people abandon ʿAlī." He wrote back
to her: "From Zayd b. Ṣūḥān to ʿĀʾishah bint Abī Bakr al-Ṣiddīq,

---

526. Correcting the ms., according to p. 44, above.
527. From Kinānah, a Medinan traditionist, d. 65–86/685–705 (Caskel and
Strenziok, I, 39, II, 155).
528. I.e., brooding and depressed.
529. I.e., armies bristling with weapons.
530. I.e., if you die.
531. In retaliation for ʿUthmān, i.e., like his son Muḥammad.
532. IA's *al-rukbān* "the travelers" is perhaps better.
533. Kūfan transmitter (mostly from al-Shaʿbī), d. 144/762 (U. Sezgin, 210).
534. In al-Kūfah. He was an ʿAbdī and had been among the Kūfan opponents of
ʿUthmān (Abbott, *Aishah*, 153). He died in the Battle of the Camel (p. 132, below).

beloved of the Messenger of God. After greetings. If you withdraw from this undertaking and return home, then I will be your devoted son. If you don't, I will be the first to break with you." "May Allāh have mercy on the Mother of the Faithful!" said Zayd b. Ṣūḥān. "She was ordered to stay at home,[535] and we were ordered to fight. But she didn't do what she was ordered and ordered us to do it, and she did what we were ordered and ordered us not to do it!"

An Account of ʿAlī b. Abī Ṭālib's Advance toward al-Baṣrah

According to al-Sarī (in writing)—Shuʿayb—Sayf—ʿUbaydah b. Muʿattib—Yazīd al-Ḍakhm:[536] While ʿAlī was in Medina news reached him that ʿĀʾishah and Ṭalḥah and al-Zubayr were headed for al-Baṣrah, so he hurriedly set off hoping to catch up with them and turn them back.[537] But on reaching al-Rabadhah he learned that they had sped on ahead, so he set up camp there for a few days. He then heard that their army was making for al-Baṣrah, so he worried no more.[538] "No one likes me more than the Kūfans," he said, "and there are Arab chiefs and leaders there." He then wrote to them: "I have chosen you specially out of all the garrison cities, in preference to the others."[539]

[3139]   According to ʿUmar—Abū al-Ḥasan—Bishr[540] b. ʿĀṣim—Muḥammad b. ʿAbd al-Raḥmān b. Abī Laylā—his father: ʿAlī wrote to the Kūfans: "In the name of Allāh, the Merciful, the Compassionate. After greetings. I have chosen you specially and to live among you because of what I know of your friendship [to me] and love for Almighty and Glorious Allāh and for His Messenger. So whoever of you joins me and assists me has

---

535. Qurʾān 33:33; cf. p. 89, below.

536. For a similar report, but from Muḥammad and Ṭalḥah, see p. 53, above.

537. To Medina.

538. *Fa-surriya bi-dhālika ʿanhu wa-qāla inna ahl al-Kūfah.* (Cf. *surra bi-dhālika wa-qāla al-Kūfah* (p. 53, above).

539. Taking *wa-innī bi-al-uthrah* to mean *wa-innī istaʾthir ʿalaykum;* cf. note 370, above, and Prym's suggested inclusion *khaṣaṣtukum.* It could also be translated as "and I am taking preference."

540. Rather than Bashīr, here and in the next *isnād,* following *Addenda,* DCXXXII.

responded to the truth and fulfilled his duty [to Allāh]."

According to ʿUmar—Abū al-Ḥasan—Ḥibbān[541] b. Mūsā—Ṭalḥah b. al-Aʿlam and Bishr b. ʿĀṣim—Ibn Abī Laylā—his father: Muḥammad b. Abī Bakr and Muḥammad b. ʿAwn[542] were sent[543] to al-Kūfah, and the people went to Abū Mūsā to ask his advice about joining up. "As for the hereafter you should stay put, but as for the here and now you should join up. It's up to you!" When the two Muḥammads heard about these words of Abū Mūsā, they dissociated themselves from him and criticized him severely. But he replied: "By Allāh!Allegiance to ʿUthmān is still binding on me and binding upon your companion who sent you. If we are required to fight,[544] then before we do so, every single one of the killers of ʿUthmān, wherever he may be, would have to be killed."

It was the last day of Rabīʿ II 36/25 October 656 when ʿAlī [b. Abī Ṭālib] left Medina, and the sister of ʿAlī b. ʿAdī[545] from Banū ʿAbd al-ʿUzzā b. ʿAbd Shams said the following verse:

O Allāh! Hamstring ʿAlī [b. ʿAdī]'s camel!
   And bless not any camel that carries him!
ʿAlī b. ʿAdī is certainly not up to it.

According to ʿUmar—Abū al-Ḥasan—Abū Mikhnaf—Numayr b. Waʿlah[546]—al-Shaʿbī:[547] When ʿAlī had stopped at al-Rabadhah, a company of Banū Ṭayyiʾ[548] came to him. "Here is a company of Banū Ṭayyiʾ that have come to you," he was told. "Some want to join up with you; some want to greet you." "May Allāh reward all of them well! But 'Allāh has favored the fighters over the stay-at-homes with a great reward.'"[549] Then they entered, and ʿAlī asked, "What would you testify our position to be?" "Whatever you wish," they replied. "May Allāh reward you well!" he said.

[3140]

---

541. Following *Addenda*, DCXXXII, Ibrāhīm.

542. Or Muḥammad b. Jaʿfar; ʿAwn was Muḥammad's uncle, according to Prym.

543. Following Ibrāhīm's vocalization.

544. Or "If he wishes us to fight," reading *arādanā* for the text's *uridnā* (*Addenda*, DCXXXII).

545. Caskel and Strenziok, I, 14, II, 152. His sister is trying to keep him back.

546. Al-Hamdānī (U. Sezgin, 215).

547. ʿĀmir b. Sharāḥīl, d. 103/721 (U. Sezgin, 136).

548. A north Arabian tribe (Caskel and Strenziok, I, 176, 249, II, 555; Watt, 87–90).

549. Qurʾān 4:95.

"You became Muslims voluntarily, you fought the apostates, and you've paid your alms to poor Muslims in full."[550] Saʿīd b. ʿUbayd al-Ṭāʾī then rose and said: "Commander of the Faithful! Some people can express exactly what's in their minds. But Allāh knows! I can't do that. But I'll try my best. Allāh gives success. I know that I'll [always] give you my best advice, both secretly and openly, and I'll fight your enemies at every engagement. I will grant claims to you that I would not grant any of your contemporaries, because of your personal merit and your relationship [to the Prophet]." "May Allāh have mercy on you!" replied ʿAlī. "You've expressed your inner thoughts perfectly." He was killed with ʿAlī at Ṣiffīn, may Allāh have mercy on him!

According to al-Sarī (in writing)—Shuʿayb—Sayf—Muḥammad and Ṭalḥah: When ʿAlī had arrived and set up camp at al-Rabadhah, he sent Muḥammad b. Abī Bakr and Muḥammad b. Jaʿfar to al-Kūfah with a letter to [the Kūfans]: "I have chosen you specially out of all the garrison cities, and I am urgently asking help from you because of what has happened. So be supporters and helpers of Allāh's religion! Give us assistance, and join with us! To set things right is what we are after, so that the community [3141] may revert to being brothers. Whoever approves of this and chooses it has approved of the truth and chosen it. Whoever disapproves of this has disapproved of the truth and belittled it." So the two men went off; ʿAlī stayed in al-Rabadhah, making preparations. He sent to Medina, requesting animals and weapons. These came to him, and his force multiplied.

He then stood up among the people and delivered this sermon:

> Through Islam Almighty and Glorious Allāh has made us great, has lifted us up,[551] and has made us brothers after lowness and fewness, after mutual dislike and distance.[552] The people progressed in this way for as long as He willed, with Islam as their religion, the right on their side, and the Book as their imām. But then this man was struck by the hands of that faction that Satan had stirred

---

550. Ṭayyiʾ were predominantly Christian (Watt, 89–90).

551. The ms. could read wa-waffaqanā "and gave us success" for the text's wa-rafaʿanā.

552. Sajʿ: baʿd dhillah wa-qillah wa-tabāghuḍ wa-tabāʿud.

up to foment discord among this community. Mark my
words! This community will not escape becoming split,
just as previous communities split up. So we take refuge
in Allāh from the evil that will be!

He then continued:

What will be must without doubt come about. Mark my
words! This community will split into seventy-three
sects, the worst one being the one who professes my
cause but doesn't perform my work. Indeed you have lived
to see [this],[553] so hold fast to your religion, go aright with
your Prophet's guidance,[554] and follow his *sunnah*. Exam-
ine what is obscure to you against the Qur'ān, and hold
fast to what the Qur'ān tallies with and abandon what it
disagrees with. Be well satisfied with Glorious and Almighty Allāh as Lord, with Islam as religion, with
Muḥammad as Prophet, and with the Qur'ān as arbiter
and imām.

According to al-Sarī (in writing)—Shu'ayb—Sayf—Muḥammad
and Ṭalḥah: As 'Alī was about to leave al-Rabadhah for Baṣrah, a
son of Rifā'ah b. Rāfi'[555] came up to him and asked, "Commander
of the Faithful! What are you intending, and where are you taking
us?" "Our aim and intention," replied 'Alī, "is *iṣlāḥ*—if they
acknowledge our right and accept that from us."[556] "And if they
don't accept that from us?" he asked. "Then," replied 'Alī, "we'll
leave them[557] to make their justification, we'll give them the
right to have it, and we'll be patient." "And if they aren't satisfied
[with that]?" "We'll leave them alone as long as they leave us
alone." "And if they don't leave us alone?" "We'll defend ourselves against them." "This is a good attitude," said Rifā'ah's son.
Al-Ḥajjāj b. Ghaziyyah, one of the Anṣār, then stood up and said,

[3142]

---

553. IA adds "them."
554. IA has "go aright with my guidance, for it is your Prophet's guidance."
555. Al-Zuraqī al-Khazrajī, who fought at Badr as an opponent of 'Uthmān (Caskel and Strenziok, I, 192, II, 487).
556. I.e., without fighting.
557. Reading *nada'uhum* with Ibrāhīm, for the text's *nada'hum*, as also in the
next line (*nu'tihim* is clearly indicative). De Goeje (*Glossarium*, ccxl) suggests
nad'uhum "we'll call on them to present their justification."

"I'm going to satisfy you with action just as you've satisfied me with words," and he recited:

Catch up with it! Catch up with it before it slips away!
    Let us hurry and go up toward the clamor.
May my soul not find refuge if I fear death!

"By Allāh! I will help Almighty and Glorious Allāh, just as He called us Helpers."[558] The Commander of the Faithful then began the march. The vanguard was led by Abū Laylā b. ʿUmar b. al-Jarrāḥ,[559] with Muḥammad b. al-Ḥanafiyyah holding the banner. ʿAbdallāh b. ʿAbbās led the right flank and ʿUmar b. Abī Salimah or ʿAmr b. Sufyān b. ʿAbd al-Asad led the left. ʿAlī marched off with 760 men, and ʿAlī's poet versified for him:

Set off in companies, and advance quickly![560]
    For [ʿAlī] has decided. So be positive about it
Until you and they encounter one another on steeds,[561]
    with which we will beat Ṭalḥah and al-Zubayr.

[3143] He was in front of the Commander of the Faithful, ʿAlī, who was on a reddish-brown she-camel of his, pulling along a dark bay horse. At Fayd[562] they were met by a *ghulām* from Banū Saʿd b. Thaʿlabah b. ʿĀmir[563] called Murrah, who asked, "Who are all these?" "The Commander of the Faithful," came the reply. "A passing journey involving blood of passing souls!" he remarked. ʿAlī heard him and called him over and asked, "What's your name?" "Murrah." "May Allāh make your life bitter!"[564] said ʿAlī. "You're playing the soothsayer[565] for today, are you?"[566] "No, I'm an augur."[567]

---

558. *Anṣār.*
559. See p. 32, above, where the same men had charge of the same positions on leaving Medina.
560. Reading either the marginal gloss *wa-khubbū* or the text's *wa-ḥuththū.*
561. *Glossarium,* CCXXXIV. It is not clear exactly who "they" and "you" (pl.) are—perhaps *ahl al-bayt* and the present company.
562. Halfway between Mecca and al-Kūfah (Yāqūt, IV, 282).
563. Or ʿAmr, of Asad (Caskel and Strenziok, I, 171, II, 497).
564. *Amarra.*
565. *Kāhin (EI²,* s.v.).
566. Reading *al-yawm* with Ibrāhīm and *Glossarium,* CCLXXXIV for the text's *al-qawm:* "You're the army's soothsayer?"
567. *ʿĀ'if (EI²,* s.v.).

When they dismounted at Fayd, Asad and Ṭayyi' came to ʿAlī and put themselves at his service, but he said: "Stay at home! The Muhājirūn are enough." A Kūfan came to Fayd before ʿAlī had left. "Who's this man?" asked ʿAlī. "ʿĀmir b. Maṭar,"568 he replied. "Al-Laythī?" "No, al-Shaybānī." "Tell me your news!" said ʿAlī. He did so, and when ʿAlī questioned him about Abū Mūsā he replied, "If you want peace,569 then Abū Mūsā is the man; but, if you want to fight, then Abū Mūsā is not the man." "By Allāh!" said ʿAlī. "All I'm after is iṣlāḥ until it's completely rejected." "I've given you the news," he said and fell silent. ʿAlī also fell silent.

According to ʿUmar—Abū al-Ḥasan—Abū Muhammad—ʿAbdallāh b. ʿUmayr—Muḥammad b. al-Ḥanafiyyah: ʿUthmān b. Ḥunayf came to ʿAlī at al-Rabadhah with the hair of his head, beard, and eyebrows all plucked out and said: "Commander of the Faithful! When you sent me I had a fine beard, but I return to you beardless." "You've earned a great reward,"570 ʿAlī told him. "The people were ruled before me by two men who acted according to the Book. But when a third ruled them they said and did things. Then the people gave me allegiance. Ṭalḥah and al-Zubayr also gave me allegiance, but then they withdrew it and incited the people against me. How strange that they should comply with Abū Bakr and ʿUmar yet oppose me. By Allāh! They know very well that I'm no less of a man than any of those who've passed on. O Allāh! Undo what the two of them have contracted, do not ratify what they have consolidated, and show them the evil of what they've done!"

[3144]

According to al-Sarī (in writing)—Shuʿayb—Sayf—Muḥammad and Ṭalḥah: When ʿAlī dismounted at al-Thaʿlabiyyah571 news came of what had befallen ʿUthmān b. Ḥunayf and his guards. So he stood up and told the men the news and then said: "O Allāh! Spare me from the killing of Muslims that You have inflicted572 on Ṭalḥah and al-Zubayr, and deliver us from all these people!"

---

568. Layth is of Kinānah and Shaybān of Bakr b. Wāʾil, both northern tribes.
569. Al-ṣulḥ.
570. Often said to someone suffering misfortune.
571. According to Yāqūt (II, 78) this is about halfway along the Mecca-Kūfah road, as it is between al-Shuqūq and al-Khuzaymah, which stand at thirds.
572. Killing a believer deliberately earns hellfire (Qurʾān 4:93).

Then when he reached al-Isād news came of what had befallen Ḥakīm b. Jabalah and the killers of 'Uthmān b. 'Affān, so he said: "Allāh is great! Now that they have got their revenge, what will save me from Ṭalḥah and al-Zubayr and them [from me]?"[573] and he recited the verses from the Qur'ān "Whatever calamity may happen on earth or to yourselves has been written down before We bring it into being."[574] He then recited the verse of poetry

Ḥakīm called with the call of courage
    and dismounted as he did onto the battleground.

Then when they reached Dhū Qār 'Uthmān b. Ḥunayf got to them, and he had not a hair on his face. When 'Alī saw him, he looked at his companions and said,[575] "He left us as an elder and returned as a youth." 'Alī stayed at Dhū Qār waiting for[576] Muḥammad and Muḥammad.[577] News then reached 'Alī of what had befallen Rabī'ah and of the departure of 'Abd al-Qays and their taking to the road, and he said, "'Abd al-Qays is the best of Rabī'ah, and Rabī'ah is all good." He then recited:

How deeply I mourn for Rabī'ah,
    Rabī'ah who always heard [me] and obeyed.
Disaster fell upon them before I reached them.[578]
    'Alī offers a prayer to be heard
That thereby they may reach the highest station.

[3145]

Bakr b. Wā'il then presented themselves to 'Alī, and he replied to them as he had to Ṭayyi' and Asad.[579]

Now, when Muḥammad and Muḥammad arrived in al-Kūfah and took Abū Mūsā the Commander of the Faithful's letter and made 'Alī's orders known among the people, they were not[580] given any [positive] response. That evening some prominent wise men went to see Abū Mūsā and asked him, "what do you think about join-

---

573. I.e., the clash is now inevitable.
574. Qur'ān 57:22.
575. Jokingly to make 'Uthmān feel better.
576. *Yalūm* "criticizing," as in the manuscript, is unlikely.
577. Ibn Abī Bakr and Ibn 'Awn/Ja'far.
578. See a variant of this hemistich, p. 125, below.
579. I.e., "Stay at home!"; see p. 85, above.
580. Reading *lam* with Ibrāhīm, for the text's *fa-lam*·

ing up [with 'Alī]?" "Reason would have been possible yesterday,"[581] he replied, "but not today. What you gave no thought to in the past[582] is what has brought what you're witnessing down upon you. So what is left is two things, and that's all. Staying here leads to the hereafter; joining up leads to this world. So make your choice!" No one responded, so the two emissaries became angry and spoke roughly to Abū Mūsā. "By Allāh!" Abū Mūsā replied. "Allegiance to 'Uthmān is still binding on me and binding upon your companion. So, if there's no way out of fighting, the killers of 'Uthmān, wherever they may be, will have to be dealt with before we fight anyone." The two of them then left for 'Alī and reached him at Dhū Qār, where they gave him the news.

Now 'Alī had gone out with al-Ashtar, who had been in a hurry to go to al-Kūfah. 'Alī said, "You, Ashtar, advised us to keep Abū Mūsā as governor, and you are always objecting. So go, you and 'Abdallāh b. 'Abbās, and repair the mess you caused!" So 'Abdallāh b. 'Abbās left with al-Ashtar and came to al-Kūfah. There they spoke with Abū Mūsā and tried to rally support against him among some of the Kūfans. But Abū Mūsā said to the Kūfans: "[Remember!] I was your leader on the day of al-Jara'ah,[583] and I am your leader today." He then assembled the people and addressed them with this sermon:

> Men! The Companions of the Prophet, those who were with him on the battlefields, know more about Glorious and Almighty Allāh and about His Messenger than those who weren't Companions. So we [Companions] owe you [non-Companions] a duty,[584] and we will definitely fulfill it. Our advice was not to take Almighty and Glorious Allāh's authority lightly or be audacious before Him. The next piece of advice was that you should take those who had come to you from Medina and send them back there until they came to an agreement among themselves. For they know better than you who is right for the imamate,

[3146]

---

581. Before 'Uthmān was killed.
582. Killing 'Uthmān.
583. A battle on a sandy hill that took place between Muslims during 'Uthmān's time (Ibn Manẓūr, IX, 397 l. 4).
584. Giving sincere advice (ḥaqq al-naṣīḥah).

and you shouldn't get involved in the matter. But, as for what's happened now, it's an endless[585] *fitnah*. The one asleep in it is better off, than the one awake in it. The one awake in it is better off than the one who stays at home from it. The one who stays at home from it is better off than the one who stands in it. The one who stands in it is better off than the one who rides in it. So be the ones all the Arabs look to![586] Sheathe your swords, take off your spearheads, cut your bowstrings, and shelter the oppressed and the persecuted until this affair is over and this *fitnah* has been dispelled.

According to al-Sarī (in writing)—Shuʿayb—Sayf—Muḥammad and Ṭalḥah: When Ibn ʿAbbās returned to ʿAlī with the news, he called his son al-Ḥasan and sent him [to al-Kūfah]. With him he sent ʿAmmār b. Yāsir,[587] saying, "Go and set right what you've messed up!" So the two headed off and entered the mosque [in al-Kūfah]. The first man to come to them was Masrūq b. al-Ajdaʿ.[588] He greeted them and turned to ʿAmmār and asked: "Abū al-Yaqẓān! Why did you all kill ʿUthmān?" "For swearing at our women and beating our bodies!" ʿAmmār replied. "By Allāh!" said Masrūq and quoted:[589] " 'You have not punished as you were punished.[590] If only you had held back! Those holding back would have benefited.' " Abū Mūsā then came out and met al-Ḥasan and embraced him. He then turned to ʿAmmār and asked: "Abū al-Yaqẓān! Were you one of those who attacked the Commander of the Faithful, making yourself, along with the other profligates, liable for capital punishment?" "No, I did not," he replied. "Why do you abuse me?" But al-Ḥasan interrupted them; he turned to Abū Mūsā and asked: "Abū Mūsā! Why are you holding the people back from us? By Allāh! All we want is *iṣlāḥ*. The Commander of the Faithful

[3147]

---

585. *Ṣammāʾ*, lit., "deaf."

586. *Jurthūmah*, a prominent place where people might congregate (Ibn Manẓūr, XIV, 362; Lane, 404c), i.e., "stay in your places, so that others will follow suit."

587. Companion of the Prophet who fell at Ṣiffīn on ʿAlī's side (Caskel and Strenziok, I, 272, II, 167; *EI²*, s.v.).

588. Al-Hamdānī, a Kūfan scholar and traditionist (Caskel and Strenziok, I, 229, II, 401).

589. Qurʾān 16:126, modified so as to refer to the past, rather than the future.

590. I.e., you have overdone the retaliation.

is not the kind to be feared over anything." "You're right, and
you're more precious to me than my father and mother," he replied, "but the adviser should be trusted. I heard the Messenger of
Allāh say: 'It will be a *fitnah*. The sitter will be better off than the
stander, the stander than the walker, the walker than the rider.'
Almighty and Glorious Allāh made us brothers. He made our
property and blood forbidden to each other when He said: 'Believers! Do not consume each other's capital in foolish pur-
suits . . . and do not kill each other! Allāh has great concern for
you.'[591] Glorious and Almighty Allāh also said the verse that
begins[592] 'Whoever kills a believer deliberately, hell is his punishment.'" 'Ammār got angry at this. He spoke harshly to him and
stood up and said: "All of you listen! It was only to him personally
that the Prophet said, 'You're better sitting in it than standing.'"[593]
"Shut up, you slave!"[594] said a Tamīmī, standing up. "Only yesterday you were with the riffraff, and today you insult our commander!" Then Zayd b. Ṣūḥān and his group got up, and so did the rest of
the people, but Abū Mūsā began restraining them. He then hurried
to the *minbar*, and the people fell silent. Meanwhile, Zayd came on
his donkey and stopped at the door of the mosque. He was carrying
ʿĀʾishah's two letters, the one to himself[595] and the one to the
Kūfan people. He had asked her to write a general public letter and
had put it with his own. He therefore was coming with both, with   [3148]
the private letter and the public one, which said: "After greetings.
Take no action, people [of al-Kūfah], and stay in your houses, except
against the killers of ʿUthmān b. ʿAffān." When he had finished
reading, he said: "She was given an order and we were given an
order. She was ordered to stay at home,[596] and we were ordered to
fight until all *fitnah* had gone.[597] But she's ordering us to do what

---

591. Qurʾān 4:29.
592. Qurʾān 4:93, which continues, "forever and ever. Allāh's anger and curse is
upon him and He has prepared an enormous punishment for him." Ibrāhīm omits
"*al-āyah.*"
593. The Prophet had had a sharp altercation with him one day, and Abū Mūsā
had repented.
594. ʿAmmār was black. He was the son of a *mawlā* of the Makhzūmī Abū
Ḥudhayfah (*EI*², s.v.).
595. See p. 79, above; Abbott, *ʿAishah*, 153.
596. Qurʾān 33:33; cf. p. 80, above.
597. Qurʾān 2:193.

she was ordered and taking on herself[598] what we were ordered to do!" But up stood Shabath b. Ribʿī[599] and called out, "You ʿUmānī!" (Zayd was from ʿAbd al-Qays of ʿUmān, not from the Baḥraynīs).[600] "You stole at Jalūlāʾ,[601] and Allāh cut off your [hand]. You've disobeyed the Mother of the Faithful, so may Allāh kill you![602] What Almighty and Glorious Allāh ordered concerning *iṣlāḥ* among the people[603] was all that she was ordered. By the Lord of the Kaʿbah! You spoke and the people became incited."[604]

Then Abū Mūsā stood up and addressed the people:

> Obey me, and be the ones all the Arabs look to![605] The oppressed will come to you for shelter, and the afraid will find safety with you. We are the Companions of Muḥammad. We're better able to understand his words "When the *fitnah* approaches it confuses; when it retreats it makes things clear. *Fitnah* rips [the community] apart like a stomach ulcer. The winds fan it, from the north and south, from the east and west. Then it dies down for a while, but where it arises from no one knows. It renders the wise man inexperienced." Sheathe your swords,[606] snap your spears, throw away your arrows, cut your bowstrings, and stay in your houses! Leave Quraysh—for[607] they've insisted on leaving Medina and on separating from those who know about the leadership—to mend its own tear and repair its own split. If it succeeds, then it will bring good things on itself; if it doesn't, then it will

[3149]

---

598. *Wa-rakibat mā umirnā bihi*. Abbott, *ʿAishah*, 154–55 translates "while she rides to carry out the orders. . . .

599. Of Tamīm; he became a Khārijī after Ṣiffīn (Caskel and Strenziok, I, 68, II, 521).

600. Shabath was probably from these. Calling Zayd ʿUmānī was derogatory.

601. He confessed. A station in Iraq on the Khurāsān road, east of the Tigris, 34°10′ N, 45° E (*EI²*, s.v.).

602. For the fulfilment of this wish, see p. 132, below.

603. Qurʾān 49:9–10.

604. Ibrāhīm notes that the text is obscure.

605. See p. 88, above.

606. Cf. p. 88, above.

607. Reading *idh*, following Ibrāhīm and Wellhausen (159), for the text's *idhā*. Leaving Quraysh means leaving ʿAlī, ʿĀʾishah, Ṭalḥah, and al-Zubayr.

bring death on themselves. Its oil[608] will flow on its skin. Trust me! Don't think I'm deceiving you! If you obey me you'll be safe spiritually and temporally, and those who caused this *fitnah* will suffer the blast of its heat.

Then Zayd stood up, lifted his handless arm, and said: "'Abdallāh b. Qays![609] Turn the Euphrates back on is course! Turn it back on itself to its source! If you can do that then you'll be able to do what you're proposing. No! Leave what you're incapable of achieving alone!" Then he recited two verses from the Qur'ān:[610] "*Alif, lam, mim*. Do the people think that they will be left alone saying 'We believe' and not be tested [by *fitnah*]?" and added, "Go and join the Commander of the Faithful and the Head of the Muslims! Do it quickly, all of you! And you'll be making the right decision."

Al-Qa'qā' b. 'Amr then stood up and said: "I give you all sincere advice. I'm concerned about you. I want[611] you to be correctly guided, so I will certainly tell you the whole truth. What the governor said is the correct course of action, if only it were possible. But as for what Zayd said—and Zayd [remember] is a part of[612] this *fitnah*—don't any of you be advised by him. No one who has launched into or embraced this *fitnah* will [be able to] extricate himself from it. The only view that really makes sense is [3150] that we have to have leadership to organize the people, to restrain the oppressor and strengthen the oppressed. Here is 'Alī. He is governing. He has been just in what he has called for, and that has been for *iṣlāḥ* and nothing else. So disperse, but keep your eyes and ears open to see how things develop!"[613]

Then Sayḥān[614] said: "Men! This situation and these people have to have a leader who will ward off the oppressor and strengthen the oppressed and unite the people. This leader of yours is calling you so that the dispute between him and his two companions

---

608. Reading *samnuhā*. Cf. Freytag, I, 614.
609. Abū Mūsā.
610. Qur'ān 29:12. Abū Mūsā's position is un-Qur'ānic.
611. The ms. has a number of questionable readings over the next few lines.
612. Ibrāhīm omits *hādhā*, and IA has *'aduww* "Zayd is totally against," requiring a different meaning for *al-amr*.
613. Be witnesses.
614. Zayd's brother. The ms. has *Ṣuḥār*.

may be looked into. He has been entrusted with the community. He is the one with insight into religion, so whoever joins up with him we'll go along with them." ʿAmmār had calmed down after his initial outburst. When Sayḥān had finished his sermon he spoke up and said: "Here is the paternal cousin of the Messenger of Allāh calling you out against the wife of the Messenger of Allāh and Ṭalḥah and al-Zubayr. I bear witness that she is his wife in the hereafter as well as this life,[615] so consider very carefully what is right, and then fight on its side!" Someone replied: "Abū al-Yaqẓān! The right is with the person about whom you bore witness that she will be in paradise and against the one about whom you didn't do so." "Desist, ʿAmmār!" said al-Ḥasan. "*Iṣlāḥ* has its proponents."[616]

Al-Ḥasan b. ʿAlī then stood up and said: "Men! Respond to the call of your commander, and go join your brothers, for there will be those who hasten to him for this affair. By Allāh! That the controllers of the affair should be those with wisdom[617] is both better in this world and more beneficial in the next. So answer our call and assist us against this affliction of ours and yours!" The people were indeed sympathetic and responded favorably to al-Ḥasan.

Then some tribesmen from Ṭayyiʾ[618] came to ʿAdī[619] and asked: "What do you think? What are your orders?" "We'll wait and see what the people do." When ʿAdī was told of al-Ḥasan's undertaking and what opinions had been voice, he said: "We gave allegiance to this man ʿAlī, and he summoned us to something good and to look into this critical new situation. So we are going along and looking." Hind b. ʿAmr[620] then stood up and spoke: "The Commander of the Faithful summoned us and sent messengers to

[3151]

---

615. ʿAmmār is here showing his impartiality.

616. I.e., my father ʿAlī and not you. ʿAmmār had not been doing too well; cf. p. 88, above.

617. I.e., ʿAlī's family or the addressees (in flattery).

618. An important north Arabian tribe (Caskel and Strenziok, I, 176, 249, II, 555).

619. Ibn Ḥātim, their leader, originally a Christian, fought at Qādisiyyah, and with ʿAlī at the battles of the Camel, Ṣiffīn, and Nahrawān (Caskel and Strenziok, I, 256, II, 139).

620. Al-Jamalī of Madhḥij, killed in the Battle of the Camel by ʿAmr b. Yathribī al-Ḍabbī (Caskel and Strenziok, I, 271, II, 283).

us, and now his son has come to us. So listen to what he says, and
join his command. Hasten to the side of your commander! Look
into this matter with him, and support him with your opinions!"
Ḥujr b. ʿAdī[621] then stood up and spoke: "Respond, all of you, to
the Commander of the Faithful. 'Hasten to fight! both light and
heavy.'[622] Agree to it! I'll be the first of you." Then al-Ashtar got
up and mentioned the Jāhiliyyah and its severity and Islam and its
ease and went on to mention ʿUthmān. Al-Muqaṭṭaʿ b. al-
Haytham b. Fujayʿ al-ʿĀmirī al-Bukkāʾī then went up to al-Ashtar
and said: "Silence! Allāh make you ugly! A dog should be left
alone with its barking!" So the people rose up and made al-Ashtar
sit down, and al-Muqaṭṭaʿ stood and said: "After this we cannot
put up with anyone coming along with bad comments about one
of our imāms. ʿAlī is sufficient in our opinion. By Allāh! If people
like this[623] disagree with ʿAlī, then let a man bite[624] his tongue in
these meetings of ours! Accept therefore what al-Ḥasan and ʿAmmār are urging you to do!" "The old man is right" said al-Ḥasan
and spoke up: "Listen, men! I set off early tomorrow morning, so   [3152]
let whoever wishes come out with me by land and whoever
wishes by water."[625] Nine thousand set off with him—some by
land, others on the water. Each seventh had its commander. Six
thousand two hundred went on land, 2,800[626] by water.

According to Naṣr b. Muzāḥim al-ʿAṭṭār—ʿUmar b. Saʿīd—Asad
b. ʿAbdallāh—a scholar contemporary with the events:[627] ʿAbd
Khayr al-Khaywānī[628] went up to Abū Mūsā and asked him,
"Were these two—that is, Ṭalḥah and al-Zubayr—among those
who gave allegiance to ʿAlī?" "Yes," he replied. "Did he do something bad to permit withdrawing allegiance to him?" "I don't
know." "May you not know! And we'll not follow you until you
do know! Abū Mūsā! Do you know anyone not involved in this

---

621. Of Kindah; he fought at Qādisiyyah, and with ʿAlī at the battles of the
Camel and Ṣiffīn (Caskel and Strenziok, I, 236, II, 329).
622. Qurʾān 9:41, a call to *jihād*.
623. Prym's possible emendation, *ḥakā*, is difficult.
624. I.e., keep tight-lipped (Freytag, II, 694).
625. The Euphrates.
626. According to IA, 2,400.
627. Cf. p. 52, above.
628. Of Hamdān (Caskel and Strenziok, II, 125).

fitnah, as you claim it to be? Only four parties[629] remain—ʿAlī behind Kūfah, Ṭalḥah and al-Zubayr in Baṣrah, Muʿāwiyah in Syria, and another party in the Ḥijāz, where no booty is gained and no enemy is fought." "There are no better people than they," replied Abū Mūsā, "where there is a *fitnah*." "Your deception has got the better of you, Abū Mūsā!" said ʿAbd Khayr.

[3153]   Now al-Ashtar had gone to ʿAlī and said, "Commander of the Faithful! I already sent a man before these two, but I didn't see him sort anything out or get control over anything. These two are the most likely of those you've sent to get the matter sorted out in the way you wish, but I don't know what will happen. So if you—may Allāh ennoble you!—were to think of sending me after them [I think it would be good], for the Kūfans are my most loyal followers. If I went to them I don't expect a single one would oppose me." "Catch them up, then!" ʿAlī told him. So al-Ashtar headed for Kūfah, and when he got there the men had all gathered in the Great Mosque. So every tribe he passed that he saw had a group sitting together or in a mosque he would invite, "Follow me to the castle!" So he reached the castle with a large following and broke in and entered. Now Abū Mūsā was standing addressing the people in the mosque and telling them to hold back. "Men!" he said. "This *fitnah* is blind and deaf. It is trampling on its halter.[630] The sleeper in it is better off than the sitter.[631] The sitter in it is better off than the stander. The stander in it is better off than the walker. The walker in it is better off than the runner. The runner in it is better off than the rider. It is a *fitnah* that rips [the community] apart like a stomach ulcer.[632] It has come at you from the place where you were safe and leaves the wise man bewildered like someone without experience.[633] We, the congregation of the Companions of Muḥammad, are better able to understand the *fitnah*—when it approaches it confuses and when it retreats it discloses."[634] ʿAmmār then heckled him, and al-Ḥasan said to

---

629. Reading *firaq* following Ibrāhīm and de Goeje (*Addenda*, DCXXXIII) for the text's *qurūn* "leaders" (*Glossarium*, CDXXII).

630. I.e., it is out of control.

631. Cf. p. 89, above.

632. Cf. p. 90, above.

633. Cf. p. 90, above.

634. Cf. p. 90, above.

him: "Resign from the governorship over us! You with no mother![635] Step down from our *minbar*!" "Did you hear this from the
Messenger of Allāh?" asked ʿAmmār. "Here's my hand to prove
what I say,"[636] replied Abū Mūsā. "The Messenger of Allāh was
saying something specifically to you," ʿAmmār said to him,
"when he said, 'You're better off sitting than you will be standing
in it.'"[637] ʿAmmār added, "Allāh overcomes whoever struggles   [3154]
against Him and rejects His words!"

According to Naṣr b. Muzāḥim al-ʿAṭṭār—ʿUmar b. Saʿīd—a
man—Nuʿaym—Abū Maryam al-Thaqafī: By Allāh! I was in the
mosque that day when ʿAmmār was addressing Abū Mūsā and
saying those words to him, when out came some of Abū Mūsā's
*ghulām*s to us. They were aggravatedly calling out: "Abū Mūsā!
This man al-Ashtar entered the castle, beat us, and threw us out."
So Abū Mūsā came down [from the *minbar*] and entered the castle, but al-Ashtar shouted at him: "Get out of our castle, mother-
less man! May Allāh eject your soul! By Allāh! You have been one
of the secret dissenters[638] for a long time!" "Just give me this
evening," he requested. "You may have it, but you're definitely
not sleeping in the castle tonight." Men then entered and were
rifling Abū Mūsā's belongings, but al-Ashtar stopped them and
sent them out of the castle. "I've expelled him,"[639] he said, and
held the men back from him.

The Commander of the Faithful Dismounts
at Dhū Qār

According to al-Sarī (in writing)—Shuʿayb—Sayf—ʿAmr—al-
Shaʿbī: When they congregated at Dhū Qār ʿAlī received them
with a group, which included Ibn ʿAbbās. He then welcomed
them. "Men of al-Kūfah!" he said. "It was you who repelled the
power of the Sasanians and their kings. You scattered their troops,
and their inheritances fell to you. You enriched[640] your territory

---

635. A milder form of *lā abā lak*!
636. I.e., you can cut it off if I'm lying.
637. Cf. p. 89, above.
638. *Munāfiqīn*; see *EI*², s.v.
639. I.e., that is sufficient.
640. IA, "protected."

and assisted the Muslims against their enemy. So I am calling you to witness our Baṣran brothers with us. What we want is that they regain their senses, but if they persist we'll treat them with gentleness and keep ourselves apart from them as long as they don't initiate any injustice against us. Allāh willing, we won't neglect any course of action that might improve the situation. We'll choose it rather than one that will make things worse. There is no power except with Allāh!"

[3155]

Seven thousand two hundred gathered at Dhū Qār. The whole of ʿAbd al-Qays also were waiting to join ʿAlī as he passed them on his way to Baṣrah, and they were . . .[641] thousand. A further 2,400 were on the river.

According to al-Sarī (in writing)—Shuʿayb—Sayf—Muḥammad and Ṭalḥah (their transmission): When ʿAlī dismounted at Dhū Qār he sent three lots of envoys [to al-Kūfah]: Muḥammad b. Abī Bakr with Muḥammad b. Jaʿfar, then Ibn ʿAbbās with al-Ashtar, then his son al-Ḥasan with ʿAmmār. Everyone who had been active rushed to join in this cause—it was not that the leaders were sending in their men. There were 5,000 of them, half going by land and half by river. Those who had not yet been active or become involved, but had given ʿAlī their obedience,[642] also rushed to join and teamed up with the moderates.[643] They were 4,000. The leaders of the moderates were al-Qaʿqāʿ b. ʿAmr, Saʿr b. Mālik,[644] Hind b. ʿAmr, and al-Haytham b. Shihāb. The leaders of the activists were Zayd b. Ṣūḥān, al-Ashtar Mālik b. al-Ḥārith, ʿAdī b. Ḥātim, al-Musayyab b. Najabah,[645] and Yazīd b. Qays.[646] These all had with them their allies and other men similar to them, who were not inferior except that they were not given actual command, like Ḥujr b. ʿAdī[647] and Ibn Maḥdūj al-

---

641. The number had fallen out of the text even before IA's time.

642. Reading *wa-kāna ʿalā ṭāʿatihi* (Ibrāhīm and *Addenda*, DCXXXIII) for the text's *wa-kāna ʿAlī ẓāʿinan*: "So ʿAlī set off."

643. *Al-jamāʿah*. For this translation and "activists" for *nuffār*, see Hinds, "Kūfan Political Alignments," 361. Both groups were early comers to Kūfah.

644. Following Ibrāhīm and *Addenda*, DCXXXIII. The text has Saʿd.

645. Al-Qurashī (Caskel and Strenziok, I, 131, II, 436).

646. Probably Ibn Tammām from Hamdān (Caskel and Strenziok, I, 231, II, 596).

647. Ibn Ḥātim. He led the Kūfans against Muʿāwiyah.

Bakrī.[648] There was no other Kūfan of another opinion, and they
hastened to war, all except a few.   [3156]

When they dismounted at Dhū Qār ʿAlī called al-Qaʿqāʿ b. ʿAmr
and sent him to the Baṣrans, saying, "Ibn al-Ḥanẓaliyyah! (al-
Qaʿqāʿ was a Companion of the Prophet) Go and see these two
men! Invite them to friendship and unity, and stress the evil of
schism. What are you going to do about any proposal from the two
of them on which you don't have my advice?" "We'll present
them with your orders. If they propose something that we don't
have your view on, we'll exert our own judgment and make our
comments on the basis of what we hear and consider necessary."
"You're the right man for the situation" replied ʿAlī.

So al-Qaʿqāʿ left and went to al-Baṣrah.[649] He first went to
ʿĀʾishah and greeted her: "Dear Mother! What compelled you to
come to this city?" "My dear son! *Iṣlāḥ* between the Muslims."
"Would you send for Ṭalḥah and al-Zubayr," he asked, "so you can
hear what I and the two of them have to say?" She did so, and they
came. "I asked the Mother of the Faithful what compelled her to
come to this region," said al-Qaʿqāʿ, "and she said '*Iṣlāḥ* between
the Muslims.' What do you two say? Do you share her opinion or
not?" "We share it," the two replied. "So describe to me what this
iṣlāḥ means. By Allāh! If we understand the same thing by it,[650]
then we will certainly be reconciled, but, if we don't understand
the same thing by it, then we will not." "Punishing the killers of
ʿUthmān," the two replied. "Neglecting that would be neglect of
the Qurʾān, but carrying it out would be giving life to the Qurʾān."
"But you've already killed those killers of ʿUthmān from Baṣrah,"
said al-Qaʿqāʿ, "and before you killed them you were nearer to the
right way than you are now. You killed 600 men bar one, and 6,000
became enraged for their sake and withdrew from your cause and
deserted you! When you then searched for the one who escaped
(meaning Ḥurqūṣ b. Zuhayr) 6,000 protected him and were ready   [3157]
to fight. So if you make an exception of him you'll be abandoning

---

648. Ḥudhayfah or Ḥassān? For Ibn Maḥdūj b. Bishr, see Caskel and Strenziok, I,
154.
649. Muir, 247; Abbott, *Aishah*, 155.
650. Ibrāhīm omits *hu* from the text's *ʿarafnāhu*.

your position,[651] and, if you fight them and those who have withdrawn from you[652] and the battle goes against you, then what you will have feared but drawn near to will be far worse, as far as I can see, than your worst fears. For you will have enraged the Muḍar and Rabī'ah of this region, such that they will gather against you in war and forsake you in support of these 6,000, just as those gathered to support the perpetrators of this huge crime and terrible sin." "So what do you suggest?" asked the Mother of the Faithful. "I say that the remedy for this situation is to quiet things down," he replied. "If it calms down, they[653] will tremble. So if you all give us allegiance then that will be a promising sign and tidings of mercy. It will cause the attainment of blood revenge for this man and well-being and safety for this community. But, if you refuse and insist strongly on your own opinion in this affair and on forcing it, then this will be an evil sign and the squandering of the blood revenge and cause Allāh to send instability through this community. So choose well-being, and you'll fare well by it and be reasons for good as you were in the past. Don't lay either us or yourselves open to disaster, lest it throw us all down. I swear to Allāh, I say this and call you to it in a state of fear that this won't end until Almighty and Glorious Allāh has taken what He wants from this community whose provisions[654] are diminishing with these events. The damage that has occurred from this affair is incalculable. It isn't like other situations. It isn't like a man killing another man or a group killing one man or even a whole tribe killing one man."[655] "Yes," they replied, "you've spoken well and you're absolutely right. So return! And if 'Alī comes with a similar position to yours, then the affair will have resolved itself." So he returned to 'Alī and told him what had happened, and he was pleased. So the armies were on the threshold of peace, some disliking it and others approving.

[3158]

The Baṣran delegations came to 'Alī while he was camped at

---

651. Of killing all of them.

652. The 6,000.

653. The killers of 'Uthmān, who will be seized and punished individually (*Glossarium*, ccxxix).

654. *Matā'*: perhaps in the hereafter.

655. But the whole community.

Dhū Qār. Before al-Qa'qā' had returned, those[656] of Tamīm and
Bakr came to find out what their fellow tribesmen from al-Kūfah
thought and why they had mobilized. They came to tell him that
their position was *islāh* and that they didn't entertain any idea of
fighting. When they told their Kūfan clansmen the opinion that
their Basran clansmen had sent them with,[657] the Kūfans replied
to them with the same words and then took them in to 'Alī and
told him their news. 'Alī then asked Jarīr b. Sharis about Talhah
and al-Zubayr. He told him everything about their situation in
detail, and quoted:

Go tell Banū Bakr as a messenger—
    because there is no way to Banū Ka'b—
"The man of virtue and long forearms[658]
    will make your oppression that came from you return back
    to you."

'Alī added at that time:

Do you not know, Abū Sim'ān, that we
    send back the chief like you with a headache?!
His mind becomes deranged from the war such that
    he stands and responds to callers who are not there.
All Bakr gathered and defended Khuzā'ah,
    but you, Surāqah, you have no defense!

Abū Ja'far [al-Tabarī] said, "Ziyād b. Ayyūb drew up a book for   [3159]
me containing reports from teachers from whom he said he had
heard directly [and then written down]. Some he read to me, and
others he did not. One of those he did not read to me but that I
copied from his book goes as follows.[659]

According to [Ziyād b. Ayyūb—] Mus'ab b. Salām al-Tamīmī—
Muhammad b. Sūqah—'Āsim b. Kulayb al-Jarmī—his father:
During the time of 'Uthmān b. 'Affān I had a dream. I saw a man
who was ruling the people while he was ill in bed, and a woman
was by his head. The people were after him and hastened toward

---

656. Reading *wufūd* with Ibrāhīm for the text's *wafd*.
657. *Islāh*.
658. I.e., good with the sword in battle.
659. Cf. Ibn 'Abd Rabbihi, II, 278.

him,[660] and had she forbidden them they would have stopped. But she did not, so they seized and killed him. I used to recount this dream of mine to everyone, whether settled or nomad, and they were surprised and did not know what it meant.

Then when ʿUthmān was killed the news reached us as we were returning from a raid, and my companions said, "Your dream, Kulayb!" We then got to Baṣrah, and we had not been there long when someone said, "Ṭalḥah and al-Zubayr are coming, and the Mother of the Faithful is with them!" This alarmed the people and they were surprised, but they were claiming to the people that they had only come out of anger over ʿUthmān and in penance over the way they had not supported him. The Mother of the Faithful spoke up: "We became angry at ʿUthmān on your behalf because of three things he did: giving command to youths, expropriating common property,[661] and beating with whip and stick. But we wouldn't be acting justly if we weren't angry at you on his account for three things that you perpetrated against him: the sanctity of the month,[662] city, and blood." The people replied, "But didn't you give allegiance to ʿAlī and agree to his command?" "We agreed," they replied, "with the sword at our necks." "Here is ʿAlī approaching you" someone said.

Our people said to me and two men with me, "Go and find ʿAlī and his men and ask them about all this. We're confused about it." So we set off. But as we neared the camp a handsome fellow on a mule was coming toward us. I asked my two companions, "Did you remember the woman I told you about, who was by the head of the ruler? She looked just like this man." He realized that we were discussing him so when he got up to us he said: "Stop! What did you say when you saw me?" We refused to say so he shouted at us, "By Allāh! You won't leave until you've told me!" At this we became frightened of him, so we told him. He then said as he went past us, "By Allāh! You saw something extraordinary." We asked the first person from the camp we came across, "Who was that?" "Muḥammad b. Abī Bakr," he replied, so we realized

[3160]

---

660. *Wa-yabhashūn ilayhi*; cf. p. 3, above.

661. *Mawqiʿ al-ghamāmah*, lit. "the place of cloud," hence herbage; see Ibn Manẓūr, XV, 340.9ff. (*iḥmāʾ*); Wellhausen, 160.

662. Dhū al-Ḥijjah.

that the woman was 'Ā'ishah[663] and our dislike of what she was doing increased. When we reached 'Alī and had greeted him, we asked him what was going on. "When the people rose against this man I kept away," he said. "Then they killed him and made me ruler against my will. But for anxiety for the religion I wouldn't have acceded to them. Then these two suddenly reneged, but I didn't let them get away with it and extracted promises from them before letting them go on the *'umrah* pilgrimage. They then came to their mother, the wife of the Messenger of Allāh, and they approved for her what they disapproved of for their own wives[664] and exposed her to things that were taboo to them and were no good. So I pursued them both to stop them ripping Islam apart and splitting the unity." Then his followers added: "By Allāh! We don't want to fight unless they do so first. *Iṣlāḥ* is all we've come out for." 'Alī's followers then shouted at us, "Give allegiance! Give allegiance!" My two companions did so but not I. I held back and said, "My people sent me for a particular purpose, so I'm not going to do anything new until I return to them." "And if they don't do it?" asked 'Alī. "Then neither will I," I replied. "Imagine they sent you out to scout," said 'Alī, "and on returning you brought them news of pasture and water but they turned away to waterless, dry areas. What would you do?" "I'd leave them," I replied, "and go to the pasture and water without them."   [3161] "Then stretch out your hand!" he replied. By Allāh! I could not resist, and I opened my hand and gave him allegiance. Afterward he used to say, "'Alī was one of the smartest of the Arabs." 'Alī then asked, "What have you heard about Ṭalḥah and al-Zubayr?" "As for al-Zubayr," I replied, "he says, 'We were forced to give allegiance,' and, as for Ṭalḥah he's keen to quote verses, and so he says:

Go tell Banū Bakr as a messenger—
    because there is no way to Banū Ka'b—
"The man of virtue and long forearms
    will make your oppression that came from you return to
    you."

---

663. Muḥammad b. Abī Bakr's sister.
664. Cf. p. 62, above, p. 126, below. There are no illicit implications (Caetani, IX, 41, n. 1).

"It wasn't like that," said ʿAlī, "but:

Do you not know, Abū Simʿān, that we
    deafen the chief like you with a headache?!
His mind becomes deranged from the war such that
    he stands and responds to callers who are not there."

Then ʿAlī marched off until he set up camp on the outskirts of Baṣrah. Ṭalḥah and al-Zubayr had had a trench dug. Our Baṣran companions asked us, "What did you hear [that] our Kūfan brothers want and say?" "They say, 'We've come for peace, and we don't want to fight,'" we replied. Suddenly while they were engaged in this way, not talking about anything other than peace, young boys emerged from the two armies, hurling insults at each other and then stones. They were followed by the slaves of the two armies, who were followed in turn by the foolhardy men. War broke out, forcing them[665] to take cover back in the trench. Fighting ensued there until they were forced to clear off[666] to the battlefield and ʿAlī's men went into the trench[667] and the others left. ʿAlī then called out aloud: "Don't pursue those who flee! Don't finish off the wounded! Don't go into any houses!" and he restrained his men. Then he sent a message to the others to come out and give allegiance, and he received allegiance under the banners. "Anyone who recognizes anything [belonging to him lying around]," said ʿAlī, "then let him take it!"[668] until nothing was left behind [3162] from the two armies. A group of young men from Qays[669] then came to him, and their spokesman said some words. "Where are your leaders?" asked ʿAlī. "They were hit under the eyes of the camel," said the spokesman and continued his speech. "This is the long-winded orator!" said ʿAlī.

The allegiance over, ʿAlī made ʿAbdallāh b. ʿAbbās governor, but he wanted to stay [there himself] until matters became stabilized.

Al-Ashtar then told me[670] to go and buy him the most expen-

---

665. Kulayb's companions.
666. Reading *ḥattā ajlaw ilā* with Ibrāhīm (cf. *Addenda*, DCXXXIII) for the text's *ḥattā aqbalā ilā*.
667. Wellhausen, 160.
668. I.e., ʿAlī let the vanquished repossess their arms, etc.
669. Who had been fighting on ʿĀʾishah's side.
670. Kulayb.

sive camel in Baṣrah. I did so, and he said, "Take it to ʿĀʾishah, and give her my greetings!" I did that, too, but she cursed him and said "Return it to him!" I then told al-Ashtar, who said, "ʿĀʾishah is blaming me for letting her sister's son[671] escape!" Then he heard the news that ʿAlī had made Ibn ʿAbbās governor, and he was angry. "For what purpose did we kill the old man?" he asked. "For[672] Yemen is ʿUbaydallāh's, the Ḥijāz is Qutham's, al-Baṣrah is ʿAbdallāh's and al-Kūfah is ʿAlī's."[673] He called for his mount and rode back.[674] When ʿAlī heard of this, he announced that they were departing. He made good speed and caught up with him, but he did not let on that he had heard about it and asked: "Why did you set off? You're way ahead of us." ʿAlī had feared that if al-Ashtar were left to go like this he would cause the people to have seditious ideas.

According to al-Sarī (in writing)—Shuʿayb—Sayf—Muḥammad and Ṭalḥah: When the Baṣran delegations had come to the Kūfans[675] and al-Qaʿqāʿ had returned from the Mother of the Faithful and Ṭalḥah and al-Zubayr with a similar view, ʿAlī gathered the people. He then stood on some sacks, praised Almighty and Glorious Allāh, and magnified Him and prayed for His blessing on the Prophet. He then mentioned the Jāhiliyyah and its misery and Islam and its happiness, and Allāh's grace toward the community in its unity in [recognizing] the first caliph after the Messenger of Allāh and the two[676] who came next. "Then there occurred this evil event brought upon this community by groups intent only on this world. They were jealous of those Allāh had given it to on account of virtue and wanted to make a complete turnaround. 'But Allāh attains His purpose'[677] and fulfills His will! Tomorrow, then, I'm setting off [toward al-Baṣrah], so all of you do likewise! All of you, that is, except anyone who helped the

[3163]

---

671. Sarcastically referring to his fight with ʿAbdallāh b. al-Zubayr (see pp. 153, 167, below).

672. Following Ibrāhīm, who has *idh* for the text's *idhā*, "if."

673. I.e., the nepotism carries on, but with Banū Hāshim rather than Umayyah.

674. Toward al-Kūfah or perhaps Medina.

675. Inserting *ahl* with Ibrāhīm and *Addenda*, DCXXXIII.

676. Ibrāhīm only has one.

677. *Bālighun amrahu* (Qurʾān 65:3), cited probably in the *qirāʾah* of Ibn ʿĀmir (cf. p. 109, below) or Abū ʿAmr, certainly not of Ḥafṣ, which has *bālighu amrihi* (Ibn al-Mujāhid, 639).

cause against ʿUthmān in any way at all; they will not set off tomorrow. Let the fools rely on themselves and do without me!"

A group then gathered,[678] among them ʿIlbāʾ b. al-Haytham,[679] ʿAdī b. Ḥātim,[680] Sālim b. Thaʿlabah al-ʿAbsī, Shurayḥ b. Awfā b. Ḍubayʿah,[681] al-Ashtar, and a number of others who had attacked ʿUthmān and approved of it. They were joined by the Egyptians, Ibn al-Sawdāʾ,[682] and Khālid b. Muljam. They conferred among themselves and asked, "What should we do? Here is ʿAlī. He understands the Book of Allāh more than those who seek ʿUthmān's killers[683] and is in the best position to act on the matter. He has stated his position and yet only they and a few others have rallied to him. So how will he react when he draws up to his opponents and they to him and they see how few we are compared to their great number? By Allāh! You will be wanted for retaliation, and you'll have no escape!" "We know Ṭalḥah and al-Zubayr's position," replied al-Ashtar, "but ʿAlī's we've only discovered today.

[3164]   Everyone's opinion about us, by Allāh! is the same, and if they and ʿAlī make amends we're dead men! So come on! let's rise up together against ʿAlī and unite him with ʿUthmān! A *fitnah* will then return in which all that will be wanted from us is to keep out of it." "This is a bad idea," said ʿAbdallāh b. al-Sawdāʾ. "You Kūfan killers of ʿUthmān at Dhū Qār, you number only 2,500 or 2,600 and Ibn al-Ḥanẓaliyyah[684] here and his men are 5,000, and they're longing to find a way of fighting you. You hardly have room to be offering advice!"[685]

"Let's go away from them and leave them," said ʿIlbāʾ b. al-

---

678. Cf. Lau, 108.

679. From Bakr b. Wāʾil (Caskel and Strenziok, I, 153, II, 354).

680. Companion of the Prophet, d. 68/687–88 (*EI*[2], s.v.).

681. Shurayḥ b. Awfā b. Yazīd al-ʿAbsī fell at Nahrawān (Caskel and Strenziok, I, 132, II, 533). Is there confusion with the Shurayḥ b. Ḍubayʿah of Qays b. Thaʿlabah of Bakr b. Wāʾil (Caskel and Strenziok, I, 155, II, 533)?

682. ʿAbdallāh b. Saba'.

683. The text is difficult, and, following *Addenda*, DCXXXIII, IA's version, 235, has been adopted here. Ibrāhīm inserts *wa-aqrabu* after *bi-kitāb Allāh* "he understands the Book of Allāh most and is closer than those who seek ʿUthmān's killers."

684. Al-Qaʿqāʿ b. ʿAmr.

685. Or "improve your position first!" (Ibrāhīm n., Lane, 1917c).

Haytham. "Then, if 'Alī's side decreases, their enemy will have more power over them,[686] whereas, if they increase, they will be more likely to make peace to your disadvantage. So leave them! Go back and stay in some town until someone comes in whom you can find protection. Pull out from this army!" "This is also a bad idea," said 'Abdallāh b. al-Sawdā'. "By Allāh! For you to be in a particular place[687] and not mixed in among innocent parties is just what the people want. If your suggestion came about, you would be easy prey." "By Allāh! I neither agree nor disagree," 'Adī b. Ḥātim replied, "but I *am* surprised at those who express any hesitation about killing ['Alī]. But, given what has happened and the position ['Alī] has achieved among the people, we have an excellent supply of horses and weapons, so if you advance we will and if you hold back we will also." "Well said!" 'Abdallāh b. al-Sawdā'. But Sālim b. Tha'labah said: "Some people do what they do out of desire for this world, but not me! By Allāh! If I meet them tomorrow I won't run home,[688] and if when I meet them in battle I stay alive let it be for no longer than the slaughtering of a camel already destined for slaughter. I swear by Allāh! You're afraid of swords like people whose affairs are only arranged by the sword." "Do you hear that?!" remarked 'Abdallāh b. al-Sawdā', but Shurayḥ b. Awfā said: "Organize yourselves before you go out! Don't delay anything that you need to do quickly, and don't rush anything that you need to delay! The people have the worst opinion of us, and I've no idea what they might do tomorrow when they come together."

[3165]

Then Ibn al-Sawdā' spoke up:[689] "Listen, men! Your strength lies in being linked with everyone else, so cultivate them. But then, when they meet tomorrow, get the fight going! Don't give them time to think; then those around you[690] will have no option but to defend themselves. Allāh will then divert 'Alī and Ṭalḥah and al-Zubayr and those who share their views from what you

---

686. And they will need us.
687. Cf. p. 27, above. Ibrāhīm suggests "of one opinion."
688. Or "I wouldn't go back on anything" if *shay'* (see Prym's n.) is read for *baytī*.
689. Cf. Lau, 108.
690. 'Alī's army.

would hate to happen."[691] They thought this plan was best[692] and went their ways agreed on it. No one else knew about it.

The next morning found 'Alī mounted and riding out with his army. When he reached 'Abd al-Qays[693] he dismounted among them and those Kūfans who had come out. 'Alī was in front.[694] Then he set off again until he dismounted at al-Zāwiyah,[695] where more men caught up with him,[696] for he had gone on ahead of them. When 'Alī's plan reached the Baṣrans and 'Alī had dismounted as just described, Abū al-Jarbā'[697] went up to al-Zubayr b. al-'Awwām and said, "The best plan is for you now to send a thousand horsemen to go against this man in the evening or[698] the morning before he meets up with his followers." "Abū al-Jarbā'," replied al-Zubayr, "we're familiar with the affairs of war, but they are fellow Muslims, and this is an unprecedented situation that has never before arisen. It's a situation in which those meeting Almighty and Glorious Allāh without an excuse now will find their excuse cut off on the Day of Resurrection also. Furthermore, their delegate[699] has left us with a kind of agreement, and I am hopeful that we'll achieve peace, so keep cheerful and patient."

[3166]

Then Ṣabrah b. Shaymān came up and said: "Ṭalḥah and al-Zubayr. Let us use this opportunity to kill this man![700] Strategy in war is better than brute force." "Ṣabrah," they replied, "we and they are Muslims and this is a situation that hasn't risen before today, that there should have been a Qur'ān revealed about it or a *Sunnah* established by the Messenger of God. No, it's something new. There are those who held that it shouldn't be set in mo-

---

691. Peace.

692. The text has "so understand this plan, and go away agreed!" as though Ibn al-Sawdā' were still speaking.

693. Near Dār al-Rizq (al-'Alī, 301; Massignon, 157).

694. The text is corrupt here, probably dittographic, but followed by Ibrāhīm. The translation follows Wellhausen, 160, and de Goeje (*Addenda*, DCXXXIII), who follows IA, 236.

695. It is not clear what this place was, but it was probably in northern Baṣrah near the road to Ābādān (al-'Alī, 290; Massignon, 157).

696. Following Ibrāhīm and text n. h.

697. Caskel and Strenziok, I, 82 or 189, II, 258.

698. Reading *aw* for *wa*.

699. Al-Qa'qā'.

700. 'Alī.

tion today—ʿAlī and his followers—but we said rather that we shouldn't leave it today or postpone it. ʿAlī said: 'What we're calling you to do—conceding to these regicides—is evil, but it's better than something yet more evil! It may seem like something unattainable, but it's about to become clear to us. The laws between Muslims entail choosing those of most general use and least damaging application.'"

Then Kaʿb b. Sūr came up and said: "What are you all waiting for? You've already made your way to their front lines, so cut off this head of their [forces]!" "Kaʿb" they replied, "this is a problem between us and our brothers, and it is far from clear. By Allāh! The Companions of Muḥammad have never taken a course of action since Almighty and Glorious Allāh sent His Prophet without knowing[701] where to put their feet, until this situation arose, but now they don't know whether they're coming or going. Today something might look good to us and bad to our brothers; tomorrow it will seem bad to us and good to them. We're producing arguments against them that they don't consider valid; then they produce similar ones.[702] We want peace if only they would respond to it and carry it out. Otherwise the final remedy is cauterization."[703]   [3167]

Some Kūfan groups went up to ʿAlī b. Abī Ṭālib and questioned him why they were advancing against the other side. Among them was al-Aʿwar b. Bunān al-Minqarī, to whom ʿAlī replied: "For iṣlāḥ and extinguishing the fire of hatred. I hope Allāh will reunify this community by us and stop their warring, if they respond to me." "And if they don't respond to us?" "We'll leave them alone as long as they leave us alone." "And if they don't leave us alone?" "We'll defend ourselves against them." "Shall we then give them as good as they gave us?" "Yes," replied ʿAlī.

Then up stood Abū Salāmah al-Daʾalānī and asked, "Do you think these people have a case for seeking revenge for this blood, if their intentions are honest before Almighty and Glorious Allāh in so doing?" "Yes," replied ʿAlī. "So do you consider you have a

---

701. Reading ʿalimū after Wellhausen, 160, and Ibrāhīm for the text's ʿalimnā. De Goeje disagrees (*Addenda*, DCXXXIII).

702. Reading *amthālihā* with Ibrāhīm for the text's *amthālinā*.

703. I.e., war.

case for delaying retaliation?" "Yes," replied ʿAlī. "In situations
that cannot be put right the ruling should be what is least damaging and of most general application." "So what will be our situation if we are afflicted tomorrow?" he asked. ʿAlī replied, "I hope
that anyone who is killed, whether from us or from them, with a
mind kept sincere to Allāh will be admitted by Allāh to paradise."[704]

Then up stood Mālik b. Ḥabīb[705] and asked, "What are you
going to do when you meet these people?" "It's perfectly clear to
us and them," replied ʿAlī, "that *iṣlāḥ* means stopping this business. If they then give us allegiance, then that will be *iṣlāḥ*; but, if
both they and we insist on fighting, then it will be a split that
won't be repaired." "And if we are afflicted tomorrow, then what
will happen to those of us who get killed?" "Whoever desires
Almighty and Glorious Allāh, then it will be his benefit and his
salvation," replied ʿAlī and stood up and delivered a sermon to the
people. He praised Allāh and magnified Him and said: "Men!
Keep control of yourselves. Restrain yourselves from doing or saying anything against these people, for they're your brothers. Be
patient over what happens to you, and beware of rushing into
anything without our guidance. If you win arguments today you'll
lose them tomorrow."[706]

ʿAlī then set off and advanced. He made his armed men and
equipment that he had come with go forward until they were in
sight of the other army. He then sent Ḥakīm b. Salāmah and
Mālik b. Ḥabīb to them, saying, "If you still hold to what was
agreed when you left al-Qaʿqāʿ b. ʿAmr, then desist and agree to our
dismounting and negotiating the whole business."

At this al-Aḥnaf b. Qays came out to him with Banū Saʿd ready
to fight—they were the ones who had protected Ḥurqūṣ b. Zuhayr
and had decided against fighting ʿAlī b. Abī Ṭālib. "ʿAlī!" he said.
"Our people are in al-Baṣrah claiming that if you overcome them
tomorrow you'll kill their men and enslave their women." "I'm
not a man to be feared so," replied ʿAlī. "Isn't that only allowed

---

704. Cf. Ibn Khaldūn, I, 440.
705. Al-Wālibī of Asad (Caskel and Strenziok, I, 52) or al-Ashjaʿī of Ghaṭafān (I,
135, II, 389).
706. In the hereafter.

with those who turn away and disbelieve? Haven't you paid attention to the words of Almighty and Glorious Allāh: 'You are not a ruler over them, except those who turn away and disbelieve'?[707] These are Muslims! Can you take care of your people for me?" "Yes, I can," replied al-Aḥnaf, "but you must choose one of two things. Either I join you, in which case it'll be just me on my own, or else I will [stay neutral and] hold back ten thousand swords from you." He then returned to his men and proposed that they abstain. "Tribesmen of Khindif!"[708] he began by saying, and a group responded to him. Then he called out, "Tribesmen of Tamīm!" and a group responded to him. Then he called out, "Tribesmen of Saʿd!" and every single Saʿdī responded to him. Then he withdrew with them and waited to see what the [remaining] forces would do. Then, when the battle took place and ʿAlī was victorious, al-Aḥnaf's men came en masse and entered into allegiance to ʿAlī, as everyone else had done.

[3169]

What the narrators[709] transmit concerning al-Aḥnaf is different from Sayf's account from his teachers. What they transmit is as was told me by Yaʿqūb b. Ibrāhīm—Ibn Idrīs—Ḥusayn—ʿAmr b. Jaʾwān—al-Aḥnaf b. Qays: We came to Medina on our way to perform the ḥajj. We were at our ḥajj places and were putting down our baggage when up came a man and said, "They are worked up and have gathered in the mosque." So off we went, and there were the people gathered around a group in the center of the mosque. ʿAlī was there, as were Ṭalḥah, al-Zubayr, and Saʿd b. Abī Waqqāṣ. As we joined them ʿUthmān b. ʿAffān arrived. "Here's ʿUthmān," someone said. "He's arrived." He was wearing a length of yellow cloth of his and had covered his head with it. "Is ʿAlī here?" he asked. "Yes," they replied. "Is al-Zubayr here?" he asked. "Yes," they replied. "Is Ṭalḥah here?" he asked. "Yes," they replied. So ʿUthmān said: "I entreat you by Allāh! There is no deity but He! Did you know that the Messenger of God said, 'Whoever buys the enclosure of such and such a tribe Allāh will

---

707. Qurʾān 88:22–23. The text has *bi-musayṭar*, which is the *qirāʾah* of Ibn ʿĀmir and a non-mainstream transmitter from al-Kisāʾī (Ibn Mujāhid, 682). Ibrāhīm has *bi-muṣayṭar*, which is the *qirāʾah* of the others.

708. A mostly western Arabian genealogical group, including Kinānah, Asad, Tamīm, Ribāb, and Ḍabbah (Caskel and Strenziok, II, 347).

709. *Al-muhaddithūn.*

[3170]   forgive him'? So I bought it for 20,000 or 25,000 dirhams. When I then came to the Prophet and said, 'Messenger of Allāh! I bought it,' he replied, 'Join it with our mosque, and the reward will be yours [in the Hereafter]!'" "Allāh be our witness! We certainly did know," they replied. He then mentioned other similar events. When I then met Ṭalḥah and al-Zubayr I asked them: "Whom do you command and wish me to give allegiance to? It's obvious this man is going to be killed." "ʿAlī," they replied.[710] "You command and wish me to give allegiance to him?" "Yes!" So I set off and went to Mecca, and while we were there the news of ʿUthmān's murder reached us. ʿĀʾishah, the Mother of the Faithful, was there, and when I met her I asked, "Whom do you command me to give allegiance to?" "ʿAlī," she replied. "You command and wish me to give allegiance to him?" "Yes!" I therefore returned to ʿAlī in Medina and gave him allegiance. I then returned to my people in Baṣrah, thinking the whole matter had been properly sorted out. But it was not long before someone came to me and said: "Here are ʿĀʾishah and Ṭalḥah and al-Zubayr. They have dismounted beside al-Khuraybah."[711] "What brings them?" I asked. "They have sent you a message calling you and asking your assistance in revenging ʿUthmān's blood," they replied. So I found myself in the most awful situation I had ever been in, and I said: "It would be extremely serious for me not to support these people, among whom are the Mother of the Faithful and the disciple of the Messenger of Allāh.[712] But it would also be extremely serious for me to fight a man who is the paternal first cousin of the Messenger of God and to whom they commanded me to give allegiance."

When I went to them they said: "We've come to find help to revenge the blood of ʿUthmān. He was unjustly killed." "Mother of the Faithful," I replied, "I entreat you by Allāh! Did I ask you, 'Whom do you command me to give allegiance to?' and you replied, 'To ʿAlī,' to which I replied, 'You command and wish me to give allegiance to him?' and you said, 'Yes'?" "I did," she replied, "but he made changes." "Zubayr, disciple of the Messenger of Allāh, and Ṭalḥah," I then said, "I entreat you both by Allāh! Did I

---

710. Ibrāhīm has "ʿAlī?"
711. Al-ʿAlī, 297; Massignon, 157.
712. Al-Zubayr.

ask you, 'Whom do you command me to give allegiance to?' and
you replied, 'To ʿAlī,' to which I replied, 'You command and wish
me to give allegiance to him?' and you said, 'Yes'?" "We did," they
replied, "but he made changes." "By Allāh!" I replied: "I will not
fight you while among you are the Mother of the Faithful and the   [3171]
disciple of the Messenger of Allāh. Nor will I fight a man who is
the paternal first cousin of the Messenger of God and to whom
you commanded me to give allegiance. So select for me one of
three courses of action. Either leave open the bridge for me, and
I'll move to the land of the Persians until Almighty and Glorious
Allāh carries through His preordained command. Or I'll move to
Mecca and stay there until Almighty and Glorious Allāh carries
through His preordained command. Or I'll withdraw but stay
nearby." "We'll discuss the matter and then send you word," they
replied.

They discussed it and said: "If we open the bridge for him and
he goes and tells the Persians your news, this isn't a good idea.
Make him stay here nearby where you can keep him under con-
trol⁷¹³ and see what he's doing." So he withdrew to al-Jalḥāʾ, two
parasangs⁷¹⁴ from al-Baṣrah, and about 6,000 did the same. Then
the armies met. The first to be killed was Ṭalḥah, and then Kaʿb b.
Sūr who was holding the Qurʾān copy and reminding these men
and those,⁷¹⁵ and then other casualties. Al-Zubayr went to Safawān,⁷¹⁶ which is as far from al-Baṣrah as you are from al-Qādisiy-
yah,⁷¹⁷ and al-Naʿir,⁷¹⁸ a Mujāshiʿī tribesman met him and asked:
"Where are you going, disciple of the Messenger of God? Come to
me and you'll be under my protection,⁷¹⁹ and no one will get
you." So al-Zubayr went with him. Someone came to al-Aḥnaf⁷²⁰
and asked him, "Al-Zubayr was met in Safawān, so what are your

---

713. Lit., "tread on his ear hole."
714. Six to eight miles (*EI*², s.v. Farsa<u>kh</u>).
715. That they should be seeking peace.
716. Al-ʿAlī, 281.
717. The name of several places in Iraq, the two most important of which are
near al-Kūfah (*EI*², s.v.).
718. Mujāshiʿ is in Tamīm (Caskel and Strenziok, I, 61).
719. *Fī dhimmatī*. Cf. Ayoub.
720. Reading (*fa-utiya*) *al-Aḥnafu* for the text's *al-Aḥnafa* but not taking "news"
to be understood (*Addenda*, DCXXXIII). Ibrāhīm inserts *khabaruhu*, "news about
him reached al-Aḥnaf."

orders?" "He brought the Muslims together so that they were hitting each other's eyebrows with swords; then he retires into his house!" He was heard by ʿUmayr b. Jurmūz, Faḍālah b. Ḥābis, and Nufayʿ, so they rode off looking for him and found him with al-Naʿir. ʿUmayr b. Jurmūz, on a weak horse of his, came at [al-Zubayr] from behind and gave him a light stab, at which al-Zubayr, on a horse of his called 'the Veiled,' bore down upon him until, just when he thought he was about to kill him, ʿUmayr b. Jurmūz shouted, "Nāfiʿ! Faḍālah!" Whereupon they bore down on al-Zubayr and killed him.

According to Yaʿqūb b. Ibrāhīm—Muʿtamir b. Sulaymān—his father—Ḥuṣayn—ʿAmr b. Jaʾwān, a Tamīmī: I (Ḥuṣayn) asked ʿAmr, "What was the situation regarding al-Aḥnaf's neutrality?" He replied, "I heard al-Aḥnaf say, 'I came to Medina on my way to perform the *ḥajj*.' He then proceeded to tell the story more or less as above, may Allāh be praised for what He has decreed and judged!"

ʿAlī b. Abī Ṭālib Sends His Son al-Ḥasan and ʿAmmār b. Yāsir from Dhū Qār to Get the Kūfans to Mobilize with Him

According to ʿUmar b. Shabbah—Abū al-Ḥasan—Bashīr b. ʿĀṣim—Ibn Abī Laylā—his father: Hāshim b. ʿUtbah[721] went out to ʿAlī at al-Rabadhah and told him about Muḥammad b. Abī Bakr's arrival and Abū Mūsā's words. "I wanted to remove him from office," said ʿAlī, "but al-Ashtar asked me to let him stay." ʿAlī then sent Hāshim back to al-Kūfah and wrote a letter to Abū Mūsā: "I have sent Hāshim b. ʿUtbah to get those Muslims with you to come and join me. So make the people come! I appointed you over your charge only so that you might join in assisting me in upholding the truth." At this Abū Mūsā called al-Sāʾib b. Mālik al-Ashʿarī[722] and asked him, "What's your opinion?" "I think," he replied, "you should do what he said in his letter." "I disagree," said Abū Mūsā. Hāshim then wrote to ʿAlī, "I came to a man,

---

721. Al-Mirqal, who fell at Ṣiffīn (Caskel and Strenziok, I, 20, II, 280).
722. From his own tribe; d. 67/687 (Caskel and Strenziok, I, 273, II, 499).

fanatical and divisive, openly full of hatred and loathing." He sent this letter with al-Muḥill b. Khalīfah al-Ṭāʾī.[723]

ʿAlī then sent his son al-Ḥasan and ʿAmmār b. Yāsir to mobilize the men for him, and he sent Qaraẓah b. Kaʿb al-Anṣārī[724] to be governor of al-Kūfah. He wrote a letter for him to take to Abū Mūsā: "After greetings. I had thought that your distance from[725] these events, in which Almighty and Glorious Allāh has not given you a part, would have stopped you from disobeying me. However, I have sent my son al-Ḥasan and ʿAmmār b. Yāsir to mobilize the men, and I have sent Qaraẓah b. Kaʿb al-Anṣārī to be governor of the garrison city.[726] So withdraw from our employment 'blamed and defeated.'[727] If you do not, then I have ordered him to oppose you. If you resist him and he overcomes you, I have ordered him to cut you to pieces."

When he delivered the letter to Abū Mūsā he withdrew. Al-Ḥasan and ʿAmmār then entered the mosque. "Men," they said, "the Commander of the Faithful says: 'I have come out in this way either as an oppressor or oppressed. So by Almighty and Glorious Allāh I now remind any man who [wishes to] fulfill his duty toward Allāh that he must come forward. If I am oppressed, he must give me his assistance; if I am an oppressor, he must punish me.[728] By Allāh! Ṭalḥah and al-Zubayr were the first to give me allegiance and the first to betray. Have I appropriated any money? Have I altered any judgment? So come forward. Enforce the good, forbid the bad!'"

According to ʿUmar—Abū al-Ḥasan—Abū Mikhnaf—Jābir[729] —al-Shaʿbī—Abū al-Ṭufayl:[730] ʿAlī said, "There will come to

---

723. There was an al-Muḥill b. al-Ashʿath al-Ṭāʾī (Caskel and Strenziok, I, 254, II, 425).

724. A companion of the Prophet (Caskel and Strenziok, I, 188, II, 466).

725. Reading *buʿdak*, following Wellhausen, 160, and Ibrāhīm for the text's *tuʿdhib*.

726. *Al-miṣr*, i.e., al-Kūfah.

727. Qurʾān 17:18. A blatant implication that Abū Mūsā is going to burn in hell.

728. *Glossarium*, CVIII.

729. Ibn Yazīd al-Juʿfī, d. c. 128/746 (U. Sezgin, 133 ff.).

730. ʿĀmir b. Wāthilah al-Kinānī. He fought with ʿAlī at Ṣiffīn and died as the last surviving Companion of the Prophet in 110/728, aged over a hundred years (U. Zezgin, 134).

[3174]   you[731] from al-Kūfah 12,001 men." So I sat on the hill at Dhū Qār and counted them and [sure enough] they numbered no more and no less.

According to ʿUmar—Abū al-Ḥasan—Bashīr b. ʿĀṣim—Ibn Abī Laylā—his father: Twelve thousand men joined up with ʿAlī, and they were organized into sevenths. Maʿqil b. Yasār al-Riyāḥī[732] was in charge of Quraysh, Kinānah, Asad, Tamīm, al-Ribāb, and Muzaynah. Saʿd b. Masʿūd al-Thaqafī was in charge of the seventh of Qays. Waʿlah b. Mahdūj al-Dhuhlī[733] was in charge of the seventh of Bakr b. Wāʾil and Taghlib.[734] Ḥujr b. ʿAdī was in charge of the seventh of Madhḥij and al-Ashʿarīn. Mikhnaf b. Sulaym al-Azdī[735] was in charge of the seventh of Bajīlah, Anmār, Khathʿam, and al-Azd.

ʿAlī Sets Up Camp at al-Zāwiyah of al-Baṣrah

According to ʿUmar b. Shabbah—Abū al-Ḥasan—Maslamah b. Muḥārib—Qatādah: ʿAlī set up camp at al-Zāwiyah for a few days, and al-Aḥnaf sent a message to him: "If you wish I personally will join you, or if you wish I will prevent 4,000 swords[736] from attacking you." "How so, considering how you have promised neutrality to your followers?" came back ʿAlī's reply. "But to fight them is to fulfill my promise to Almighty and Glorious Allāh," replied al-Aḥnaf. So ʿAlī sent a message to him: "Prevent whomever you can from fighting [me]!" ʿAlī then left al-Zāwiyah, and Ṭalḥah and al-Zubayr and ʿĀʾishah left al-Furḍah,[737] and they all met at the place where ʿUbaydallāh (or ʿAbdallāh) b. Ziyād's[738]

---

731. I.e., his forces.

732. Most probably of Muzaynah, the Companion of the Prophet, d. 60/680 (Caskel and Strenziok, I, 88, II, 399).

733. Probably Waʿlah b. al-Mujāhid al-Dhuhlī (Caskel and Strenziok, I, 152, II, 586). Ibrāhīm has Makhdūj here but Mahduj in the next report.

734. Up to here all northern Arabs. From here all southern Arabs.

735. Head of a famous Kūfan Azd family and great-grandfather of Abū Mikhnaf, the historian (Caskel and Strenziok, I, 218, II, 407).

736. Cf. the 10,000, p. 109, above.

737. Massignon, 157.

738. Ibn Abīhi, governor of al-Baṣrah in the mid-50s/670s and later also of al-Kūfah, sent troops against Ḥusayn at Karbalāʾ in 61/680; he was killed in 67/686 (EI[1], s.v.).

castle was [later situated]. When the armies had gathered, Shaqīq
b. Thawr[739] sent a message to ʿAmr b. Marjūm al-ʿAbdī:[740] "Advance! and lead us toward ʿAlī's army!" So they both advanced
through the quarters of ʿAbd al-Qays and Bakr b. Wāʾil.[741] They
then turned toward the army of the Commander of the Faithful.
"Whoever these men are with," said the people, "has won." Shaqīq b. Thawr handed their banner to a *mawlā* of his called   [3175]
Rashrāshah. So Waʿlah b. Maḥdūj al-Dhuhlī sent him a message:
"Nobility has perished! You have handed the honor of your tribe
over to Rashrāshah!" "Mind your own business and we'll mind
ours!" Shaqīq's reply came back. They remained three days, and
no fighting occurred between them. ʿAlī continued to send mes-
sages to them, speak with them, and restrain them.

According to ʿUmar—Abū Bakr al-Hudhalī—Qatādah: ʿAlī left
al-Zāwiyah, heading for Ṭalḥah, and al-Zubayr and ʿĀʾishah left al-
Furḍah, heading for ʿAlī, and they all met at the place of the castle
of ʿUbaydallāh b. Ziyād on Thursday, 14 Jumādā II 36/8 December
656.[742] "When the two armies came in sight of each other"[743] al-
Zubayr rode out on a horse, heavily armed. "Here comes al-
Zubayr!" ʿAlī was told. "If Allāh is to be called to mind,"[744] said
ʿAlī, "then he's the more probable of the two to take heed."[745]
Ṭalḥah also rode out. ʿAlī then went out to them, near enough for
the necks of their mounts to cross each other. "By my life!" exclaimed ʿAlī. "You've prepared weapons and horses and men. If
you have prepared an excuse before Allāh then fear Allāh,[746] may
He be praised! 'Do not be[747] like the woman who undoes what

---

739. Of Bakr b. Wāʾil, leader in the conquests (Caskel and Strenziok, I, 153, II,
526).

740. Leader of ʿAbd al-Qays for ʿAlī (Caskel and Strenziok, I, 169, II, 179), for the
text's and Ibrāhīm's Ibn Marḥūm.

741. Al-ʿAlī, 291; Massignon, 157.

742. Cf. p. 158, above, where al-Wāqidī dates it 10 Jumādā II.

743. Qurʾān 26:61, where Moses was fighting Pharaoh.

744. By quoting the Qurʾān, as in what follows.

745. Reading either *yadhdhakkaru* in the fifth stem, as in Qurʾān 80:4 ("Or take
heed and benefit by it"), or *yadhdhakiru* in the eighth stem, with Nöldeke (*Addenda*, DCXXXIII) and Wellhausen, 160, meaning more or less the same. The text has
yudhakkaru "be reminded," which Ibrāhīm emends to *yadhkuruhu* "to remember."

746. Because the excuse cannot be good.

747. Dual, rather than plural, as in the Qurʾān.

she has spun tightly into separate threads.'[748] Am I not brother in religion to you both, you holding my blood sacred and me yours?[749] Has a crime occurred allowing you to kill me?" "You incited the people against ʿUthmān," replied Ṭalḥah. "'On that Day Allāh will show them their true religion fully, and they will know that it is Allāh who is the plain truth,'"[750] quoted ʿAlī. "You, Ṭalḥah! You are seeking revenge for the blood of ʿUthmān! May Allāh curse ʿUthmān's killers![751] Al-Zubayr! do you remember the day you passed me in Banū Ghanm[752] territory with the Messenger of Allāh and he looked at me and laughed and I laughed with him, and you said, 'Ibn Abī Ṭālib is always proud!' and the Messenger of Allāh said to you, 'Quiet! He is not conceited. Believe me, you're going to fight him, and you'll be the aggressor'?" "O Allāh! I do, and had I remembered I wouldn't have come out like this. By Allāh! I will never fight you!" So ʿAlī left [them and returned] to his followers and said, "Al-Zubayr has just made a pledge to Allāh not to fight you." Al-Zubayr returned to ʿĀʾishah and said to her, "This is the only important situation I've been in since being able to reason when I haven't known what I was doing." "What do you want to do?" she asked. "I want to leave them and go," he replied, but his son ʿAbdallāh said to him: "You've brought these two armies[753] face to face and they've set up their lines of battle against each other, and you want to leave them and go! You've caught sight of Ibn Abī Ṭālib's banners and realized that strong young men are carrying them." "I have sworn an oath not to fight him," he replied, and what his son said to him angered him. ʿAbdallāh said, "Redeem your oath and fight him!"

[3176]

---

748. Qurʾān 16:92. The context concerns the importance of keeping oaths and that they should not be broken for political reasons.

749. Reading *tuharrimāni . . . wa-uḥarrimu*, following Ibrāhīm, for the text's *tuḥramāni . . . wa-uḥramu* "you're forbidden my blood, and I'm forbidden yours."

750. Qurʾān 24:25. While the immediate context in the Qurʾān refers to those who slander Muslim women and is interpreted as referring to ʿĀʾishah, ʿAlī is saying that Allāh will punish Ṭalḥah for slandering him. The implicit reference to ʿĀʾishah may be an ironic twist.

751. I.e., you; cf. the parallel passage, p. 126, below.

752. The name of a number of clans (Caskel and Strenziok, II, 272), perhaps Ghanm b. Dūdān of Asad in Mecca.

753. *Al-gharayn*; see p. 118, below; Ibrāhīm 502, n. 2; Lane, 2308a. The reading *al-ʿarrayn* (*Addenda*, DCXXXIII) means "favor-seekers" or "guests" (Lane, 1991b).

So al-Zubayr called for a slave of his called Makhūl and freed him.[754] 'Abd al-Raḥmān b. Sulaymān al-Taymī[755] then said the verses

I have never seen, as I have today, a brother of brothers[756]
    more astonishing[757] than one redeeming his oaths
By freeing a slave, but in disobedience to the Merciful.[758]

One of their poets added the verses

He sets Makhūl free to save his religion
    as an expiation to Allāh for his oath,
Perfidy[759] written all over his face!

Return to Sayf's account from Muhammad and Ṭalḥah   [3177]

'Imrān b. Ḥusayn[760] sent a message to the people, urging them all to leave both the armies, as al-Aḥnaf had done. Among those to whom he sent a message were Banū 'Adī, and his messenger approached until he called out at the door of their mosque, "Listen! Abū Nujayd 'Imrān b. Ḥusayn sends you his greetings. He says to you, 'I would far prefer to be [away] at the base of some mountain[761] among nanny goats with lopsided udders[762] and sheep, shearing their fleeces and drinking their milk, than to shoot one arrow at anyone from these two battle lines!'" With a single voice Banū 'Adī all replied: "By Allāh! We are not going to leave the household of the Messenger of God (meaning the Mother of the Faithful) for anything!"

According to 'Amr b. 'Alī—Yazīd b. Zuray'—Abū Na'āmah al-'Adawī—Ḥujayr b. al-Rabī': 'Imrān b. Ḥusayn told me, "Go to

---

754. Cf. p. 126, below.
755. Following Ibrāhīm and *Addenda*, DCXXXIII, instead of the text's al-Tamīmī.
756. Al-Zubayr.
757. Reading *a'jaba* (*Addenda*, DCXXXIII) for the text's *a'jabu*.
758. A proper redeeming of an oath would have to be in obedience.
759. Because of his promises to Muḥammad and 'Alī.
760. Of Khuzā'ah, a Compaion of the Prophet, d. 52/673 (Caskel and Strenziok, I, 197, II, 357).
761. Reading *jabal ḥadan*, following Nöldeke (*Addenda*, DCXXXIII) and Ibrāhīm.
762. Reading *a'nuz ḥudun* (Lane, 591a,b), following Nöldeke (*Addenda*, DCXXXIII). According to *Glossarium*, CXCV, it may mean "very red/black nanny goats." The text and Ibrāhīm have *a'nuz khuḍr*, "tawny nanny goats." Cf. also the next report.

your tribe, when they have all gathered together, and stand up among them and say: ''Imrān b. Ḥusayn, Companion of the Messenger of Allāh, has sent me to you to give you his greetings and ask for Allāh's mercy on you. He has sworn an oath by Allāh, apart from Whom there is no other god, that he would far prefer to be a mutilated Ethiopian slave pasturing nanny goats with lopsided udders[763] on some mountain top until the day he dies than for a single arrow to be shot between the two armies.'" The leaders of the tribe lifted their heads to him[764] and said, "We are never going to leave the household of the Messenger of God for anything!"

[3178]   *Return to Sayf's account from Muḥammad and Ṭalḥah*

The Baṣrans were in factions: One sided with Ṭalḥah and al-Zubayr, one with 'Alī, and a third did not agree with fighting anyone from either side. 'Ā'ishah came out from the house where she was staying and moved down to the mosque of al-Ḥuddān[765] in the Azd quarter—the battle took place in their compound. The chief of the Azd at that time was Ṣabrah b. Shaymān, and Ka'b b. Sūr said to him: "When the armies see each other you won't be able to hold them back. It will be like torrents gushing forth. So obey me, and don't be there with them! Withdraw with your tribe! I fear that peace won't prevail. So keep behind this deluge, and leave these two armies of Muḍar and Rabī'ah. After all, they are two brothers.[766] If they make amends, then peace is what we've been wanting; if they fight, then we can be their judges tomorrow." Now Ka'b had been a Christian in the Jāhiliyyah, so Ṣabrah said to him: "I fear there is some Christianity in you—are you telling me to abstain from *iṣlāḥ* between Muslims?! And to desert the Mother of the Faithful, Ṭalḥah, and al-Zubayr if they reject ['Alī's] peace offer?! And to leave seeking revenge for 'Uth-

---

763. Reading *a'nuzan ḥaḍaniyyāt*, following Nöldeke (*Addenda*, DCXXXIII); *Glossariium*, CXCV, and Ibrāhīm. Cf. also the previous report. The text has *a'nuzan ḥaṣīnāt*, "inaccessible?/pregnant? nanny goats."

764. Signifying readiness to reply after listening.

765. Massignon, 157.

766. They should make peace. They shared an eponymous "father," Nizār, as opposed to the Yamanīs here being addressed.

mān?! By Allāh! I'd never do such a thing!" So the Yamanīs[767] agreed to be present at the battle.

According to al-Sarī (in writing)—Shuʿayb—Sayf—al-Durays al-Bajalī—Ibn Yaʿmar: When al-Aḥnaf b. Qays returned from being with ʿAlī he was met by Hilāl b. Wakīʿ b. Mālik b. ʿAmr,[768] who asked him, "What's your decision?" "To withdraw. What's yours?" "To protect the Mother of the Faithful. Are you going to leave us and you're our chief?" "I will be your chief only tomorrow when you are killed and I remain," replied al-Aḥnaf. "You're saying all this, and you're our elder!" said Hilāl. Al-Aḥnaf replied, "I'm the elder who is disobeyed, and you're the youth who is obeyed." Banū Saʿd then followed al-Aḥnaf, and he withdrew with them to Wādī al-Sibāʿ.[769] Banū Ḥanẓalah followed Hilāl, and Banū ʿAmr[770] agreed with Abū al-Jarbāʾ and fought. [3179]

According to al-Sarī (in writing)—Shuʿayb—Sayf—Muḥammad —Abū ʿUthmān: When al-Aḥnaf came, he called out, "Tribesmen of Udd,[771] withdraw from this business, and leave these two armies to be quick or slow!"[772] But al-Minjāb b. Rāshid[773] called out: "Tribesmen of al-Ribāb,[774] don't withdraw! Witness this business, and take it on yourselves to be the quick ones!" So they separated. Then al-Aḥnaf called out, "Tribesmen of Tamīm, withdraw from this business, and leave these two armies to be quick or slow!" But Abū al-Jarbāʾ (who belonged to Banū Ghaylān[775] b. Mālik b. ʿAmr b. Tamīm) got up and called out: "Tribesmen of ʿAmr, don't withdraw from this business! Take it on yourselves to be the quick ones!" Abū al-Jarbāʾ was leading Banū ʿAmr b. Ta-

---

767. Following the lead of Azd, Ṣabrah's people.

768. From the same tribe.

769. Five miles from Baṣrah on the Mecca road (Yāqūt, V, 343).

770. These three groups were all part of Tamīm.

771. Reading *yā la-Udd* following Ibrāhīm, who notes that this is Udd b. Ṭābikhah (see Caskel and Strenziok, I, 59). He was a major eponym for northern Arabs, comprising, among others, all the tribes and men in this *khabar*. Prym notes that the text's *yā la-Zayd* is incorrect; for the emendation *yā la-Wudd*, see *Addenda*, DCXXXIII.

772. *Glossarium*, CDLXI.

773. Of Ḍabbah; see Caskel and Strenziok, I, 90, II, 408.

774. Part of Udd; see Caskel and Strenziok, I, 85–87.

775. For the text's ʿUthmān, see Caskel and Strenziok, II, 203. Abū al-Jarbāʾ was ʿĀṣim b. Dulaf (Caskel and Strenziok, I, 82, II, 203).

mīm, and al-Minjāb b. Rāshid was leading Banū Ḍabbah.[776] Then, when al-Aḥnaf called out, "Tribesmen of Zayd Manāh,[777] withdraw from this business, and leave these two armies to be quick or slow!" Hilāl b. Wakīʿ replied, "Don't withdraw from this business!" and called out, "Tribesmen of Ḥanẓalah,[778] take it on yourselves to be the quick ones!" Hilāl was leading Ḥanẓalah. Banū Saʿd[779] did obey al-Aḥnaf and withdrew to Wādī al-Sibāʿ.

According to al-Sarī (in writing)—Shuʿayb—Sayf—Muḥammad and Ṭalḥah: Mujāshiʿ b. Masʿūd al-Sulamī[780] led Hawāzin,[781] Banū Sulaym,[782] and al-Aʿjaz. Zufar b. al-Ḥārith[783] led ʿĀmir.[784] Aʿṣur b. al-Nuʿmān al-Bāhilī led Ghaṭafān.[785] Mālik b. Mismaʿ[786] led Bakr b. Wāʾil. The whole of ʿAbd al-Qays withdrew to ʿAlī, except for one man who stayed back. There were those who stayed back from Bakr b. Wāʾil, those that withdrew equaling those that stayed. They were led by Sinān.

[3180]   Al-Azd had three leaders: Ṣabrah b. Shaymān,[787] Masʿūd,[788] and Ziyād b. ʿAmr.[789] Al-Shawādhib had two leaders. Al-Khirrīt b. Rāshid[790] led Muḍar. Al-Ruʿbī (nicknamed) al-Jarmī[791] led Quḍā-ʿah and its followers, and Dhū al-Ājurah al-Ḥimyarī[792] led the rest of Yaman.

---

776. Caskel and Strenziok, I, 89 ff.

777. Who included Ḥanẓalah and Saʿd; see Caskel and Strenziok, I, 59.

778. Caskel and Strenziok, I, 59.

779. Caskel and Strenziok, I, 75. Al-Aḥnaf belonged to the ʿAmr branch; see Caskel and Strenziok, I, 76.

780. Caskel and Strenziok, II, 419.

781. All tribes in this paragraph are northern.

782. Caskel and Strenziok, I, 122 ff.

783. Of Banū ʿĀmir; he fought with Muʿāwiyah at Ṣiffīn (Caskel, pl. 96 no. 609).

784. Caskel and Strenziok, I, 93 ff.

785. Caskel and Strenziok, I, 127 ff.

786. A prominent Qays and Bakr leader (Caskel and Strenziok, I, 155, II, 391; Pellat, 33, 152, 196).

787. Al-Ḥuddānī (on ʿĀʾishah's side); see Caskel and Strenziok, I, 216, II, 534. All tribes and identified men in this paragraph were southern Arabs, apart from Khirrīt.

788. Ibn ʿAmr al-Qamar; see Caskel and Strenziok, I, 213, II, 402.

789. Caskel and Strenziok, I, 203, II, 606.

790. Chief of the Banū Nājiyah. He fought with ʿAlī again at Ṣiffīn but later broke with him, so ʿAlī sent after him, and he was killed (EI², s.v.). He belonged to ʿAbd al-Bayt b. al-Ḥārith (Caskel and Strenziok, I, 29, II, 347, 123). See also I, 3418 ff.

791. Jarm b. Rabbān were reckoned among Quḍāʿah; see Caskel and Strenziok, I, 327, II, 259.

792. Dhū al-ʿAshīrah b. Dallāl; see Caskel and Strenziok, I, 278, II, 236?

Ṭalḥah and al-Zubayr came out and took up a position with the army at al-Zābūqah,[793] in the location of Qaryat al-Arzāq. Then the whole of Muḍar took up a position there, and they were in no doubt that peace would prevail. The whole of Rabīʿah took up a position above them, and they were in no doubt that peace would prevail. The whole of Yaman took up a position below them, and they also were in no doubt that peace would prevail. ʿĀʾishah was in al-Ḥuddān; the army, 30,000 strong, was at al-Zābūqah, led by those just mentioned. They sent Ḥakīm[794] [b. Salāmah] and Mālik [b. Ḥabīb] back to ʿAlī with the message "We stand by what we agreed to when we left al-Qaʿqāʿ,[795] so come forward!"[796] The two of them left and came to ʿAlī with the message, so he mounted and [went and] took up a position opposite them. The tribes took up positions opposite their own tribes, Muḍar facing Muḍar, Rabīʿah facing Rabīʿah, and Yaman facing Yaman,[797] and they were in no doubt that peace would prevail. Some stood opposite others, and some went across to others, and all they talked about and intended was peace.

The Commander of the Faithful had come out with his 20,000 followers. The Kūfans were led by the same men who had come with them to Dhū Qār. ʿAbd al-Qays had three leaders: Jadhīmah[798] and Bakr were led by Ibn al-Jārūd,[799] al-ʿUmūr were led by ʿAbdallāh b. al-Sawdāʾ, and Ahl Hajar were led by Ibn al-Ashajj.[800] Bakr b. Wāʾil from the Baṣrans were led by Ibn al-Ḥārith b. Nahār, and the Zuṭṭ and Sayābijah were led by Danūr b. ʿAlī. [3181] ʿAlī had come to Dhū Qār with 10,000 and a further 10,000 had joined him.

According to ʿUmar b. Shabbah—Abū al-Ḥasan—Bashīr b.

---

793. Al-ʿAlī, 292; Massignon, 157.

794. For the text's Ḥukaym, see p. 13, above; *Addenda*, DCXXXIV; Wellhausen, 160, and Ibrāhīm.

795. Following Ibrāhīm's vocalization.

796. To make peace.

797. Cf. Muir, 249: "The Beni Ar-Rabiʿa of Al-Kufa fought against the Beni Ar-Rabiʿa of Al-Basra, the Beni Modar of the one against the Beni Modar of the other." Muḍar and Rabīʿah were reckoned as constituting the northern Arabs, Yamaniyyah the southern.

798. Caskel, pl. 169.

799. Probably al-Mundhir b. Bishr, governor of Iṣṭakhr for ʿAlī, d. 61/680–81; see Caskel and Strenziok, I, 169, II, 429.

800. The son of al-Mundhir b. al-Ḥārith al-Ashajj? See Caskel and Strenziok, I, 169, II, 429. Therefore amend Ahl Hajar to Ahl ʿAṣar?

ʿĀṣim—Fiṭr b. Khalīfah—Mundhir al-Thawrī—Muḥammad b. al-Ḥanafiyyah: We set off from Medina with 700 men, and 7,000[801] joined us from Kūfah. A further 2,000 sided with us from[802] round about Baṣrah, most of them Bakr b. Wāʾil; some say 6,000.

Return to Muḥammad and Ṭalḥah's account

When everyone had taken up position and was calm, ʿAlī, Ṭalḥah, and al-Zubayr came out, and they stood facing one another. They discussed their differences and realized that peace and cessation of hostilities were the only appropriate course of action, as they saw that authority had begun to disintegrate and that it might not be regained. So they dispersed from that place on that understanding. ʿAlī returning to his camp, Ṭalḥah and al-Zubayr to theirs.

The Battle

According to al-Sarī (in writing)—Shuʿayb—Sayf—Muḥammad and Ṭalḥah: At dusk ʿAlī sent ʿAbdallāh b. ʿAbbās to Ṭalḥah and al-Zubayr, and at the same time they sent Muḥammad b. Ṭalḥah to ʿAlī with the advice that each side should talk with its followers, and they agreed. So that evening—in Jumādā II—Ṭalḥah and al-Zubayr sent a message to the chiefs of their followers, and ʿAlī did so to his, apart from those who had rebelled against ʿUthmān. So when they retired to bed there was peace. They slept that night as they never had before, because they were free from what they were on the point of and because they had withdrawn from the demands and plans that some of them had been making.[803]

But those who had stirred up the question of ʿUthmān spent the worst night of their lives, for they were on the verge of destruction.[804] All night they were busy in discussion until they decided secretly to open hostilities. They kept it secret for fear that their evil machinations would be found out. Before dawn the next day

[3182]

---

801. Cf. Conrad.
802. Ibrāhīm has *man* for the text's *min*.
803. Lau, 108.
804. Peace would lead to their being brought to justice.

they got up, unnoticed by those nearby, and slipped out on their mission in the dark. Their Muḍar went to[805] their Muḍar, their Rabīʿah to their Rabīʿah, their Yamaniyyah to their Yamaniyyah and began using their weapons [against them]. So the Baṣrans rose up, and so did each fighting group against those of their fellows who had launched a surprise attack against them.[806]

Al-Zubayr and Ṭalḥah then came out with the chiefs of Muḍar and sent ʿAbd al-Raḥmān b. al-Ḥārith b. Hishām[807] to lead the right flank (who were Rabīʿah) and sent ʿAbd al-Raḥmān b. ʿAttāb b. Asīd[808] to the left flank, themselves remaining in the center, and asked,[809] "What is all this?" "The Kūfans came upon us at night" was the reply. At this they said, "We knew that ʿAlī wouldn't stop until he had spilled blood and desecrated what is sacred and that he would never come to an agreement with us." The two of them then returned with the Baṣrans, who repelled those Kūfans[810] [who had launched the surprise attack] and forced them back to their camp. ʿAlī and the Kūfans heard the noise. A man had been placed[811] near ʿAlī to tell him what they wanted him to hear. So when he asked, "What's going on?" this man replied: "A force of theirs made a surprise attack on us at night, but we sent them back to where they came from. We then found them ready for battle, and they began attacking, so everyone rose up to fight." ʿAlī then said to the commander of the right wing of his army, "Engage the right flank!" and to the commander of the left wing: "Engage the left flank! I knew[812] that Ṭalḥah and al-Zubayr wouldn't stop until they had spilled blood and desecrated what is sacred and that they would never come to an agreement with us and that the Sabaʾiyyah would not cease causing trou-

[3183]

---

805. Caetani, IX, 178.

806. *Bahatūhum*, mistranslated by Lau (108) as "had lied to them."

807. From Quraysh; see Caskel and Strenziok, I, 23, II, 129.

808. From Quraysh; killed in the Battle of the Camel; see Caskel and Strenziok, I, 8, II, 128.

809. *Qāla*. Ibrāhīm's *qāla* is a misprint.

810. Following IA, 232.

811. By the attackers. According to IA, 232, by the Sabaʾiyyah, and to Caetani, IX, 179, by ʿUthmān's murderers. That the troublemakers were the Sabaʾiyyah is not specified in this report from Sayf until ʿAlī's remark, which looks like an interpolation; see note 813.

812. Following the text's *ʿalimtu* for Ibrāhīm's *ʿalimta*.

ble."[813] ʿAlī then shouted out to the people: "Hold back! It's nothing!"

Now it had been their unanimous decision regarding this *fitnah* not to be the first aggressor. In that way, they could produce proof and demand rights against the others. [They agreed that] they would not kill anyone running away, nor would they finish off any wounded, nor would they pursue. This was some of what the two sides decided upon and then proclaimed publicly.[814]

According to Al-Sarī (in writing)—Shuʿayb—Sayf—Muḥammad and Ṭalḥah and Abū ʿAmr: Kaʿb b. Sūr came up to ʿĀʾishah and said: "Do something [to save the situation], for the troops are intent on fighting! May Allāh give you success in restoring peace!" So she mounted, and they covered her howdah with protective armor; then they sent her camel named ʿAskar, forward. Yaʿlā b. Umayyah, who had bought it for 200 dinars,[815] had lifted her up on to it. When she emerged from the houses she could hear a commotion, so she halted and soon heard an even louder commotion. "What is it?" she asked, and they replied, "It is the clamor of the army." "For good or for bad?" she asked. "For bad." "Whichever of the parties this clamor comes from," she said, "they will be defeated." By Allāh! She was still standing when defeat surprised her. Al-Zubayr headed off in the direction he happened to be facing and took the road to Wādī al-Sibāʿ. As for Ṭalḥah, an arrow from an unknown archer[816] pinned his knee to the side of his horse. When his boot filled with blood and he became drowsy,[817] he said to his *ghulām*: "Get up behind me on the horse. Hold on to me tightly, and find me a place where I can get off." So they went to al-Baṣrah, and he represented his and al-Zubayr's case in the following poem:

[3184]

Events have hit and killed me [with their arrow],
    while I, on shooting my arrow, have missed them.

---

813. This last phrase appears to have been tagged on (a little awkwardly) to ʿAlī's criticism of Ṭalḥah and al-Zubayr, or perhaps it means "so long as the Sabaʾiyyah keep causing trouble."
814. Caetani, IX, 179.
815. Caskel and Strenziok, I, 67, II, 590.
816. See pp. 127, 150, below.
817. Lane, 343c.

I was lost when I pursued a share[818]
    out of a foolishness I committed, having lost my good
    sense.
I was like al-Kusaʿī[819] in my regret when,
    against my better judgment, I bought the approval of Banū
    Sahm.[820]
I obeyed them by separating from Āl Laʾy,[821]
    who then threw my meat and blood to the wild animals.

Another Account of the Battle of the Camel

According to Abū Jaʿfar [al-Ṭabarī]: Others have given accounts of
this battle and of al-Zubayr and how he left his post that day,
which differ from Sayf's account from his two informants. Some
of them gave the account of that which Aḥmad b. Zuhayr (—his
father Abū Khaythamah—Wahb b. Jarīr b. Ḥāzim—his father—
Yūnus b. Yazīd al-Aylī—al-Zuhrī) told me[822] in an account of the
story of ʿAlī, Ṭalḥah and al-Zubayr, and ʿĀʾishah, which we are in
the process of relating: The news, that is, of the seventy who were
killed with al-ʿAbdī[823] at al-Baṣrah, reached ʿAlī, so he advanced   [3185]
with 12,000 men and came to al-Baṣrah and said:

How deeply I mourn for Rabīʿah,[824]
Rabīʿah who always heard [me] and obeyed.
    This tradition of theirs[825] was what caused this disaster.

When the [forces] confronted each other ʿAlī went out on his horse
and called out to al-Zubayr, and the two of them confronted each
other. ʿAlī asked al-Zubayr, "What has brought you [to this]?"

---

818. A pun on the word *sahm*, which also means "arrow," as in the previous
line.

819. Who regretted the harm he did to himself through his own stupidity
(Thaʿālibi, s.v. *nadāmat al-Kusaʿā*; Fretag, II, 776).

820. I.e., Banū Umayyah. A further pun on the word.

821. I.e., Banū Hāshim.

822. I.e., Abū Jaʿfar al-Ṭabarī.

823. Al-Ḥakīm b. Jabalah.

824. ʿAbd al-Qays was part of Rabīʿah. Cf. p. 86, above.

825. Reading *sunnatuhā* with Ibrāhīm, i.e., a tradition of obedience to ʿAlī. De
Goeje suggests *nubbiʾtuhā* "I have been given the news that they have had a
disaster" (*Addenda*, DCXXXIV).

"You," he replied. "I don't find you[826] suitable for this leadership or more entitled to it than we." "After ʿUthmān," replied ʿAlī, "it is certainly not you who are suitable for it. We considered you one of Banū ʿAbd al-Muṭṭalib[827] until your son,[828] the son of evil, reached maturity and created a division between us and you." ʿAlī then said how bad the evil he had done was and mentioned how the Prophet had passed by the two of them and had said to ʿAlī: "What did the son of your father's sister[829] say? He will fight you, being the aggressor." Al-Zubayr then left him, saying, "I will not fight you." He returned to his son ʿAbdallāh and said, "I have no firm conviction about this war." "When you set out you did have," replied his son, "but you saw the banners of Ibn Abī Ṭālib and you realized that that meant death, so you lost heart." These words angered him so that he shook with rage and said angrily: "Woe betide you! I have sworn him an oath not to fight him." "Expiate your oath by freeing your *ghulām* Sarjis," his son replied. So he freed him, and he joined the ranks alongside them. ʿAlī had said to al-Zubayr: "Are you asking me for compensation for the blood of ʿUthmān, when it was you who killed him? I ask Allāh in His power right now to give a hateful punishment[830] to he among us who was the severest in opposing ʿUthmān." ʿAlī said to Ṭalḥah: "You have brought the Messenger of Allāh's wife to make her fight while you hide your wife at home.[831] Didn't you give me allegiance?" "I did," he replied, "but with the sword at my neck."

[3186]   ʿAlī then said to those around him:[832] "Which of you will hold up this copy of the Qurʾān and what is in it before them? Should his hand be cut off, he will then take it with his other one; if that is cut off, he will take it with his teeth." A young boy[833] said, "I will." ʿAlī put this to everyone around him, but none volunteered

---

826. Reading *lā arāka* for the text's *lā urāka*.

827. Ṣafiyyah, al-Zubayr's mother, was the daughter of ʿAbd al-Muṭṭalib, the grandfather of the Prophet and ʿAlī.

828. ʿAbdallāh, who became anticaliph during Yazīd b. Muʿāwiyah's rule.

829. Ṣafiyyah.

830. E.g., be killed.

831. Cf. pp. 62, 101, above.

832. For this motif, see Nöldeke, *Geschichte*, 126; *Addenda*, DCXXXIV; Noth, *Quellenkristische Studien*, 154. Cf. also p. 129, below.

833. Called Muslim on p. 130, below.

except the boy, so ʿAlī said to him, "Hold this up before them and say, 'Every word in this shall judge between you and us, and I beg of you for Allāh's sake to stop shedding our blood and yours.'" But, with the copy of the Qurʾān in his hand, the boy was attacked. His hands were cut off, so he took it in his teeth until he was killed. ʿAlī then said, "Battle is now justified, so fight them!"

Seventy[834] men were killed that day, each holding in turn the nose rein of ʿĀʾishah's camel. After the camel was hamstrung and the force was routed, an arrow hit Ṭalḥah and killed him. Some say that it was fired by Marwān b. al-Ḥakam.[835] At one stage Ibn al-Zubayr had taken hold of the camel's nose rein and ʿĀʾishah had said, "Who is this?" When he told her she said, "Weep for the bereavement of Asmāʾ!"[836] Indeed he did get wounded and threw himself down among the other wounded and was pulled out and recovered from his wound.

Muḥammad b. Abī Bakr carried ʿĀʾishah[837] away and erected a large tent over her. ʿAlī came and stood in front of her and said: "You roused the people, and they became excited.[838] You stirred up discord among them such that some killed others," and he went on at length. ʿĀʾishah replied: "Ibn Abī Ṭālib! You have gained your victory. Give me an honorable pardon.[839] You have put your forces to the test very well today." ʿAlī then let her go free and sent a group of men and women with her, equipped her, and ordered her to be given 12,000 dirhams.[840] ʿAbdallāh b. Jaʿfar thought that was too little and brought out a huge sum for her, saying, "If the Commander of the Faithful does not authorize it, then I will pay it myself."   [3187]

It was alleged that al-Zubayr was killed by Ibn Jurmūz and that he was standing by the door of the Commander of the Faithful and said to the doorkeeper, "Ask leave for the killer of al-Zubayr to

---

834. Cf. Conrad.

835. See Hinds, "Murder," 469 n. 3.

836. Her sister and Ibn al-Zubayr's mother; see p. 55, above. I.e., "you are also going to get killed."

837. His sister.

838. *Istafzazti . . . fazzū.* IA has *istanfarti . . . farrū,* "You mobilized the people and they rushed to fight."

839. Lane, 1306b.

840. Caetani, IX, 137.

enter." ʿAlī said, "Let him in and give him the good news that he is going to hell."[841]

According to Muḥammad b. ʿUmārah—ʿUbaydallāh b. Mūsā—Fuḍayl—Sufyān b. ʿUqbah—Qurrah b. al-Ḥārith: I was siding with al-Aḥnaf b. Qays, and Jawn b. Qatādah, my father's brother's son, was siding with al-Zubayr b. al-ʿAwwām, and Jawn told me: While they were hailing al-Zubayr as amir a horseman came riding up and greeted him as amir also. After al-Zubayr had returned the greeting, the man said, "That force of ʿAlī has reached such and such a place, and of the armies that have come against you I've never seen one with shabbier weapons and smaller numbers and more fearful." Then he left. Another horseman then came and greeted him as amir. After al-Zubayr had returned the greeting the man said, "The force has reached such and such a place, and they have heard of the numbers, equipment, and arms that Almighty and Glorious Allāh has amassed for you, and Allāh has put fear in their hearts, so they have turned back in retreat." "That's enough from you just now," said al-Zubayr. "By Allāh! If all Ibn Abī Ṭālib could find was ʿarfaj he would walk against us holding it."[842] Then he left. A third horseman came as the horses were on the point of emerging from the dust cloud, and greeted him as amir. After al-Zubayr had returned the greeting, the man [3188] said, "That force has come out against you, and I met ʿAmmār b. Yāsir among them and talked with him." "He's not on their side!" exclaimed al-Zubayr. "Yes he is. By Allāh! He is on their side," replied the horseman. "I swear Allāh would not have put him on their side," said al-Zubayr. "I swear Allāh has put him on their side." "I swear Allāh would not have put him on their side."[843] Seeing the man contradict him al-Zubayr said to one of his followers: "Mount! See whether he's speaking the truth!" So he mounted with him, and they set off, and I watched them until they stopped for a short while next to the cavalry. Then they returned to us, and al-Zubayr said to this man, "Well?" "He spoke

---

841. See p. 159, below.

842. ʿArfaj is a small shrub the size of a sitting man, with many soft shoots but no leaves (Ibn Manẓūr, III, 147f.), i.e., ʿAlī is unbeatable; he does not even need weapons.

843. Al-Zubayr's anxiety is because he had been present when the Prophet predicted that oppressors would kill ʿAmmār.

the truth," he replied, and al-Zubayr exclaimed, "It feels as though my nose has been cut off!" or "It feels as though my back has been cut in two!" (Muḥammad b. ʿUmārah—ʿUbaydallāh [b. Mūsā]—Fuḍayl: I do not know which he actually said.) He began to tremble such that his weapon shook, and Jawn said: "May my mother be bereaved of me! This is the man[844] I wanted to die with or live with. I swear by He Who holds my soul in His hand that this fear I see that has taken hold of him is [only] because of something he heard or saw from the Messenger of God."

While these men were thus occupied [al-Zubayr] turned to go, mounted, and left. Jawn did the same[845] and caught up with al-Aḥnaf. Two horsemen then appeared and came to al-Aḥnaf and his companions, dismounted, and urgently demanded his attention. They conferred secretly with him for an hour and then departed. ʿAmr b. Jurmūz[846] then came to al-Aḥnaf and said, "I caught up with al-Zubayr in Wādī al-Sibāʿ and killed him." Jawn used to say, "I swear by He Who holds my soul in His hand, al-Aḥnaf was the one who planned to kill al-Zubayr."

According to ʿUmar b. Shabbah—Abū al-Ḥasan [al-Madāʾinī]—Bashīr[847] b. ʿĀṣim—al-Ḥajjāj b. Arṭāh—ʿAmmār b. Muʿāwiyah al-Duhnī—[Duhn being] a branch of Aḥmas Bajīlah:[848] On the day of the Battle of the Camel ʿAlī took a copy of the Qurʾān and took it around his companions, asking, "Who will face death and take this copy of the Qurʾān to call them to what it contains?" A Kūfan youth came forward wearing a padded white tunic[849] and said, "I will." But ʿAlī ignored him. ʿAlī asked again, "Who will face death and take this copy of the Qurʾān to call them to what it contains?" The youth said, "I will." But ʿAlī again ignored him. ʿAlī asked a third time, "Who will face death and take this copy of the Qurʾān to call them to what it contains?" The youth again said, "I will," so ʿAlī handed it to him. He then called them, but they cut off his right hand. So he took it with his left and called them, and they

[3189]

---

844. Al-Zubayr.
845. Having decided that al-Zubayr was a lost cause.
846. ʿUmayr on p. 112, above.
847. Caetani, IX, 139, has Bishr.
848. Caskel, pl. 223.
849. *Qabāʾ*; Lane, Supp. 2984. Similar to a *qafṭān*; Dozy, 352–62.

cut that off as well. So he held it to his chest, with the blood flowing down over his tunic, and he was killed. ʿAlī then said, "Fighting them is now lawful." Among the youth's mother's verses in mourning were

O Allāh! Muslim[850] called them,
    reciting the Book of Allāh without fearing them.
Their mother[851] was standing looking on,
    not restraining them as they plotted folly together.[852]
Their beards are dyed with clots of blood.

According to ʿUmar b. Shabbah—Abū al-Ḥasan [al-Madāʾinī]—Abū Mikhnaf—Jābir—al-Shaʿbī: The right flank of the army of the Commander of the Faithful attacked the Baṣran left flank and fought, and the enemy troops took refuge with ʿĀʾishah, most of them being Ḍabbah and Azd. The fighting lasted from late morning until nearly midafternoon; some say until nearer sunset.[853] When they were routed an Azd tribesman called out, "Turn!" But Muḥammad b. ʿAlī[854] struck him and cut his hand off, so the man called out: "Men of Azd! Flee!" A large number of Azd were killed, and they cried out [as they fled], "We follow the way[855] of ʿAlī b. Abī Ṭālib." A man from Banū Layth[856] later said:

[3190]   Ask about us on the day when we met the Azd,
    when the horses were running yellow and red—
We sliced their livers and forearms.
    May they be far away in their [foolish] opinion and be
    distant!

According to ʿUmar b. Shabbah—Abū al-Ḥasan [al-Madāʾinī]—Jaʿfar b. Sulaymān—Mālik b. Dīnār: ʿAmmār attacked al-Zubayr on the day of the Battle of the Camel and had begun to drive a spear at him when he said, "Do you want to kill me?" "No! Leave!" he said.

---

850. Ibn ʿAbdallāh (see p. 152, below), rather than "a Muslim" (Caetani, IX, 139).
851. ʿĀʾishah.
852. IA: "ordering them to kill and not restraining them."
853. See Lane, 1271, 906.
854. Ibn al-Ḥanafiyyah.
855. *Dīn*.
856. A follower of ʿAlī.

According to ʿĀmir b. Ḥafṣ: On the day of the Battle of the Camel ʿAmmār approached and drove the spear at al-Zubayr, who said, "Are you going to kill me, Abū al-Yaqẓān?" "No, Abū ʿAbdallāh," he replied.

Return to Sayf's account

According to Muḥammad and Ṭalḥah: When the army was routed at the height of the morning al-Zubayr called out to them: "Al-Zubayr is over here! Come to me!" A *mawlā* of his was with him calling out, "Are you running away from the disciple of the Messenger of God?!" But then al-Zubayr set off toward Wādī al-Sibāʿ, pursued by some horsemen. The armies did not notice him, busy in combat with each other, so when he saw the horsemen after him he turned and attacked them and split them up. They charged again, but when they recognized him they said: "It's al-Zubayr! Let him be!" A group including ʿIlbāʾ b. al-Haytham . . .[857] and al-Qaʿqāʿ with a group then passed Ṭalḥah, who was saying: "To me, servants of Allāh! Hold fast! Hold fast!" But he[858] said to him, "Abū Muḥammad, you're wounded and cannot achieve what you want, so go back to the tents!" Then he said, *"Ghulām,* take me [into the city], and find me a place [to rest]!" So he was taken to al-Baṣrah, accompanied by a *ghulām* and two men. The fight went on after he had left, and in the rout the men retreated toward al-Baṣrah. But when they saw that the camel had been encircled by Muḍar[859] they rallied and reformed as a center [of the army],[860] as they had been when they [first] engaged in battle, and returned to fight anew, while Rabīʿah of al-Baṣrah held their ground, some as a right flank, some as a left. "Kaʿb! Leave the camel, and go forward holding the Book of Almighty and Glorious Allāh, and call them to it!" said ʿĀʾishah and thrust the Qurʾān copy at him. Then up came the forces headed by the Sabaʾiyyah, fearing that peace would be made, and Kaʿb met them with the Qurʾān copy. ʿAlī was behind them, restraining them, but they insisted on advancing, and then when Kaʿb called them they all shot [their ar-

[3191]

---

857. There is a lacuna in the text here; supply "approached"?
858. Perhaps the *ghulām,* who may have appeared in the lacuna.
859. I.e., to protect ʿĀʾishah.
860. Muir, 249; Caetani, IX, 180; cf. p. 151, below.

rows] at him at the same time[861] and killed him. They then shot at 'Ā'ishah in her howdah, and she started calling out: "My sons! [Remember] the recompense [of Allāh]![862] The recompense!" She raised her voice very loud, "Allāh! Allāh! Remember Almighty and Glorious Allāh and the reckoning!" But they insisted on advancing. So the next thing she did when they insisted was to cry out: "You men! Curse the killers of 'Uthmān and their various supporters!" She began to imprecate [them], and the people of Baṣrah filled the air with the noise of imprecation. 'Alī heard the imprecation and asked, "What's all that shouting?" "It's 'Ā'ishah imprecating the killers of 'Uthmān and their various supporters," they replied, "and [her army] imprecating them with her." So 'Alī also began to imprecate: "O Allāh! Curse the killers of 'Uthmān and their various supporters!"

She then sent a message to 'Abd al-Raḥmān b. 'Attāb and 'Abd al-Raḥmān b. al-Ḥārith: "Keep up your positions!" She then urged her people to fight when she saw that 'Alī's army wanted only her and were not holding back from [her] men. Then Muḍar of al-Baṣrah advanced and attacked Muḍar of al-Kūfah, so that 'Alī became hard pressed and pushed on the nape of [his son] Muḥammad's neck and told him, "Attack!" But he shrank back, so 'Alī stretched out his hand to the banner to take it from him. Then [Muḥammad] attacked, so ['Alī] left the banner in [Muḥammad's] hand. Muḍar of al-Kūfah then attacked. Swords were clashing in front of the camel, and the [battle] grew hot, while the outer flanks stayed as they were, accomplishing nothing. Now 'Alī had tribes with him other than Muḍar. Zayd b. Ṣūḥān[863] was from one of these, and a man from his tribe said to him: "Go back to your tribe! What's this situation got to do with you? Don't you see that Muḍar [of al-Baṣrah] are over against you and that the camel is before your very eyes and that death is this side of it?!" "Death is better than life; death is what I want," he replied. So he was shot and his brother Sayḥān[864] also. Ṣa'ṣa'ah[865] was brought away

[3192]

---

861. Reading *rishqan* with Ibrāhīm (cf. Lane, 1090b) for the text's *rashqan*. Cf. p. 152, below.

862. *Baqiyyat Allāh* (Qur'ān 11:87; Lane, 238c).

863. From 'Abd al-Qays; see Caskel and Strenziok, I, 170, II, 603.

864. Caskel and Strenziok, I, 170, II, 502.

865. Another brother; see Caskel and Strenziok, I, 170, II, 538.

wounded. The battle raged fiercely, and when ʿAlī saw this he sent word to Yaman and Rabīʿah: "Join those next to you!"[866]

A tribesman from ʿAbd al-Qays stood forward and said, "We are calling you to the Book of Almighty and Glorious Allāh." "And how can someone call us to the Book of Allāh," they[867] replied, "who doesn't carry out the punishments of Allāh (may He be praised!) and who killed the one who called for Allāh, Kaʿb b. Sūr?" At this Rabīʿah all shot [their arrows] at him at the same time and killed him. Muslim b. ʿAbdallāh al-ʿIjlī then stood where he had been, and they all shot [their arrows] at him at the same time and killed him. Yaman of al-Kūfah then called Yaman of al-Baṣrah, but they shot [arrows] at them.

According to al-Sarī (in writing)—Shuʿayb—Sayf—Muḥammad and Ṭalḥah: The first engagement raged fiercely until midday. During it Ṭalḥah was wounded and al-Zubayr was lost. When the others then gathered round ʿĀʾishah, and the Kūfans were insisting on fighting, with ʿĀʾishah as their only target, she urged on her own men, and they fought on until they called out to one another and made a truce. But they returned to fighting in the afternoon. This was Thursday[868] in Jumādā II. They fought the early part of the day with Ṭalḥah and al-Zubayr and the middle part with ʿĀʾishah. The fighters advanced against each other, and Yaman of al-Baṣrah routed Yaman of al-Kūfah and Rabīʿah of al-Baṣrah routed Rabīʿah of al-Kūfah. ʿAlī then rushed with Muḍar of al-Kūfah against Muḍar of al-Baṣrah and said: "Death has no escape. It catches up with the fleer and does not abandon the one who holds his ground!"

According to ʿUmar—Abū al-Ḥasan—Abū ʿAbdallāh al-Qurashī —Yūnus b. Arqam—ʿAlī b. ʿAmr al-Kindī—Zayd b. Ḥisās[869]— Muḥammad b. al-Ḥanafiyyah: My father thrust the banner at me on the Day of the Camel and said, "Advance!" So I did until I could find no way forward except against a spear. "Advance!" he

[3193]

---

866. *Ijtamiʿū ʿalā man yalīkum*: perhaps "Fight together against those facing you!" or "Gather behind one leader!"
867. On ʿĀʾishah's side.
868. This is at least a month different from the date given on pp. 76 and 81, above.
869. Ibn Jassās or Ḥassān (*Addenda*, DCXXXIV) or Ḥashās (Caskel, I, 185, II, 601)?

said, "you without a mother!" But I drew back and said, "I find no way forward except against the head of a spear." So another person took hold of the banner from me—I don't know who he was—and I looked up and there was my father in front of me, saying:

You are the one whom my good will has tempted [to take
        more].[870]
        O ʿAysha![871] the people around you are actually enemies.
Giving in is better than to have one's sons fighting.

According to al-Sarī (in writing)—Shuʿayb—Sayf—Muḥammad and Ṭalḥah: The two flanks fought a fierce fight as they advanced against each other, as had happened with the two centers. The Yamanīs fought from both sides, and ten of them from al-Kūfah were killed by the banner of the Commander of the Faithful— every time a man took it he was killed—five of these were from Hamdān[872] and five from the rest of Yaman. When Yazīd b. Qays[873] saw this, he took it and held it tightly in his hand, saying:

[3194] Soul of mine! you have lived and have become rich
        for a long while. The length you have remained is enough
        for you today!
Will you always be seeking[874] long life?

In fact, he was quoting this from an earlier poet. Nimrān b. Abī Nimrān al-Hamdānī then said:

I bared my blade into the tribesmen from Azd.[875]
        I struck into their old men and beardless youths,
All of them with long forearms[876] and eager to fight.

Then Rabīʿah of al-Kūfah advanced, and among them killed round the banner of the left flank was Zayd. Then Ṣaʿṣaʿah was thrown

---

870. Reading al-ʿutbā for al-ḥusnā, following Nöldeke (Addenda, DCXXXIV).
871. I.e., ʿĀʾishah.
872. A southern Arab tribe (EI², q.v.).
873. Ibn Tammām of Hamdān, ʿAlī's governor of Iṣfahān and al-Rayy and involved in the murder of ʿUthmān; see Caskel and Strenziok, I, 231, II, 596.
874. Following the text's aṭalbu (=aṭalabu) ṭūliʾl-ʿumri for Ibrāhīm's aṭlabu ṭūlaʾl-ʿumri.
875. Defending ʿĀʾishah. See these verses again on p. 144, below.
876. I.e., good with swords.

down, then Sayḥān, then ʿAbdallāh b. Raqabah[877] b. al-Mughīrah.
Abū ʿUbaydah b. Rāshid b. Sulmā[878] said as he was thrown down:
"O Allāh! You led us out of error, You rescued us from ignorance,
You afflicted us with *fitnah*, and we became confused and in
doubt." Then he was killed. Then al-Ḥusayn b. Maʿbad b. al-
Nuʿmān was thrown down, too, and he handed the banner to his
son Maʿbad, as he began to say: "Maʿbad! Take her young camel
near her,[879] and she'll become affectionate,"[880] and it remained
firm in his grip.

According to al-Sarī (in writing)—Shuʿayb—Sayf—Muḥammad
and Ṭalḥah: When the armored warriors of Muḍar of al-Baṣrah and
Muḍar of al-Kūfah saw that no one was giving in, they called out
among the armies of ʿĀʾishah and ʿAlī: "Men! Attack the extremities when your endurance is running out and when victory is
elusive!" So they began stabbing extremities—arms and legs. No
battle has ever been seen before or after, or been heard of, in which   [3195]
there were more cut-off arms and legs whose owners were not
known than this one. ʿAbd al-Raḥmān b. ʿAttāb lost a hand that
day before he was killed, and, when a fighter from this group or
that lost any extremity, he would fight like a martyr until he was
killed.

According to al-Sarī (in writing)—Shuʿayb—Sayf—al-Ṣaʿb b.
ʿAṭiyyah b. Bilāl—his father: The situation got very bad, so the
Kūfan right flank retreated to the center and stayed there. The
Baṣran left flank stayed close to their center and prevented the
Kūfan right flank from penetrating there, but they came very
close. The same thing happened with the Kūfan left flank and
the Baṣran right flank. ʿĀʾishah then asked the man on her left,
"Who are these?" "Your sons al-Azd," replied Ṣabrah b. Shaymān.
"Tribesmen of Ghassān!"[881] she called out, "we used to hear tell
of your prowess with the sword; keep it up today!" and she quoted
the verses

---

877. For the text's Ruqayyah (*Addenda*, DCXXXIV). Probably Ibn Khawṭaʿah, rather than Ibn al-Mughīrah; see p. 142, below, as also for the others that follows.
878. Or Rāshid; see p. 143, below.
879. War.
880. I.e., fight hard, and the battle will go in your favor.
881. Southern Arabian confederation (Caskel and Strenziok, II, 35, 273).

The Ghassānī protectors fought with their swords,
     as did Hinb[882] and Aws[883] and Shabīb.[884]

She then asked the man on her right, "Who are these?" "Bakr b. Wāʾil," they replied. She said, "It was of you the poet said:

They came at us with swords and armor as though they were,
     judging from their impenetrable strength, Bakr b. Wāʾil.

It's only ʿAbd al-Qays in front of you!" So they fought their fiercest engagement[885] until then. Then she went up to the squadron in front of her and asked, "Who are these?" "Banū Nājiyah,"[886] they replied. "Bravo! Bravo! Abṭaḥiyyah[887] swords and Qurashī swords!" said she. And they clashed swords in a way anyone would want to avoid. Then Banū Ḍabbah circled round, [protecting] her, and she said, "Go to it! The choicest coalition[888] [has come]!" Then, when they became thinned out,[889] Banū ʿAdī joined them and many people were around ʿĀʾishah, and she asked, "Who are you?" "Banū ʿAdī," they replied. "We've come to join our brothers." "The head of the camel remained steady," she said, "until Banū Ḍabbah were killed around me." So Banū ʿAdī kept the camel's head upright and fought in such a way—not trying to make excuses or turning aside when losing the ends of limbs—until, when this increased and became widespread in both camps together, [the enemy forces] went for the camel, saying, "The enemy will not be removed unless it's killed," and ʿAlī's two flanks then shifted and joined the center. The Baṣrans did the same, and the fighters were filled with hatred toward one another. Then they all came together in their two centers, and Ibn Yathribī took hold of the camel's head and said the following *rajaz* verses, claiming that he had killed ʿIlbāʾ b. al-Haytham, Zayd b. Ṣūḥān, and Hind b. ʿAmr:

[3196]

---

882. Southern Arabian tribe (Caskel and Strenziok, I, 328, II, 283).
883. Southern Arabian tribe (Caskel and Strenziok, II, 35, 214).
884. Southern Arabian tribe (Caskel and Strenziok, I, 202, II, 522).
885. Reading *qitāl* (*Addenda*, DCXXXIV) for the text's *al-qitāl*.
886. From Quraysh.
887. From Mecca.
888. *Jamrat al-jamarāt*, i.e., Banū Ḍabbah b. Udd, Banū al-Ḥārith b. Kaʿb, and Banū Numayr b. ʿĀmir; see Lane, 453b; Caskel and Strenziok, I, 247.
889. Through being killed.

For those that don't know me, I am Ibn Yathribī,
   the killer of ʿIlbāʾ and of Hind al-Jamalī,
And of a son of Ṣūḥān, who followed the way of ʿAlī.[890]

ʿAmmār then called out to him:[891] "By my life! You've taken refuge in a secure stronghold, and there's no way to get at you. If you're speaking truthfully, come out from this squadron, and come near me!" So Ibn Yathribī left the halter in the hand of a Banū ʿAdī tribesman and moved into a position between ʿĀʾishah's army and ʿAlī's. The people then thronged round ʿAmmār until he approached Ibn Yathribī. ʿAmmār warded him off with his shield, and Ibn Yathribī struck ʿAmmār. His sword got embedded in the shield, and he tried to pull it out but could not. ʿAmmār then went out against him, completely out of control. He stooped down and cut off Ibn Yathribī's legs, and he[892] fell down on his backside. His companions put him on a horse, and he was later carried off the battlefield near death; he was brought to ʿAlī, who ordered his head to be cut off. When Ibn Yathribī was wounded that ʿAdawī tribesman left the halter and came out to fight, calling out, "Who will come out to fight?" ʿAmmār held back, but Rabīʿah al-ʿUqaylī[893] appeared in front of him. (The ʿAdawī tribesman's name was ʿAmrah b. Bajrah.[894]) Rabīʿah had the strongest voice in the army, and he declaimed the verses [3197]

O Mother of ours! the most refractory[895] mother we know!
   A mother [normally] feeds a son and shows him mercy.
Have you not seen how many a brave is being wounded,
   his hand and wrist made lonely?

Then they clashed, and each one of them wounded his opponent, and they both died.

ʿAṭiyyah b. Bilāl continued: At the end of the day a man called al-Ḥārith of Banū Ḍabbah joined us and took the place of the ʿAdawī, and we have never, ever seen a stronger man than he, and he began to recite the verses

---

890. ʿAlā dīn ʿAlī. See p. 154, below.
891. Ibn Yathribī.
892. Ibn Yathribī.
893. Caskel and Strenziok, I, 102?
894. Following Ibrāhīm; the text has no diacritics, except on the final letter.
895. See p. 141, below, for a variant of these verses.

We, Banū[896] Ḍabbah, are the allies of the camel;
  we lament the death of Ibn ʿAffān with tips of spears.
[3198]   Death is sweeter to us than honey!
  Send back our chief[897] to us, and that will be enough.[898]

According to ʿUmar b. Shabbah—Abū[899] al-Ḥasan—al-Mufaḍḍal b. Muḥammad—ʿAdī b. Abī ʿAdī—Abū Rajāʾ al-ʿUṭāridī: I was watching a man on the Day of the Camel. He was turning his sword this way and that in his hand, as though it were a toy,[900] reciting all the while:

We, Banū Ḍabbah, are the allies of the camel;
  we take the field against death whenever death dismounts.
Death, we want it more than honey!
  We lament the death of Ibn ʿAffān with tips of spears.
Send back our chief to us, and that will be enough.

According to ʿUmar—Abū al-Ḥasan—al-Mufaḍḍal al-Ḍabbī: The man was Wasīm b. ʿAmr b. Ḍirār al-Ḍabbī.
According to ʿUmar—Abū al-Ḥasan—al-Hudhalī: ʿAmr b. Yathribī was urging on his tribe on the Day of the Camel. They took their turns holding the nose rope and said the *rajaz* verses

We, Banū Ḍabbah, will not flee
  until we see [our own] skulls tumble
And boiling red blood tumbling from them.

Mother of ours, ʿAysha! Do not fear!
  All your sons are heroes brave.[901]
Mother of ours, wife of the Prophet,
  wife of the blessed and the guided!

This continued until forty men had been killed holding the nose rope. ʿĀʾishah said, "My camel remained steady until I no longer

---

896. *Banū* in the text, *banī* in Ibrāhīm (see his note), as also in following occurrences.
897. ʿUthmān.
898. Ibn Manẓūr, XIII, 48.17. An impossible demand meaning therefore "fight to the end!" These verses come again on p. 153, below.
899. Following *Addenda*, DCXXXIV.
900. *Mikhrāq*—either a wooden or plaited-rag sword (Lane, 729c).
901. Cf. p. 149, below.

heard the cries of Banū Ḍabbah." On that day 'Amr b. Yathribī [3199]
killed 'Ilbā' b. al-Haytham al-Sadūsī, Hind b. 'Amr al-Jamalī, and
Zayd b. Ṣūḥān, while reciting these *rajaz* verses:

I strike out at them but I do not see[902] Abū Ḥasan.[903]
    This is the biggest grief that could be!
We are setting the leadership the way we fix a nose rein.[904]

Al-Hudhalī, however, maintained that this poem was recited at
the Battle of Ṣiffīn.[905]

'Ammār then confronted 'Amr b. Yathribī. 'Ammār was then
ninety years old and was wearing a fur garment with a rope of
palm fiber tied around his waist. 'Amr b. Yathribī rushed toward
him, but ['Ammār] turned his leather shield toward him, and
['Amr] drove into it with his sword, and the people shot at him
until he was knocked down, while reciting:

If you kill me, I am still Ibn Yathribī,
    the killer of 'Ilbā' and Hind al-Jamalī,
And then of Ibn Ṣūḥān, whose cause was the way of 'Alī.

He was taken prisoner and then brought to 'Alī. "Spare me!" he
asked. "After those three whom you advanced against with your
sword," replied 'Alī, "and struck their faces with it?" So 'Alī ordered him to be killed.

According to 'Umar—Abū al-Ḥasan—Abū Mikhnaf—Isḥāq b.
Rāshid—'Abbād b. 'Abdallāh b. al-Zubayr—his father: I came out
of the day of the Camel with thirty-seven wounds from blows and
stabs. I never saw anything like the Day of the Camel. Not a
single one of us fled; we were as solid as rock.[906] All who took
hold of the camel's nose rein were killed. 'Abd al-Raḥmān b. 'Attāb took it and was killed; al-Aswad b. Abī al-Bakhtarī took it and
was thrown to the ground; then I came and took hold of the nose
rein. "Who are you?" asked 'Ā'ishah. "'Abdallāh b. al-Zubayr," I

---

902. Reading *arā* with Ibrāhīm and Nöldeke (*Addenda*, DCXXXIV) for the text's
urā.
903. 'Alī was perhaps in the fray elsewhere.
904. "We are doing our best to control the situation." This line also occurs on
p. 16, above.
905. *EI*[1], s.v.
906. Lit., "like the black mountain."

[3200]

replied. "Weep for the bereavement of Asmāʾ!"[907] exclaimed ʿĀʾishah. At this point al-Ashtar passed me. I recognized him, so I got hold of him round the chest, and we fell down together. "Kill me and Mālik!" I called out to those around. Men from both armies came and fought on behalf of each of us. When we stopped fighting, the nose rein was no longer being held. "Hamstring the camel!"[908] cried out ʿAlī. "If it's hamstrung they'll disperse." So a man struck it, and it fell, and I have never heard a sound more noisy than the bellowing of that camel. ʿAlī then ordered Muḥammad b. Abī Bakr to set up a tent over ʿĀʾishah. "See if anything has hit her," he said, so Muḥammad put his head in. "Damn you! Who are you?" she cried. "The member of your family you hate most!" "Ibn al-Khathʿamiyyah?"[909] "That's right." "You're more precious to me than my father and my mother," she replied. "Praise to Allāh, Who has spared you!"

According to Isḥāq b. Ibrāhīm b. Ḥabīb b. al-Shahīd—Abū Bakr b. ʿAyyāsh—ʿAlqamah: I said to al-Ashtar, "But you were very much against the killing of ʿUthmān, so what made you come out to al-Baṣrah?" "These men gave allegiance to him and then reneged, and it was Ibn al-Zubayr who forced ʿĀʾishah to come out. So I was praying to Almighty and Glorious Allāh to make me meet him to fight. He did meet me, and we fought hand to hand. But I was not satisfied simply with the strength of my arm. So I stood up in the stirrup, struck him on his head, and threw him down." We[910] asked, "So it was he who said, 'Kill me and Mālik!'" "No. I didn't leave him needing anything more done to him. The one you mean is ʿAbd al-Raḥmān b. ʿAttāb b. Asīd. He met me, and we each hit the other. He knocked me down, and I knocked him down, so he began saying, 'Kill me and Mālik!' But they didn't know who Mālik was.[911] Had they known they would have killed me."

Abū Bakr b. ʿAyyāsh said: "Here is your documentary evidence

---

907. See p. 127, above.
908. Cf. Abbot, "Women," 263.
909. Al-Khathʿamiyyah is Asmāʾ bt. ʿUmays of Khathʿam, Abū Bakr's third wife (*EI*[2], s.v. Abū Bakr). ʿAlī married her when Abū Bakr died, which is perhaps part of the reason why Muḥammad was "most hated." ʿĀʾishah's mother was Umm Rūmān bint ʿĀmir of Kinānah. The mother of Asmāʾ (al-Zubayr's wife) was Qutaylah bt. ʿAbd al-ʿUzzā of ʿĀmir, and Umm Kulthūm's mother was Ḥabībah bt. Khārijah of al-Ḥārith b. al-Khazraj.
910. ʿAlqamah and others.
911. He was always known as al-Ashtar.

for this story.[912] Al-Mughīrah told me it, from[913] Ibrāhīm from
ʿAlqamah, who said, 'I said to al-Ashtar' and so on."

According to ʿAbdallāh b. Aḥmad—his father—Sulaymān—
ʿAbdallāh—Ṭalḥah b. al-Nadr—ʿUthmān b. Sulaymān—ʿAbdallāh   [3201]
b. al-Zubayr: A young man stood in front of us and said, "Beware
of these two men!"[914] He then mentioned him[915] [that] the char-
acteristic trait of al-Ashtar was that one of his feet was exposed
because of a pain he felt in it. "So when we met up," he continued, "al-Ashtar said, 'When [ʿAbdallāh b. al-Zubayr] came at me
he leveled his spear at my foot, so I said: "This man is stupid.
What could he achieve from me even if he cut it right off? Aren't I
going to kill him?"[916] But when [ʿAbdallāh b. al-Zubayr] got near
me he grabbed [his] spear with both hands and searched out my
face with it. I said, "He's some opponent!"'"

According to ʿUmar b. Shabbah—Abū al-Ḥasan—Abū Mikhnaf
—Ibn ʿAbd al-Raḥmān b. Jundab—his father—his grandfather:
ʿAmr b. al-Ashraf[917] took hold of the camel's nose rein, and no one
came near him without being struck by his sword, until al-Ḥārith
b. Zuhayr al-Azdī[918] approached, saying the verses

O Mother of ours! O best Mother we know!
    Do you not see how many a brave is being wounded,
His head and wrist made lonely?[919]

They exchanged a couple of blows and I saw them both thrashing
the ground with their legs[920] until they died. Later I (Jundab) went
to visit ʿĀʾishah in Medina. "Who are you?" she asked. "An Azdī

---

912. *Hādhā kitābuka shāhiduhu.*

913. ʿAn—following Ibrāhīm and *Addenda*, DCXXXIII, and ignoring Prym's suggestion in his n. c to substitute *ibn* for ʿan, i.e., al-Mughīrah ibn Ibrāhīm. According to Ibrāhīm's index, the missing links between Ibn ʿAyyāsh and ʿAlqamah (see
the *isnād* at the beginning of the preceding paragraph) are al-Mughīrah b. Miqsam
and Ibrāhīm al-Nakhaʿī.

914. Al-Ashtar and ʿAbdallāh b. al-Zubayr, who were both renowned for their
strength.

915. The text of this report is difficult, perhaps corrupt, in places. Here it is most
probably referring to al-Ashtar.

916. Ibrāhīm's paragraph break here is not helpful.

917. Al-ʿAtakī al-Azdī—his tribe had not yet emigrated to al-Baṣrah (Caskel and
Strenziok, I, 203, II, 171).

918. Of the Kabīr branch (Caskel and Strenziok, I, 218, II, 315).

919. See p. 137, above, for a variant of these verses.

920. Having been wounded and knocked over.

tribesman living in Kūfah." "Were you present with us on the Day of the Camel?" "Yes." "For us or against us?" "Against," I replied. "Do you know then who it was who said: 'Mother of ours! O best Mother we know?'" "I do," I replied. "It was my paternal cousin," and she wept so bitterly I thought she was not going to stop.

According to ʿUmar—Abū al-Ḥasan—Abū Laylā[921]—Dīnār b. al-ʿAyzār—al-Ashtar: When I met ʿAbd al-Raḥmān b. ʿAttāb b. Asīd I met the strongest and most cunning of men. I got hold of him round the neck, and we fell to the ground together, and he called out to those around, "Kill me and Mālik!"

[3202]

According to ʿUmar—Abū al-Ḥasan—Ibn Abī Laylā—Dīnār b. al-ʿAyzār—al-Ashtar: I saw ʿAbdallāh b. Ḥakīm b. Ḥizām[922] with the banner of Quraysh, and ʿAdī b. Ḥātim al-Ṭāʾī attacking each other like two male camels. So [ʿAdī and I] took turns against him and killed him. ʿAbdallāh, that is, after he had stabbed ʿAdī and put out his eye.

According to ʿUmar—Abū al-Ḥasan—Abū Mikhnaf—his paternal uncle, Muḥammad b. Mikhnaf[923]—a number of the elders of the tribe, all of whom had been at the Battle of the Camel: The banner of the Kūfan Azd[924] was held by Mikhnaf b. Sulaym,[925] but he was killed that day. So from his close family al-Ṣaqʿab[926] and his brother ʿAbdallāh b. Sulaym took hold of it, but they killed him too. So al-ʿAlāʾ b. ʿUrwah took it, and victory came while it was in his hand.

The banner of the Kūfan ʿAbd al-Qays was held by al-Qāsim b. Muslim, but he was killed, as were Zayd b. Ṣūḥān and Sayḥān b. Ṣūḥān with him. A number of others of them took the banner and were killed too, among them ʿAbdallāh b. Raqabah[927] and

---

921. Following Ibrāhīm for the text's Ibn Abī Laylā; cf. the *isnād* on p. 144, below.

922. Al-Qurashī (Caskel and Strenziok, I, 19, II, 111).

923. Ibn Sulaym (see note 925), born perhaps in 19/640 (U. Sezgin, 225).

924. On ʿAlī's side.

925. Of the Thaʿlabah branch (Caskel and Strenziok, I, 218, II, 407). Contrary to his death, reported here, he is said to have held their banner at Ṣiffīn also and was appointed governor of Isfahan and Hamadhān by ʿAlī (U. Sezgin, 225 n. 128; Hinds, "Banners," 42).

926. Ibn Sulaym, his brother (Caskel and Strenziok, I, 218, II, 538).

927. For the text's Ruqayyah. Ibn Khawṭaʿah (*Addenda*, DCXXXIV); cf. p. 135, above; Caskel and Strenziok, I, 170, II, 117.

Rāshid.[928] Then Munqidh b. al-Nuʿmān[929] took hold of it and
passed it to his son, Murrah b. Munqidh,[930] and the battle finished while it was in his hand.

The banner of the Kūfan Bakr b. Wāʾil was with Banū Dhuhl,
and was held by al-Ḥārith b. Ḥassān b. Ḥawṭ[931] al-Dhuhlī, and
Abū al-ʿArfāʾ al-Raqāshī said, "Take care of yourself and your
tribe!" But he advanced and said: "Tribesmen of Bakr b. Wāʾil!
Nobody had the standing with the Messenger of God that your   [3203]
companion[932] had, so support him!" So he[933] advanced and was
killed, as were his son and five of his brothers. Bishr b. Ḥassān b.
Ḥawṭ[934] said these verses to him that day as he was fighting:

I am Ibn Ḥassān b. Ḥawṭ,[935] and my father
    was the messenger of all Bakr to the Prophet.[936]

His son recited:

I announce and lament the death of chief al-Ḥārith b. Ḥassān
    to the clans of Dhuhl and Shaybān!

A tribesman from Dhuhl then recited:

You announce to us the death of the best man from ʿAdnān;[937]
    [he was glorious when there was] stabbing and confronting
    opponents.

Men were killed from Banū Maḥdūj who were prominent among
the Kūfans, and thirty-five were killed from Banū Dhuhl. One
tribesman said to his brother as he fought: "Brother of mine! How
superb our fighting would be if we were in the right." "We are in
the right!" he replied. "Others have wandered right and left, but
we've maintained our loyalty to our Prophet's household."[938] The

---

928. Or Abū ʿUbaydah b. Rāshid; see p. 135, above.
929. See p. 135, above.
930. See p. 135, above.
931. For the text's Khūṭ (Caskel and Strenziok, I, 154, II, 307).
932. I.e., ʿAlī.
933. Al-Ḥārith.
934. For the text's Khūṭ, al-Ḥārith's brother (Caskel and Strenziok, I, 154).
935. For the text's Khūṭ.
936. At the time of the *wufūd;* see Watt, 141.
937. The northern Arabs.
938. *Ahl bayt nabiyyinā.*

two of them fought to the death. The Baṣran ʿAbd al-Qays—who were with ʿAlī—were headed by ʿAmr b. Marḥūm. Bakr b. Wāʾil were headed by Shaqīq b. Thawr, and their banner was held by Rashrāshah, his *mawlā*. The Baṣran Azd—who were with ʿĀʾishah—were headed by ʿAbd al-Raḥmān b. Jusham b. Abī Ḥunayn al-Ḥamāmī. So ʿĀmir b. Ḥafṣ told me, but others say it was Ṣabrah b. Shaymān al-Ḥuddānī.[939] Their banner was held by ʿAmr b. al-Ashraf al-ʿAtakī, who was killed and along with him thirteen men from his close family.

[3204]

According to ʿUmar—Abū al-Ḥasan—Abū Laylā—Abū ʿUk-kāshah al-Hamdānī—Rifāʿah al-Bajalī—Abū al-Bakhtarī al-Ṭāʾī: Ḍabbah and Azd circled around ʿĀʾishah on the Day of the Camel. Some Azdī tribesmen were picking up the dung of her camel, breaking it up, smelling it, and saying, "The dung of our mother's camel smells of musk!" At the same time a man[940] from ʿAlī's companions was fighting, reciting as he did so:

I bared my blade [and thrust it] into the tribesmen from Azd.
    I struck into their old men and beardless youths,
All of them with long forearms and eager to fight.

Waves of men jostled each other, and then someone yelled, "Hamstring the camel!" So Bujayr b. Duljah from the Kūfan Ḍabbah struck it. "Why did you hamstring it?" he was asked. "I saw my tribe[941] being killed, and I feared they would all perish. I hoped by hamstringing it that at least some of them would remain alive."

According to ʿUmar—Abū al-Ḥasan—al-Ṣalt b. Dīnār: A tribesman from Banū ʿUqayl went up to the dead Kaʿb b. Sūr.[942] He thrust the butt of his spear into his eyes, jerked it round, and said, "I've never seen property produce better cash than you!"[943]

According to ʿUmar—Abū al-Ḥasan—ʿAwānah: They fought all day until nightfall on the Day of the Camel, and someone[944] said the verses

---

939. See p. 120, above.
940. Nimrān, according to p. 134, above.
941. I.e., the Baṣran branch.
942. Shot as he tried to get the two sides to make peace (Caskel and Strenziok, I, 211, II, 366; p. 132, above).
943. He was a valuable asset and good to get rid of.
944. On ʿĀʾishah's side.

The sword healed us of Zayd and Hind[945]
  completely and of the two eyes of ʿAdī.
We kept fighting them all day until nightfall
  with sturdy spears and sharp swords.

Ibn al-Ṣāmit said the verses   [3205]

Go off Ḍabbah! for the land is wide
  to your left. Death lurks in the valley, [namely, we,]
A fighting force like the rays of the rising sun,
  a force with a torrent that flows with force.
So we will stand up to you[946] in every battle,
  holding Mashrafiyyah swords, striking and not weakening.

According to al-ʿAbbās b. Muḥammad—Rawḥ b. ʿUbādah—
Rawḥ—Abū Rajāʾ: I saw a man whose ear had been cut off. "Have
you always been like that, or were you wounded by something?" I
asked. "Let me tell you," he replied. "As I was walking among the
corpses on the day of the Battle of the Camel, I came upon a man
thrashing [the ground with] his leg and reciting:

Our mother brought us to drink at the pool of death,
  and we did not leave until our thirst was quenched.
When we obeyed Quraysh our senses had gone awry,
  and our support for the Ḥijāzīs caused us pain."[947]

I said: "ʿAbdallāh! Say, 'There is no god but Allāh!'"[948] "Come
nearer, and dictate [it] to me; my ear's blocked," he replied. I went
nearer, and he asked me, "Who are you?" A tribesman from al-
Kūfah," I replied, at which he jumped on me and cut off my ear, as
you see, and said, "When you meet your mother, tell her that
ʿUmayr b. al-Ahlab al-Ḍabbī did this to you."

According to ʿUmar—Abū al-Ḥasan—al-Mufaḍḍal the great
narrator and ʿĀmir b. Ḥafṣ and ʿAbd al-Majīd al-Asadī: ʿUmayr
b. al-Ahlab al-Ḍabbī was wounded on the Day of the Camel.
One of ʿAlī's men passed by him as he lay among the wounded.
ʿUmayr said to him, "Come over here!" and when he did so

---

945. I.e., killed them.
946. *Nuqīmu lakum* "we will wait for you" (*Glossarium*, CDXL).
947. Reading *ʿanāʾu* (*Addenda*, DCXXXIV).
948. Before you die.

he cut off his ear. ʿUmayr b. al-Ahlab recited the verses

Our mother brought us to drink at the pool of death,
    and we did not leave until our thirst was quenched.
It would have been better if Ibn Ḍabbah's[949] support for his mother
    and her allies[950] had been found elsewhere and done without.[951]

[3206]   It was bad luck when we obeyed Banū Taym b. Murrah.[952]
    What are Taym but slaves, male and female?![953]

According to al-Sarī (in writing)—Shuʿayb—Sayf—al-Miqdām al-Ḥārithī:[954] There was a man from our tribe called Hāniʾ b. Khaṭṭāb. He had been among those who attacked ʿUthmān but was not at the Battle of the Camel. When he heard the *rajaz* poem on the lips of the people back in al-Kūfah, the one that goes

We, Banū Ḍabbah, are the allies of the camel,[955]

he riposted with the verses

The chief of Madhḥij and Hamdān refused
    to return Naʿthal[956] to how he was,
A new creation after that of the Merciful.[957]

According to al-Sarī (in writing)—Shuʿayb—Sayf—al-Ṣaʿb b. ʿAṭiyyah—his father: On that day Abū al-Jarbāʾ[958] began reciting *rajaz* verses:

Are you listening to ʿAlī and obeying [him]
    before tasting the edge of the Mashrafī sword

---

949. I.e., his own.

950. *Shīʿatahā.*

951. Disregarding Wellhausen's emendation of *waghanāʾu* to *waʿanāʾu* (*Addenda*, DCXXXIV).

952. I.e., Ṭalḥah.

953. *Taym* means servant (*EI*[1], s.v.).

954. Probably Ibn Rabīʿah, the Kūfan notable (Caskel and Strenziok, I, 230, II, 408).

955. See p. 138, above, where one of the verses says *ruddū ʿalaynā shaykhanā* "Make ʿUthmān come back to us!"

956. I.e., ʿUthmān.

957. I.e., Banū Ḍabbah's request was impossible, so it was pointless to fight.

958. A member of ʿĀʾishah's army. It is as though in these verses he is sending a message to everyone in ʿAlī's army.

And forsaking the wives of the Prophet who are in the right?
  I know a people I do not care about![959]

According to al-Sarī (in writing)—Shuʿayb—Sayf—Muḥammad
and Ṭalḥah: The Mother of the Faithful was encircled by courageous and clearsighted Muḍarī clansmen.[960] No one would take
hold of the rein unless he was holding the banner and the flag and
was unwilling to give it up. Nor would anyone take hold of it
unless he was well known among those encircling the camel and
could state his genealogy to her, "I'm so-and-so, son of so-and-so."
By Allāh! They would [then] fight fiercely in its defense, and
death could not be brought to it except with great endeavor and
difficulty. Every follower of ʿAlī who tried to reach it was either   [3207]
killed or fled and did not return. When the center of ʿAlī's army
became mixed with the flanks, ʿAdī b. Ḥātim came and attacked
it, but his eye was gouged out, so he shrank back. Then al-Ashtar
came and ʿAbd al-Raḥmān b. ʿAttāb b. Asīd tried to push him
away—he was badly cut and weak with loss of blood—but al-
Ashtar grabbed him round his chest and threw him off his mount
onto the ground. But he jerked around beneath him and managed
to run away half dead.
  According to al-Sarī (in writing)—Shuʿayb—Sayf—Hishām b.
ʿUrwah—his father: No one would come and take hold of the rein
unless he said, "I'm so-and-so, son of so-and-so, Mother of the
Faithful." So when ʿAbdallāh b. al-Zubayr came up but said nothing she asked, "Who are you?" "I'm ʿAbdallāh, your sister's son."
"Weep for the bereavement of Asmāʾ" replied ʿĀʾishah, meaning
her sister. Al-Ashtar and ʿAdī b. Ḥātim reached the camel, so
ʿAbdallāh b. Ḥakīm b. Ḥizām[961] came out against al-Ashtar, who
advanced toward him. They each struck the other but al-Ashtar
killed [ʿAbdallāh b. Ḥakīm], so ʿAbdallāh b. al-Zubayr advanced
toward him, but al-Ashtar dealt him a blow on the head and
severely wounded him. ʿAbdallāh then hit al-Ashtar lightly; each
grabbed the other round the chest, and they fell to the ground
fighting. "Kill me and Mālik!" exclaimed ʿAbdallāh b. al-Zubayr.

---

959. Yours. This is a threat.
960. *Afnāʾ*, perhaps "splinter groups" (Hinds, "Murder," 452).
961. Caskel and Strenziok, I, 19, II, 111.

Mālik used to say later, "Not for red camels[962] would I have wanted him to say, 'And al-Ashtar.'" Then some of ʿAlī's followers and some of ʿĀʾishah's rushed toward them and the two men separated; each side saved its man from his opponent.

According to al-Sarī (in writing)—Shuʿayb—Sayf—al-Saʿb b. ʿAṭiyyah—his father: Muḥammad b. Ṭalḥah then came up and took hold of the camel's nose rein. "Dear Mother!" he said. "Give me your order!" "I order you," she replied, "to be like the best son of Adam if you're spared." So he took hold of the nose rein. Then whenever anyone attacked him he would attack them, quoting the Qurʾān "*Ḥāʾ mīm*! They will not be given victory by Allāh!"[963] A number of men then gathered and attacked him, each of them claiming to have killed him—al-Mukaʿbir al-Asadī, al-Mukaʿbir al-Ḍabbī, Muʿāwiyah b. Shaddād al-ʿAbsī, and ʿAffān b. al-Ashqar al-Naṣrī. One of them thrust him through with a spear, and his killer said these verses about it:

He was disheveled through spending nights reciting verses from
    his Lord.
    By all appearances he had done little harm and was a good
    Muslim.
I ripped the neck opening of his shirt with a spear,
    and he fell down, dying, his hands and face thrown to the
    ground.
He was reminding me of the verse *ḥāʾ mīm* while the spear was
    driving.
    Why did he not recite *ḥāʾ mīm* before coming out to fight?!
[He fought me] over nothing, except that he was not a follower
    of ʿAlī. Those who do not follow the right regret it.

According to al-Sarī (in writing)—Shuʿayb—Sayf—al-Saʿb b. ʿAṭiyyah—his father: On that day al-Qaʿqāʿ b. ʿAmr said, provoking al-Ashtar, "Are you going to attack again?" But he made no reply, so he said: "Al-Ashtar! Some of us know how to fight others

[3208]

---

962. I.e., the best camels (Wensinck, I, 513b)—similar to our saying "Not for all the tea in China."

963. Qurʾān 41:1, 41:16. By implication the enemies of ʿĀʾishah are being likened to ʿĀd, whom Allāh destroyed.

better than you." So al-Qaʿqāʿ attacked. The rein was being held by Zufar b. al-Ḥārith,[964] who was the last to take his turn with the rein. No, by Allāh! Every single elder from Banū ʿĀmir was struck down that day in front of the camel. Among those killed on that day was Rabīʿah,[965] the grandfather of Isḥāq b. Muslim, while Zufar[966] recited the *rajaz* verses:

O Mother of ours, ʿAysha! Do not fear!
    All your sons are heroes brave.[967]
No one among us is anxious[968] or [over]cautious.   [3209]

Al-Qaʿqāʿ replied with the *rajaz* verses

If we come to drink at a stagnant pool we clean it up,[969]
    but others are unable to drink the water we protect.[970]

In fact, he was quoting these verses.

According to al-Sarī (in writing)—Shuʿayb—Sayf—Muḥammad and Ṭalḥah: One of the last to fight on that Day was Zufar b. al-Ḥārith. Al-Qaʿqāʿ marched toward him. Around the camel no fully grown ʿĀmirī[971] tribesman remained without being struck down; they hastened to meet death.

Al-Qaʿqāʿ said: "Bujayr b. Duljah![972] Shout to your tribesmen [in ʿĀʾishah's army] that they should hamstring the camel before they get struck down and the Mother of the Faithful gets struck down!" So he called out" "Tribesmen of Ḍabbah! ʿAmr b. Duljah![973] Call me to come to you!" So ʿAmr called to him. "Am I safe to go and return?" asked [Bujayr]. "You are," replied [ʿAmr]. So [Bujayr] cut the camel's leg right off, and [the camel] threw itself down on its side and growled. Al-Qaʿqāʿ called out to those

---

964. Fought at Ṣiffīn under Muʿāwiyah (Caskel and Strenziok, I, 96, II, 609).
965. Ibn ʿĀṣim (Caskel and Strenziok, I, 102, II, 477).
966. Zufar belonged to Banū ʿĀmir (Caskel and Strenziok, I, 96).
967. Cf. p. 138, above.
968. *Wahhām*—or "Thinks too much and becomes afraid" (Prym, *Glossarium*, DLXVIII). IA has *bi-wahwāhin* "weak-spirited."
969. However bitter the battle, we fight and win; cf. Ibn Manẓūr, V, 222.
970. They are unable to fight us.
971. Zufar belonged to Banū ʿĀmir (see previous *khabar*). Fully grown means over forty.
972. A relative of al-Qaʿqāʿ.
973. His cousin on ʿĀʾishah's side.

next to [the camel], "You won't be attacked." Then he and Zufar joined in cutting the camel's girth. The two of them then lifted the howdah off and put it down and took up [protective] positions around it.[974] Those soldiers of ʿĀʾishah behind that position fled.

According to al-Sarī (in writing)—Shuʿayb—Sayf—al-Ṣaʿb b. ʿAṭiyyah—his father: In the evening, when ʿAlī had arrived, the camel and those around it had been surrounded, Bujayr b. Duljah had hamstrung it and said, "You won't be attacked," the soldiers stopped fighting. When evening came and fighting had completely stopped, ʿAlī said the following verses about it:

[3210]   I complain to You about my sorrows, those obvious and those
                hidden,
           and about a group who have drawn a curtain over my sight.
           I have killed their Muḍar with my Muḍar.
           I have healed my own wounds, but I have killed my people.

According to al-Sarī (in writing)—Shuʿayb—Sayf—Ismāʿīl b. Abī Khālid—Ḥakīm b. Jābir: Ṭalḥah said that day: "O Allāh! Give ʿUthmān what he wants from me [for my former sins]!" Then, as his horse was standing still, an arrow from an unknown archer[975] pinned his knee to the saddle. He kept his position, and his boot filled with blood. But when he became drowsy he said to his *mawlā*: "Get up behind me on the horse, and find me a place where no one knows me. I've never seen an old man lose so much blood as today."[976] So his *mawlā* mounted and held him tightly and said, "The enemy is catching up with us." He finally brought him to one of the ruined houses of Baṣrah and put him down in its shade. He died in that ruin and was buried in the quarter of Banū Saʿd.[977]

According to al-Sarī (in writing)—Shuʿayb—Sayf—al-Bakhtarī al-ʿAbdī—his father: Rabīʿah fought with ʿAlī on the Day of the Camel, comprising a third of the Kūfans. The Muslims split into two[978] on the Day. They were lined up Muḍar opposite Muḍar,

---

974. Taking the camel and the howdah, surrounding ʿĀʾishah protectively, and saying "You won't be attacked" all mean that the battle has been won and is over.

975. Cf. p. 124, above.

976. IA has "as I have today."

977. To the east of al-Baṣrah? (Massignon, 157).

978. Reading *wa-nuṣṣifa* for the text's *wa-niṣfa*.

Rabī'ah opposite Rabī'ah, and Yaman opposite Yaman.

"Commander of the Faithful! Allow us to stand against Muḍar," requested Banū Ṣūḥān,[979] and 'Alī let them. Then Zayd [b. Ṣūḥān] went forward. Someone said to him: "What makes you stand over against the camel and Muḍar? Death is next to you and opposite you. Withdraw to us!" "It's death we want!" he replied, and that Day they were struck down, although Ṣa'ṣa'ah.[980] escaped from among them.

According to al-Sarī (in writing)—Shu'ayb—Sayf—al-Ṣa'b b. 'Aṭiyyah: A man on our side called al-Ḥārith said that day: "Tribesmen of Muḍar! For what are you killing each other? You're rushing we don't know where, except that we'll be judged there. No one will stand in for you!"

According to 'Abdallāh b. Aḥmad—his father—Sulaymān— [3211] 'Abdallāh b. al-Mubārak—Jarīr—al-Zubayr b. al-Khirrīt[981]—a sheikh from al-Ḥaramayn[982] called Abū Jubayr: On the Day of the Camel I passed Ka'b b. Sūr as he was taking hold of the nose rein of 'Ā'ishah's camel, and he said, "Abū Jubayr! By Allāh! The verses a woman once said [to her son] apply to me:

My dear son, do not go away, and do not fight!"

According to al-Zubayr b. al-Khirrīt: 'Alī passed by his corpse, stood over him, and said: "By Allāh! Well I know, you are steadfast for truth, judging justly," and he praised him for these and other things.

According to al-Sarī (in writing)—Shu'ayb—Sayf—Ibn Ṣa'ṣa'ah al-Muzanī or Ṣa'ṣa'ah—'Amr b. Ja'wān—Jarīr b. Ashras:[983] Ṭalḥah and al-Zubayr's action was at the height of the morning of that day, and then their army fled. 'Ā'ishah was therefore looking for peace, but the army surprised her by returning, and Muḍar protected her all around.[984] So the army stood for battle, and

---

979. From 'Abd al-Qays, who belonged to Rabī'ah (Caskel and Strenziok, I, 170).
980. Zayd b. Ṣūḥān's brother (Caskel and Strenziok, I, 170, II, 538).
981. Following *Addenda*, DCXXXIV, and Ibrāhīm, for the text's al-Ḥurayth.
982. The two sacred enclaves, Mecca and Medina, following *Addenda*, DCXXXIV, for the text's al-Ḥarāmayn.
983. Perhaps Ibn Sharis, as p. 99, above (*Addenda*, DCXXXIV).
984. Cf. p. 131, above.

ʿĀʾishah's action was in the middle of the day. Now ʿAlī. . . .[985] Kaʿb b. Sūr took ʿĀʾishah's Qurʾān copy[986] and rushed out between the two lines, imploring them by Almighty and Glorious Allāh to stop the bloodshed. He was handed his armor, but he threw it down at his feet. His shield was brought, but he pushed it away. So they all shot [their arrows] at him at the same time[987] and killed him. They did not give him time to think, and suddenly they intensified their attack against them and fought more closely. From both Baṣrans[988] and Kūfans he was the first to be killed in front of ʿĀʾishah.

[3212]

According to al-Sarī (in writing)—Shuʿayb—Sayf—Makhlad b. Kathīr—his father: We sent Muslim b. ʿAbdallāh[989] to call our brothers[990] to stop, but they all shot [their arrows] at him and killed him, as the center of the army did to Kaʿb. So *he* was the first to be killed in front of the Commander of the Faithful and ʿĀʾishah. The mother of Muslim said the following verses mourning him:[991]

O Allāh! Muslim went to them,
    submitting to death when he called them
To the Book of Allāh without fearing them.
    They smeared him with blood when he went to them,
And their mother[992] was standing, looking on,
    not restraining them as they plotted folly together.

According to al-Sarī (in writing)—Shuʿayb—Sayf—al-Ṣaʿb b. Ḥakīm b. Sharīk—his father—his grandfather: By the evening of the Day of the Camel the two flanks of the Kūfan army had been routed and then had merged with the center. Now Ibn Yathribī had been *qāḍī* of al-Baṣrah before Kaʿb b. Sūr, and he, ʿAbdallāh,

---

985. Lacuna in the text. Prym suggests inserting "was behind them" as on p. 131, above.

986. Omitting *wa-ʿAlī* from Ibrāhīm.

987. Reading *rishqan* with Ibrāhīm (cf. Lane, 1090b) for the text's *rashqan*, as on p. 132, above.

988. Ibrāhīm omits the Baṣrans.

989. Probably Ibn Ḥiyay/Ḥuyayy, from ʿAlaqat Bajīlah (Caskel and Strenziok, I, 222, II, 436). The authority for the variant account, p. 129, above, was from Aḥmas Bajīlah.

990. On the other side.

991. Cf. p. 130, above.

992. ʿĀʾishah.

and his brother ʿAmr were with them on the Day of the Camel. He was on horseback, standing in front of the camel. "Where is a man to attack the camel?" asked ʿAlī. Hind b. ʿAmr al-Murādī responded, but Ibn Yathribī intercepted him. So they exchanged blows, and Ibn Yathribī killed him. Then Sayḥān b. Ṣūḥān attacked, but Ibn Yathribī intercepted him. So they exchanged blows, and Ibn Yathribī killed him. Then ʿIlbāʾ b. al-Haytham attacked, but Ibn Yathribī intercepted him and killed him. Then Ṣaʿṣaʿah attacked, and [Ibn Yathribī] struck him. So Ibn Yathribī killed three, finishing them off in the battle—ʿIlbāʾ, Hind, and Sayḥān. Ṣaʿṣaʿah and Zayd were taken away wounded—one[993] died, and the other survived.

[3213]

According to al-Sarī (in writing)—Shuʿayb—Sayf—ʿAmr b. Muḥammad—al-Shaʿbī: On the day of the Camel seventy[994] tribesmen from Quraysh took hold of the nose rein, and each one was killed as he held it. Al-Ashtar attacked, so ʿAbdallāh b. al-Zubayr intercepted him, and they exchanged blows. Al-Ashtar struck him down and made for him, but ʿAbdallāh leaped on him, grabbed him round the chest, and fell down with him to the ground, saying, "Kill me and Mālik!" The people did not know him as Mālik. Had he said, "and al-Ashtar," and had a million lives not one of them would have been spared. He carried on, struggling to get out of ʿAbdallāh's grip, until he managed to escape.

Whenever someone attacked the camel and escaped, he did not make a second attempt. Both Marwān and ʿAbdallāh b. al-Zubayr were wounded that day.

According to ʿAbdallāh b. Aḥmad—his paternal uncle—Sulaymān—ʿAbdallāh—Jarīr b. Ḥāzim—Muḥammad b. Abī Yaʿqūb and Ibn ʿAwn—Abū Rajāʾ: ʿAmr b. Yathribī al-Ḍabbī, the brother of ʿAmīrah[995] the qāḍī, recited the following verses that day:

We, Banū Ḍabbah, are the allies of the camel,
  we take the field against death whenever death
  dismounts.[996]

---

993. Zayd.
994. Cf. Conrad.
995. As vocalized by Prym. Perhaps ʿUmayrah?
996. See p. 138, above.

Ibn ʿAwn added the verses (not in Ibn Abī Yaʿqūb's version):

Killing is sweeter to us than honey!
    We lament the death of Ibn ʿAffān with the tips of spears.
Send back our chief to us, and that will be enough.

[3214]   According to al-Sarī (in writing)—Shuʿayb—Sayf—Dāwūd b. Abī Hind—an elder from Banū Ḍabbah: Ibn Yathribī said some *rajaz* verses that day:

For those that don't know me, I am Ibn Yathribī,
    the killer of ʿIlbāʾ and Hind al-Jamalī
And of a son of Ṣūḥān, who followed the way of ʿAlī.[997]

"Who'll come and fight?" Ibn Yathribī called out. A man went out, but he killed him. Another came out, and he killed him too. He then said some more *rajaz* verses:

I kill them, and I can see ʿAlī,
    [so that] if I wished I could thrust an ʿUmrī[998] spear into
    his mouth!

Then ʿAmmār b. Yāsir came out against him—and he was the weakest who had done so.[999] As ʿAmmār stood forward, the men said, "We belong to Allāh, and to him we return."[1000] I also said about ʿAmmār because of his weakness: "By Allāh! This man will be joining those who preceded him!" He was slender and thin-legged, and he was carrying a sword of which the shoulder belt was too short for him[1001] and of which the hilt [therefore] was near his armpit. Ibn Yathribī struck him with his sword, but it became embedded in his leather shield. So ʿAmmār struck him and injured him. ʿAlī's companions then threw stones at Ibn Yathribī and heavily wounded him, and he was carried off badly injured.

    According to al-Sarī (in writing)—Shuʿayb—Sayf—Ḥammād al-Burjumī—Khārijah b. al-Ṣalt: On the Day of the Camel when al-Ḍabbī recited:

---

997. *ʿAlā dīn ʿAlī*. See the same verses on p. 137, above.
998. *Glossarium*, CCCLXXVII. Ibrāhīm has *ʿAmrī*.
999. He was very old.
1000. Qurʾān 2:156. Said on the death of someone.
1001. Reading *tashiffu* [*ʿanhu*] (*Addenda*, DCXXXIV and Ibrāhīm) for the text's *bi-shiqqihi* "by his side."

We, the Banū Ḍabbah, are the allies of the Camel;
    we lament the death of Ibn ʿAffān with the tips of spears.
Send back our chief to us, and that will be enough.

ʿUmayr b. Abī al-Ḥārith recited in reply:

How can we send back your chief when his bones have become
    old?[1002]
We struck his chest until he fell.

According to al-Sarī (in writing)—Shuʿayb—Sayf—al-Ṣaʿb b.
Ḥakīm—his father—his grandfather: A tribesman from Banū
Ḍabbah hamstrung the camel. He was called Ibn Duljah, ʿAmr or   [3215]
Bujayr. Al-Ḥārith b. Qays, one of ʿĀʾishah's followers, said the
following verses about this:

We struck his leg so he fell down dead
    from one hit during the surge that was decisive.
If we had not been created for the sake of [protecting] the
    Prophet's household
    and his wife's sanctity, they would have divided us among
    themselves very quickly.

They were falsely attributed to ʿAlī's follower al-Muthannnā b.
Makhramah.[1003]

*The Severity of the Battle on the Day of the Camel
and the Account of Aʿyan b. Ḍubayʿah's[1004]
Looking into the Howdah*

According to al-Sarī (in writing)—Shuʿayb—Sayf—Muḥammad b.
Nuwayrah—Abū ʿUthmān—al-Qaʿqāʿ: The way the center of the
army fought on the Day of the Camel was more like the Battle of
Ṣiffīn than anything I have seen. I saw us defending ourselves
against them with the points of our spears and leaning against the
butts of our spears. They were doing likewise, so that had the men
walked on them they would have supported them.[1005]

1002. I.e., he has died, as Ibrāhīm notes.
1003. Al-Muthannā b. Mukharrabah? (Caskel and Strenziok, I, 168, II, 438).
1004. Al-Mujāshiʿī.
1005. Like a bridge.

According to 'Īsā b. 'Abd al-Raḥmān al-Marwazī—al-Ḥasan b. al-Ḥusayn al-'Uranī—Yaḥyā b. Ya'lā al-Aslamī—Sulaymān b. Qarm[1006]—al-A'mash[1007]—'Abdallāh b. Sinān al-Kāhilī: On the Day of the Camel we shot arrows at each other until there were no more to shoot, and we stabbed each other with spears until they were enmeshed in our chests and theirs. Had horses been made to walk over them they could have. Then 'Alī called out, "Use swords, sons of the Muhājirūn!" The old man[1008] said, "I never entered Dār al-Walīd[1009] without remembering that day."

[3216]   According to 'Abd al-A'lā b. Wāṣil—Abū Fuqaym—Fiṭr—Abū Bashīr: I was with my *mawlā* at the time of the Camel, and since then I have never passed Dār al-Walīd and heard the sounds of the washermen beating[1010] without remembering how they fought.

According to 'Īsā b. 'Abd al-Raḥmān al-Marwazī—al-Ḥasan b. al-Ḥusayn—Yaḥyā b. Ya'lā—'Abd al-Malik b. Muslim—'Īsā b. Ḥiṭṭān: The army made a retreat; then we returned, and 'Ā'ishah was [seated] on a red camel in a red howdah, which I could describe only as a hedgehog because of the arrows.

According to 'Abdallāh b. Aḥmad—his father—Sulaymān—'Abdallāh—Ibn 'Awn—Abū Rajā: Some people were recalling the Day of the Camel. It's as if I can see 'Ā'ishah's howdah now. It was as though it was a hedgehog from the arrows that had been shot into it. "Did you fight that day?" I asked Abū Rajā'. "By Allāh!" he replied. "I fired arrows, and I don't know what effect they had."

According to al-Sarī (in writing)—Shu'ayb—Sayf—Muḥammad b. Rāshid al-Sulamī—Maysarah Abū Jamīlah: After the Camel had been hamstrung Muḥammad b. Abī Bakr and 'Ammār b. Yā-sir came to 'Ā'ishah and cut the saddle girth. They lifted off the howdah and put it to one side until 'Alī had given them further instructions about it. "Take her into al-Baṣrah!" he told the two of

---

1006. Prym notes that this name is also spelled Qadam and Qazam.

1007. If this is the famous al-A'mash, then it is Abū Muḥammad Sulaymān b. Mihrān, traditionist and Qur'ān reader, b.c. 60/679–80, d. probably 148/765 (*EI*[2], s.v.).

1008. Presumably 'Abdallāh b. Sinān.

1009. In the market of al-Kūfah (Caetani, IX, 147).

1010. They beat the clothes with wood against wood; Ibn Manẓūr, V, 415; cf. Muir, 249 n. 1.

them, and they took it into the house of ʿAbdallāh b. Khalaf al-
Khuzāʿī.[1011]

According to al-Sarī (in writing)—Shuʿayb—Sayf—Muḥammad
and Ṭalḥah: ʿAlī ordered a group of men to carry the howdah out
from the dead bodies. Al-Qaʿqāʿ and Zufar b. al-Ḥārith had already
removed it from the back of the camel and put it down at its side.
Muḥammad b. Abī Bakr then came up to it with a group of men,   [3217]
and he put his hand in. "Who's this?" said ʿĀʾishah. "Your dutiful
brother," he replied. "Undutiful!"[1012] "How do you feel about
your sons' beating today, Mother?" asked ʿAmmār b. Yāsir. "Who
are you?" asked ʿĀʾishah. "Your dutiful son, ʿAmmār,"[1013] he replied. "I'm no mother of yours!" "You are, even though you loathe
the idea." "You're boasting that you're victorious and doing just
what you reproved [others for doing]. By Allāh! This is totally
wrong! Those who do this sort of thing are never victorious."
They then brought her out in her howdah from the corpses and
put her down away from everyone. It was as though her howdah
was sprouting[1014] suckers from the arrows stuck in it. Aʿyan b.
Ḍubayʿah al-Mujāshiʿī[1015] then came up to look down into the
howdah, and she exclaimed: "Clear off! Allāh curse you!" "By
Allāh!" he replied. "I can see little rosy!"[1016] "May Allāh disgrace
you![1017] May He cut off your hand! May He expose your geni-
tals!"[1018] He was indeed killed in al-Baṣrah, and stripped, his hand
was cut off, and he was thrown naked into one of the ruins in the Azd

1011. A prominent Baṣran, killed on the side of ʿAlī at the Battle of the Camel
(Caskel and Strenziok, I, 196, II, 112).

1012. *Akhūk . . . ʿaqūq*. Muḥammad was being sarcastic.

1013. *ʿAmmār al-bārr*.

1014. Reading *muqaṣṣib* (*Addenda*, DCXXXIV) for the text's *muqaḍḍab*
"pruned."

1015. Of Tamīm and a friend of ʿAlī's (Caskel and Strenziok, I, 61, II, 217).

1016. *Ḥumayrāʾ*, a term of endearment to a wife. The Prophet is said to have
called ʿĀʾishah so.

1017. *Hatak Allāhu sitrak*. The translation (cf. Lane, 1304c) refers to the next
sentence's triple fulfillment of the curse; however, it could refer back to Aʿyan's
looking into the howdah and mean, "May Allāh rip down *your* curtain!" i.e., and
expose the women of *your* family, although this is not fulfilled in what follows.

1018. A Muslim woman could hardly say anything nearer the bone. It could be
translated more mildly "and show up your deficiency," but this would not fit what
follows.

quarter. 'Alī then came to her and exclaimed: "O Mother! May Allāh forgive us and you!" "May He forgive us and you!" she replied.

According to al-Sarī (in writing)—Shuʿayb—Sayf—al-Ṣaʿb b. Ḥakīm b. Sharīk—his father—his grandfather: Muḥammad b. Abī Bakr arrived with ʿAmmār, and cut the thongs of the girth from the howdah, and the two of them then lifted it off. When they had put it down, Muḥammad put in his hand and said, "Your brother Muḥammad!" "The most blameworthy!"[1019] she replied. "Dear sister, have you been hit?" he asked. "That's no business of yours!" she replied. "Whose is it then? Those who've gone astray?"[1020] "No, those who guide right."[1021] 'Alī then arrived. "How are you, Mother?" he asked her. "Fine." "May Allāh forgive you!" he said. "And you," she replied.

[3218] According to al-Sarī (in writing)—Shuʿayb—Sayf—Muḥammad and Ṭalḥah: When it was nearly the end of the night Muḥammad took 'Āʾishah out to al-Baṣrah to stay in the house of 'Abdallāh b. Khalaf al-Khuzāʿī as a guest of Ṣafiyyah bt. al-Ḥārith b. Ṭalḥah b. Abī Ṭalḥah b. ʿAbd al-ʿUzzā b. ʿUthmān b. ʿAbd al-Dār,[1022] the mother of Ṭalḥah al-Ṭalaḥāt b. 'Abdallāh b. Khalaf.[1023]

According to al-Wāqidī, the battle took place on Thursday 10 Jumādā II 36 (December 4, 656).[1024]

The Killing of al-Zubayr b. al-ʿAwwām

According to al-Sarī (in writing)—Shuʿayb—Sayf—al-Walīd b. 'Abdallāh—his father: When Ṭalḥah and al-Zubayr's army was routed on the Day of the Camel, al-Zubayr left. He passed the army of al-Aḥnaf, who, when he saw him and was told who he was, remarked: "By Allāh! He's been forced to do this"[1025] and

---

1019. *Mudhammam*, the opposite of *Muḥammad*. Cf. p. 37, above.

1020. Sarcastic criticism of Ṭalḥah and al-Zubayr.

1021. 'Āʾishah ripostes that Muḥammad has gone astray.

1022. His Qurashī wife (Caskel and Strenziok, II, 555).

1023. Called so because of all the Ṭalḥahs on his mother's side; later governor of Sijistan (Caskel and Strenziok, I, 196, II, 555).

1024. Caetani, IX, 131. According to Caetani, IX, 2, this 10 Jumādā II was a Sunday. See p. 115, above, where the date is given as Thursday, 14 Jumādā II.

1025. Reading *bi-khiyār*, following Ibrāhīm and closer to the ms. for the text's *anḥiyāz*, perhaps "What's this? Desertion?"

asked his men, "Who'll keep us informed about him?" "I will,"
replied 'Amr b. Jurmūz to his companions, and he followed him.
When he caught up with him al-Zubayr looked at him furiously
and asked, "Why are you here?" "That's just what I wanted to ask
you,"[1026] he replied. A *ghulām* of al-Zubayr's who was with him,
called 'Aṭiyyah, said, "He's armed!" "Why be frightened by [such]
a man?" replied al-Zubayr. It was time for prayer, so Ibn Jurmūz
said, "Let's do the prayer!" Al-Zubayr also said, "Let's do the
prayer!" So they dismounted. Ibn Jurmūz stood behind him and
then stabbed him from behind through the neck opening of his
armored coat and killed him. He then took his horse, his signet
ring, and his weapons and returned to the army with the news,
leaving the *ghulām*, who buried him in Wādī al-Sibāʿ.[1027]

"By Allāh! I don't know whether what you've done is good or
bad," said al-Aḥnaf and went down to 'Alī, Ibn Jurmūz accom-
panying him. They went up to him and told him the news. He
asked for al-Zubayr's sword and said, "A sword that many times
dispelled distress from the face of the Messenger of God!"[1028] and
sent it to 'Ā'ishah.[1029] Then he turned to al-Aḥnaf and said, "You
held out [on me]!" "I thought that I was doing everything right,"
he replied, "and that what happened coincided with your orders,
Commander of the Faithful. So be lenient! You've come a long
way, and you'll need me in the future more than you have done in
the past. So acknowledge the good I've done, and recognize my
sincere devotion for the sake of the future, and don't say things
like that,[1030] for I'll always give you my sincere support."

[3219]

Those Routed on the Day of the Camel Who Hid and Went off into the Surrounding Towns

According to al-Sarī (in writing)—Shuʿayb—Sayf—Muḥammad
and Ṭalḥah: At the height of the morning of the rout al-Zubayr
went off on foot toward Medina, but he was killed by Ibn Jurmūz.
ʿUtbah b. Abī Sufyān and the two sons of al-Ḥakam, ʿAbd al-

1026. Or "I just wanted to ask you [how you were/what you were doing.]"
1027. Presumably in the modern area of Baṣrah called al-Zubayr.
1028. E.g., at Uḥud and Ḥunayn.
1029. Sister of Ṣafiyyah, al-Zubayr's wife.
1030. "You thought this was a good opportunity to impress me."

Raḥmān and Yaḥyā, also left for the surrounding area on the day of the rout, their heads badly wounded.[1031] They met ʿIṣmah b. Ubayr al-Taymī, who asked, "Are you looking for protection?"[1032] "Who are you?" they replied. "ʿIṣmah b. Ubayr." So they said, "Yes, we are." "You may have my protection for twelve months." So he took them and guarded them and looked after them until they recovered. "Choose the area you most prefer," he then said, "and I'll take you there." "Syria," they replied. So with 400 riders from Taym al-Ribāb he escorted them until they had entered well into Kalb territory at Dūmah. "You've now fulfilled your obligation to yourself and to them," said the Kalbīs. "You've carried out your duty, so return!" So he did. A poet composed a verse about this:

[3220]
When the spears were being aimed Ibn Ubayr was loyal
      to Āl Abī al-ʿĀṣ. His loyalty was memorable.

As for Ibn ʿĀmir,[1033] he also left wounded in the head, and a man from Banū Ḥurqūs[1034] called Murayy[1035] met him and offered to give him protection. He accepted, so he gave him protection, and he stayed with him. "Which territory would you most prefer?" he then asked. "Damascus," he replied. So with riders from Banū Ḥurqūṣ he escorted him until they got him to Damascus.

Ḥārithah b. Badr,[1036] who had been on ʿĀʾishah's side and whose son or brother, Zirāʿ (or in another copy, Dirāʿ[1037]) had been hit in the battle, said the verses

Some news has reached me that Ibn ʿĀmir
      has made his camel kneel and thrown down his ropes[1038]
      in Damascus.

Marwān b. al-Ḥakam took refuge on the day of the rout with a family from ʿAnazah. "Inform Mālik b. Mismaʿ where I am," he

---

1031. For this translation of *shujjijū*, see "until they recovered," below. Ibrāhīm, 535 n., glosses it "to cross the desert."

1032. *EI²*, s.v. Djiwār.

1033. ʿAbdallāh b. ʿĀmir b. Kurayz.

1034. Of Ṭayyiʾ? Cf. Caskel and Strenziok, I, 249.

1035. Following Wellhausen, 160; cf. *Addenda*, DCXXXIV.

1036. Caskel and Strenziok, I, 71, II, 316.

1037. A marginal gloss crept into the text, as Prym notes. Ḥārithah's brother's name was Dhirāʿ (Caskel and Strenziok, I, 71, II, 316).

1038. Settled.

asked them, so they went to Mālik and told him where he was. Mālik asked his brother Muqātil, "How shall we deal with this man who has sent us a message saying where he is?" "Send my brother's son, and give him protection," he replied, "and then seek assurance of protection for him from ʿAlī. If he gives him it, then that's what we want. If he doesn't, then we'll come out with him and with our swords. If he obstructs, then we'll fight on his behalf with our swords. We'll either come through or perish honorably." He had previously asked the opinion of others in his family on this same question that he was asking Muqātil, but they had told him not to [protect Marwān], but he took the advice of his brother and not theirs. He therefore sent a message to Marwān and put him up in his house, determining to defend him if forced to do so, saying, "Death for protection is loyalty." Marwān's descendants remembered this of them later, and they benefited by it from them, and the Marwānids honored them because of it.

ʿAbdallāh b. al-Zubayr took refuge in the house of a man from al-Azd called Wazīr and said, "Go to the Mother of the Faithful and tell her where I am, but make sure Muḥammad b. Abī Bakr[1039] doesn't find out!" So he went to ʿĀʾishah and told her. "Bring Muḥammad to me!" she said. "Mother of the Faithful!" replied Wazīr. "ʿAbdallāh has forbidden me to let Muḥammad know." But she sent a message to Muḥammad: "Go with this man, and bring me your sister's son!" So he set off with the Azdī and went with him to Ibn al-Zubayr. "By Allāh!" [the Azdī] said. "I've brought you what you didn't want, but the Mother of the Faithful was insistent." Muḥammad and ʿAbdallāh then came out, abusing each other. Muḥammad was mentioning ʿUthmān and abusing him, and ʿAbdallāh was abusing Muḥammad, until they reached ʿĀʾishah at ʿAbdallāh b. Khalaf's house. ʿAbdallāh b. Khalaf was on ʿĀʾishah's side before the Day of the Camel; his brother ʿUthmān was killed with ʿAlī. ʿĀʾishah sent out [men] to look for the wounded, and she had a number of them stay [where she was]. One of those she did this with was Marwān. They stayed in rooms in the house.

[3221]

1039. Who had been given charge of ʿĀʾishah by ʿAlī.

According to al-Sarī (in writing)—Shuʿayb—Sayf—Muḥammad and Ṭalḥah: While ʿAlī was in his camp tribal leaders came to visit ʿĀʾishah. One of the first to do so was al-Qaʿqāʿ b. ʿAmr. She said to him when he had greeted her: "I saw two men battling in front of me yesterday, and they recited such-and-such *rajaz* verses. Of the two, do you know who was the Kūfan, from your side?" "Yes," he replied, "the one who said, 'The most refractory mother we know.'[1040] By Allāh! He was lying; you're the most dutiful mother we know, but you weren't obeyed." "By Allāh!" she said. "Had I but died two decades before this day!" Al-Qaʿqāʿ then left and went to ʿAlī and told him that ʿĀʾishah had questioned him. "Alas for you!" said ʿAlī. "Who are the two men?" "The other one was Abu Hālah,[1041] who said:

So that I could see his companion ʿAlī."

"By Allāh!" said ʿAlī. "Had I but died two decades before this day!" Their response was thus exactly the same.

According to al-Sarī (in writing)—Shuʿayb—Sayf—Muḥammad and Ṭalḥah: Those of the wounded who were able to get up again stole away in the middle of the night into al-Baṣrah. ʿĀʾishah asked about a number of people on that day, both allies and opponents, as people came to visit her while she was in the house of ʿAbdallāh b. Khalaf. Whenever she was told of the death of one of them, she said, "May Allāh be merciful to him!" "Why do you say this?" asked one of her followers. "It's what the Messenger of God used to say. 'So-and-so is in paradise; so-and-so is in paradise,'" she replied. That day ʿAlī b. Abī Ṭālib said, "I fervently hope that there is not one of these who has purified himself whom Allāh has not taken into paradise."

According to al-Sarī (in writing)—Shuʿayb—Sayf—ʿAṭiyyah—Abū Ayyūb—ʿAlī: No verse of the Qurʾān was revealed to the Prophet that gave him more joy than Almighty and Glorious Allāh's words: "Whatever calamity afflicts you you have earned, but He forgives much."[1042] The Prophet said: "Whatever a Muslim suffers in this world by way of calamity to himself is in payment

[3222]

1040. Rabīʿah al-ʿUqaylī; see p. 137, above.
1041. ʿAlī's man in the fight.
1042. Qurʾān 42:30.

for a wrongdoing, but what Almighty and Glorious Allāh forgives
is more. So whatever afflicts him in this world deletes his wrongdoing and is a forgiveness for him. It will not be counted against   [3223]
him in punishment on the Day of Resurrection. What Almighty
and Glorious Allāh has forgiven him in this world He has forgiven
forever. Allāh is far above going back on His forgiveness."

*'Alī's Grief over Those Killed at the Battle
of the Camel, Their Burial, and His Gathering What
Was in the Camp and Its Despatch to al-Baṣrah*

According to al-Sarī (in writing)—Shu'ayb—Sayf—Muḥammad
and Ṭalḥah: 'Alī b. Abī Ṭālib remained in his camp for three days
and did not enter al-Baṣrah while the people were sent out to their
dead. They went out to them and buried them, and 'Alī went
around with them among the bodies. When Ka'b b. Sūr was
brought to him, he said, "You told me it was only fools who had
joined up with them, and here you see the learned man." He then
came upon 'Abd al-Raḥmān b. 'Attāb and said, "And here is the
chief of them!"[1043] (The [informant] they were going around with
says, "This[1044] means they had all agreed on him and approved
that he should lead their prayer.")
Whenever 'Alī passed a man with some good points he would
say, "There were those who claimed that only the riffraff came
out against us, but here is a strenuously devout Muslim." He
prayed over both their Baṣran and their Kūfan dead, and he prayed
over the Quraysh of both camps. They were both Medinans and
Meccans. 'Alī then buried the severed limbs in a huge grave and
collected everything that was left in the camp. He sent it to the
mosque in al-Baṣrah, saying: "Whoever recognizes anything [of
his own] should take it, except any weapon that was in the stores
with the mark of the government[1045] on it. For indeed,[1046] there is
still [there] what [the government] has not yet recognized [as belonging to it, so] take that property belonging to Almighty and   [3224]

1043. *Ya'sūb al-qawm.*
1044. *Ya'sūb al-qawm.*
1045. *Sulṭān.*
1046. Reading *la-mā* with the ms. and *Addenda*, DCXXXIV for the text's *mimmā*.

Glorious Allāh that they had collected in order to fight you with. A Muslim is not entitled to the property of any deceased Muslim, and they had taken possession of those weapons without their being given them as booty[1047] by the government."

The Number of Fatalities at the Battle of the Camel

According to al-Sarī (in writing)—Shuʿayb—Sayf—Muḥammad and Ṭalḥah: Those killed at the Battle of the Camel around the camel numbered 10,000, half from 'Alī's followers and half from 'Āʾishah's. Two thousand Azdīs fell plus 500 from the rest of al-Yaman. Two thousand from Muḍar fell plus 500 from Qays, 500 from Tamīm, 1,000 from Banū Ḍabbah, and 500 from Bakr b. Wāʾil.

It was said that in the first battle 5,000 Baṣrans were killed and a further 5,000 in the second battle, totaling 10,000 Baṣran fatalities and 5,000 Kūfans.

Seventy elders of Banū 'Adī were killed that day, all of whom were well versed in the Qurʾān. Youths and men who were not so well versed in the Qurʾān were also killed. 'Āʾishah said, "I was still hoping for victory until I heard the voices of Banū 'Adī subside."

'Alī's Visit to 'Āʾishah and the Punishment He Ordered for Those Who Offended Her

According to al-Sarī (in writing)—Shuʿayb—Sayf—Muḥammad and Ṭalḥah: On Monday 'Alī entered al-Baṣrah, went to the mosque, and prayed there. Then he went into al-Baṣrah itself, and the people came to him. Later he went to 'Āʾishah on his she-mule. When he arrived at the house of 'Abdallāh b. Khalaf—the largest house in al-Baṣrah—he found the women weeping with 'Āʾishah over the two sons of Khalaf, 'Abdallāh and 'Uthmān.[1048] Ṣafiyyah bint al-Ḥārith[1049] had veiled her face and was weeping,

[3225]

1047. *Tanafful*; Maqrīzī and Ibrāhīm have *tanfīl* (*Addenda*, DCXXXV), but this would not alter the sense.

1048. Fought on 'Alī's side in the Battle of the Camel (Caskel and Strenziok, I, 196, II, 579).

1049. Wife of 'Abdallāh b. Khalaf.

but when she saw him she said: "'Alī! Killer of loved ones! Splitter of groups! May Allāh make your sons fatherless, as you have done to the sons of 'Abdallāh!" He made her no reply and remained silent until he went into 'Ā'ishah, greeted her, sat down next to her, and said, "Ṣafiyyah just met me with some harsh words, but up until today I haven't seen her since she was a little girl." Then, as 'Alī left, Ṣafiyyah turned to him and repeated what she had said to him, so he halted his she-mule and said, "In truth, I had a mind," and he pointed to the doors of the house, "to open this door and kill those inside, and then this one and kill those inside, and then this one and kill those inside." Some of the wounded had taken refuge with 'Ā'ishah, and 'Alī had been told that they were with her there, but he pretended not to know. [At this, Ṣafiyyah] fell silent, and 'Alī left. "By Allāh!" said an Azdī. "This woman[1050] won't get away from us!" But 'Alī got angry. "Silence!" he said. "Don't any of you dishonor women! Don't force your way into any house! Don't stir up discord with any woman by hurting her, even if they shout abuse at your womenfolk and call your leaders and your honest men fools. They are weak. We have been commanded to hold back from them, [even if] they are polytheists.[1051] A man who recompenses a woman by beating her will have his descendants after him reproached for it. So let me not hear of anyone that he has confronted a woman. I will punish him as the most wicked of people." 'Alī then left and was met by a man who said: "Commander of the Faithful! Two men I had met previously stood up at the door and were offensive to someone whose abuse [of you] is more painful to you than that of Ṣafiyyah." "Alas! Do you mean 'Ā'ishah?" "Yes," he replied, "two of their men stood at the door of the house. One of them recited   [3226]

May you, our mother, be repaid for [what you did to] us in
    disobedience!

And the other recited:

Mother of ours! Repent, for you have made a mistake."

So ['Alī] sent al-Qaʿqāʿ b. 'Amr to the door, and he sent those

---

1050. Ṣafiyyah.
1051. IA substitutes "Muslims."

guarding it to get control of the two men. "I'm going to cut off their heads!" said al-Qaʿqāʿ but then added, "I will punish them very severely [instead]." So he gave them each a hundred lashes and had their tunics stripped off them.

According to al-Sarī (in writing)—Shuʿayb—Sayf—al-Ḥārith b. Ḥaṣīrah—Abū al-Kunūd: They were two Azdīs from al-Kūfah called ʿIjl and Saʿd, sons of ʿAbdallāh.

The Baṣrans' Allegiance to ʿAlī and His Division of the Contents of the Treasury among Them

According to al-Sarī (in writing)—Shuʿayb—Sayf—Muḥammad and Ṭalḥah: Al-Aḥnaf gave allegiance in the evening because he had been absent, he and Banū Saʿd. Then they all entered al-Baṣrah, and the Baṣrans gave allegiance under their banners. ʿAlī gave allegiance to the Baṣrans, even the wounded and those who had sought protection. But when Marwān returned [to Medina][1052] he went and joined Muʿāwiyah. But others said, "He stayed in Medina until Ṣiffīn was over."

[3227] When ʿAlī had completed the allegiance with the Baṣrans, he investigated the treasury and found more than 600,000 dirhams. So he divided it up among those who had fought with him,[1053] 500 dirhams going to each of them, saying, "You'll get the same again on top of your wages if Almighty and Glorious Allāh lets you conquer Syria." The Sabaʾiyyah murmured against this and secretly criticized ʿAlī.

ʿAlī's Conduct toward Those Who Fought Him on the Day of the Camel

According to al-Sarī (in writing)—Shuʿayb—Sayf—Muḥammad b. Rāshid—his father: It was part of ʿAlī's practice not to kill those who fled or to finish off the wounded or to dishonor women, or to take money. So on that day some men asked, "What allows us to kill them but forbids us their money?" "Those who fought you

---

1052. He was one who had sought protection.
1053. Ibrāhīm, following Maqrīzī (*Addenda*, DCXXXV), adds "at the battle."

are like you," replied ʿAlī. "Those who make peace with us are one
with us, and we are one with them, but, for those who persist
until they get struck by us, I fight them to the death. You are in no
need of their fifth."[1054] It was on that day the Khawārij[1055] began
talking among themselves.

Al-Ashtar Sends ʿĀʾishah a He-Camel
He Had Bought for Her and Her Exit
from al-Baṣrah to Mecca

According to Abū Kurayb Muḥammad b. al-ʿAlāʾ—Yaḥyā b.
Ādam—Abū Bakr b. ʿAyyāsh—ʿĀṣim b. Kulayb—his father: When
they had finished on the Day of the Camel al-Ashtar ordered me
to go and buy him a he-camel for 700 dirhams from a man from
Mahrah.[1056] "Take it to ʿĀʾishah," said al-Ashtar, "and tell her, ʾAl-
Ashtar Mālik b. al-Ḥārith has sent it to you, and he says, "This is
to take the place of your camel.""" So I took it to her and said,   [3228]
"Mālik sends you greetings, and says that this camel is in place of
your camel." "May Allāh not give him peace! For he has killed the
chief of the Arabs (by which she meant Ibn Ṭalḥah) and committed crimes against my sister's son." So I took it back to al-Ashtar
and informed him, at which he uncovered two hirsute forearms
and said, "They wanted to kill me, so what else could I do?"

According to al-Sarī (in writing)—Shuʿayb—Sayf—Muḥammad
and Ṭalḥah: ʿĀʾishah headed for Mecca, taking the road[1057] from
al-Baṣrah. Marwān and al-Aswad b. Abī al-Bakhtarī left the road
and went to Medina. ʿĀʾishah stayed in Mecca until the ḥajj[1058]
and then returned to Medina.

1054. The fifth was reserved for Allāh, His Messenger, relatives, orphans, the
poor, and travelers (Qurʾān 8:42).

1055. Seceders from ʿAlī's cause, principally after the Battle of Ṣiffīn; see *EI²*, s.v.
Khāridjites.

1056. In the southeastern Arabian peninsula, famed for its camels.

1057. Reading *fa-kāna wajhuhā*. Prym's *fa-kāna wajjahahā* has no explicit subject, but could be ʿAlī—"so he sent her away [from al-Baṣrah]." The text may be
corrupt, and, like IA, 258, Prym's proposed reconstruction, "ʿĀʾishah left al-Baṣrah
and headed toward Mecca," corresponds with the translation above.

1058. A little over seven months later, if the end of Rabīʿ II is taken as the date of
the battle, and five or six if Jumādā II is taken; see pp. 81, 133, above.

What 'Alī b. Abī Ṭālib Wrote about the Victory to His Governor of al-Kūfah

According to al-Sarī (in writing)—Shu'ayb—Sayf—Muḥammad and Ṭalḥah: 'Alī wrote to his governor of al-Kūfah about the victory, in a letter concerning al-Kūfah, while the governor was in Mecca.

> From 'Allāh's servant 'Alī, Commander of the Faithful. After greetings. We fought in the middle of Jumādā II in Khuraybah, one of the open areas in al-Baṣrah. Almighty and Glorious Allāh gave them the *sunnah* of the Muslims.[1059] There were many killed from our side and theirs. Among those killed from our side were Thumāmah b. al-Muthannā, Hind b. 'Amr, 'Ilbā' b. al-Haytham, Sayḥān and Zayd, the two sons of Ṣūḥān, and Mahdūj. 'Ubaydallāh b. Rāfi'[1060] was the scribe. Zufar b. Qays was the messenger who brought the good news to Kūfah, still in Jumādā II.

[3229]
'Alī Accepts Allegiance from the People and the Account of Ziyād b. Abī Sufyān[1061] and 'Abd al-Raḥmān b. Abī Bakrah

These words were said in the allegiance: "The fulfillment of Allāh's promise and covenant is obligatory on you. Our peace will be your peace, and our war will be your war. You will restrain your tongue and hand from attacking us."

Now Ziyād b. Abī Sufyān was one of those who withdrew and did not take part in the battle. He stayed back in the house of Nāfi' b. al-Ḥārith. 'Abd al-Raḥmān b. Abī Bakrah came with those seeking protection after 'Alī had finished with the allegiance and gave himself up. 'Alī asked him, "What about your father's brother,[1062]

1059. I.e., put an end to their deviation by trying to reason with them before taking up arms (*Glossarium*, CCCLXVII, and p. 73, above).

1060. For the text's 'Abdallāh, following Ibrāhīm, although there is no entry in Caskel, while there is one for an 'Abdallāh (Caskel and Strenziok, I, 195, II, 117). De Goeje suggests 'Ubaydallāh b. Abī Rāfi' (*Addenda*, DCXXXV).

1061. Settled early in al-Baṣrah with Abū Bakrah, probably a brother by the same mother, Sumayyah (*EI²*, s.v. Abū Bakrah; and Prym's n. c to the text); later Mu'āwiyah's viceroy in Iraq. See *EI¹*, s.v. Ziyād b. Abīhi.

1062. I.e., Ziyād.

the one who held out and refused to join me?"[1063] "By Allāh, Commander of the Faithful!" he replied. "He loves you and is very eager to please you, but I heard that he's ill. So I'll find out his news and come back to you." He was keeping his whereabouts a secret from 'Alī until he had consulted him, but [Ziyād] ordered him to tell him, so he did. "Walk in front of me!" said 'Alī, "and lead me to him!" He did so, and when he reached where he was he said, "You refused to join me and held out [on me]!" and 'Alī put his hand on his chest and said, "There's a sharp pain here." Ziyād then made apologies to him, and he accepted them. 'Alī then consulted with him and wanted him to govern al-Baṣrah. But Ziyād said: "Let it be a man from your close family, and the people will be content with him and more likely to be reassured or easily led. I will support him for you and advise him." So 'Alī and Ziyād parted, having decided on Ibn 'Abbās, and 'Alī returned to where he was staying.

The Appointment of Ibn 'Abbās as Governor of al-Baṣrah and Ziyād over the Kharāj Tax

'Alī appointed Ibn 'Abbās governor of al-Baṣrah and Ziyād over the [3230] kharāj tax and the treasury, and he ordered Ibn 'Abbās to listen to Ziyād's advice. "I consulted him about some small thing concerning the people," Ibn 'Abbās used to say, "and he replied, 'If you know you're in the right and that your opponent is in the wrong, I'll give you proper advice; if you don't know, I'll give you proper advice just the same.' 'I'm in the right,' I replied, 'and they're in the wrong.' So he said, 'Use those who obey you to beat those who disobey you and go against your orders! And, if it brings more strength and benefit to Islam that their heads be cut off, then cut them off!' I asked Ziyād to write this down, and when he left I looked at what he had done and realized that he had given me a well thought out opinion.'"

The Saba'iyyah set off without 'Alī's permission, which caused 'Alī to leave in haste and set off on their tracks to foil any plan they might be making. He had stayed in [al-Baṣrah] a while.

According to al-Sarī (in writing)—Shu'ayb—Sayf—Muḥammad

1063. *Al-mutaqā'id bī* or, in Ibrāhīm, *al-muqā'id bī.*

and Ṭalḥah: The people of Medina learned about the Day of the Camel before sunset on the Thursday from a vulture that circled around Medina with something hanging down. They were staring at it when it fell. To their surprise, it was a human hand wearing a signet ring engraved with the name of 'Abd al-Raḥmān b. 'Attāb. All Baṣrans between Mecca and Medina, whether near al-Baṣrah or far, then became frightened, having learned of the battle from the hands and feet carried to them by vultures.

[3231]
'Alī Equips 'Ā'ishah to Leave al-Baṣrah

According to al-Sarī (in writing)—Shu'ayb—Sayf—Muḥammad and Ṭalḥah: 'Alī equipped 'Ā'ishah with everything she needed in the way of riding beasts, provisions, and other baggage and sent with her all those who had fought on her side and had survived, except for anyone who wished to stay behind. He also selected forty prominent Baṣran women to go with her. "Get ready for the journey, Muḥammad!"[1064] he said, "and see that she arrives."[1065] So on the day she was to set off he came to her to stand and bid her farewell. The people were there so she went out to them, and they said their farewells to her and she to them. "My sons," she said, "some of us criticized others of us, saying they were slow or excessive.[1066] But don't let any of you hold it against any others over anything you might hear about this. By Allāh! There was never anything in the past between me and 'Alī other than what usually happens between a woman and her male in-laws. In my opinion he has shown himself one of the best of men, despite my criticism." "By Allāh, men!" replied 'Alī. "She has spoken the truth and nothing but the truth. That was all there was between us. She's the wife of your Prophet now and forever."[1067]

The day she left was Saturday 1 Rajab, 36/December 24, 656. 'Alī escorted her some miles and then left his sons to accompany her for a day.

1064. Ibn Abī Bakr.
1065. At Medina.
1066. In dealing with 'Uthmān.
1067. I.e., 'Alī has forgiven her.

Accounts of the Carnage on the Day of the Camel

According to 'Umar b. Shabbah—Abū al-Ḥasan—Muḥammad b. al-Faḍl b. 'Aṭiyyah al-Khurāsānī—Saʿīd al-Quṭaʿī: We used to recount the number of dead at the Battle of the Camel as exceeding 6,000.

According to 'Abdallāh b. Aḥmad b. Shabbawayh—his father— [3232] Sulaymān b. Ṣāliḥ—'Abdallāh—Jarīr b. Ḥāzim—al-Zubayr b. al-Khirrīt[1068]—Abū Labīd Limāzah b. Ziyād: I asked him,[1069] "Why do you curse 'Alī?" He replied, "Should I not curse a man who killed 2,500 of us by the time the sun was over our heads?"

According to Jarīr b. Ḥāzim—Ibn Abī Yaʿqūb: On the Day of the Camel 'Alī b. Abī Ṭālib killed 2,500 men—1,350 of them were from Azd, 800 from Banū Ḍabbah, and 350 from the rest of the people.

According to ['Abdallāh b. Aḥmad b. Shabbawayh]—his father — Sulaymān—'Abdallāh—Jarīr: When Al-Muʿarriḍ b. 'Ilāṭ[1070] was killed on the Day of the Camel his brother al-Ḥajjāj recited the verses

Never did I see a day when more men hastened to fight
  with only a left hand, because they had lost their right.

According to Muʿādh—'Abdallāh—Jarīr: When Al-Muʿarriḍ b. 'Ilāṭ was killed on the Day of the Camel his brother al-Ḥajjāj recited the verses

Never did I see a day when more men hastened to fight
  with[1071] only a left hand, because they had lost their right.

What 'Ammār b. Yāsir Told 'Āʾishah When the Battle of the Camel Was Over

According to 'Abdallāh b. Aḥmad—his father—Sulaymān—'Abdallāh—Jarīr b. Ḥāzim—Abū Yazīd al-Madīnī: When the

---

1068. Following Ibrāhīm and *Addenda*, DCXXXV, for the text's Ibn al-Ḥurayth.
1069. I.e., al-Zubayr b. al-Khirrīt asked Abū Labīd.
1070. Of Sulaym. Only his brother al-Ḥajjāj is mentioned in Caskel and Strenziok, I, 122, II, 291). Al-Ḥajjāj was involved in the expedition against Khaybar (Ibn Hishām, 770 ff.; tr., 519 ff.; see also Watt, 97).
1071. *Bi-kaffi shimālin* for *li-kaffi* . . . in the preceding version. Prym points out that in the ms. this line comes at the end of the next *khabar*, but it appears that it belongs here.

[3233]   people had finished fighting, ʿAmmār b. Yāsir said to ʿĀʾishah, "Mother of the Faithful, how far this march is from the pact that was made for you!"[1072] "Abū al-Yaqẓān!" she replied. "Yes?" he asked. "By Allāh! As I always knew, you're a great speaker of the truth!" "Praise be to Allāh!" he replied, "Who has judged in my favor by your tongue!"

1072. Not to leave her house (Qurʾān 33:33).

The End of the Account of the Battle of the Camel

'Alī b. Abī Ṭālib Sends Qays b. Sa'd b. 'Ubādah to Be Ruler of Egypt

In this year—that is, 36—Muḥammad b. Abī Ḥudhayfah[1073] was killed. This was because, when the Egyptians had left to go to 'Uthmān with Muḥammad b. Abī Bakr, he stayed in Egypt, expelled 'Abdallāh b. Sa'd b. Abī Sarḥ,[1074] and took control of the country. There he remained until 'Uthmān was killed and allegiance was given to 'Alī. Mu'āwiyah then rebelled, and 'Amr b. al-'Āṣ gave him allegiance. The two of them then went to Muḥammad b. Abī Ḥudhayfah before Qays b. Sa'd reached Egypt. They tried without success to enter Egypt, so they continued to practice deceit on Muḥammad b. Abī Ḥudhayfah until he came out with 1,000 men to 'Arīsh of Egypt and set up fortifications. 'Amr then went to him there and set up mangonels against him. This made Muḥammad come out with thirty of his men, whereupon they were captured and put to death, may they rest in peace.

According to Hishām b. Muḥammad[1075]—Abū Mikhnaf Lūṭ b. Yaḥyā b. Sa'īd b. Mikhnaf b. Sulaym—Muḥammad b. Yūsuf[1076] al-Anṣārī of Banū al-Ḥārith b. al-Khazraj—'Abbās b. Sahl[1077] al-Sā'idī: It was Muḥammad b. Abī Ḥudhayfah b. 'Utbah b. Rabī'ah b.   [3234] 'Abd Shams b. 'Abd Manāf who sent the Egyptians to 'Uthmān b. 'Affān, and then, once they had gone to 'Uthmān and besieged him, he (back in Egypt) seized 'Abdallāh b. Sa'd b. Abī Sarḥ, one of Banū 'Āmir b. Lu'ayy[1078] of Quraysh and 'Uthmān's governor of Egypt at the time. Muḥammad then expelled him and made himself leader of the prayer. So 'Abdallāh b. Sa'd left Egypt and encamped at the border between Egypt and Palestine, awaiting the outcome of the business over 'Uthmān.

A rider appeared and 'Abdallāh b. Sa'd asked: "What's your news, 'Abdallāh?[1079] Tell us what's been happening to the people

---

1073. Ibn 'Utbah b. Rabī'ah b. 'Abd Shams b. 'Abd Manāf, a paternal cousin of 'Uthmān but against him; Caetani, IX, 307–8.

1074. A scribe of the Prophet and a milk brother of 'Uthmān (Caskel and Strenziok, I, 27, II, 117).

1075. Al-Kalbī (Caetani, IX, 308–9).

1076. Ibn Thābit Abū Yūsuf (U. Sezgin, 212).

1077. Ibn Sa'd (U. Sezgin, 212).

1078. Caskel and Strenziok, I, 27.

1079. 'Abdallāh is the address to a Muslim whose name is not known.

where you came from." "I will," he replied. "The Muslims have killed ʿUthmān." "ʿWe belong to Allāh, and to Him we return,'"[1080] said ʿAbdallāh b. Saʿd. "And then what did they do, ʿAbdallāh?" "Then they gave allegiance to the paternal cousin of the Messenger of God, ʿAlī b. Abī Ṭālib." "ʿWe belong to Allāh, and to Him we return,'" said ʿAbdallāh b. Saʿd again. "It seems that you think that ʿAlī b. Abī Ṭālib's becoming ruler is as bad as the killing of ʿUthmān," the man said to him, [astonished]. "That's right," he replied. The man then gave him a searching look and realized that he knew him. "You look like ʿAbdallāh [b. Saʿd] b. Abī Sarḥ, ruler of Egypt," he said. "That's right," he replied. "If you've any desire for life left," the man said to him, "then escape fast! The Commander of the Faithful's opinion about you and your followers is bad. If he overcomes you, he'll kill you or banish you from Muslim territory, and here on my heels is a new ruler[1081] coming instead of you." "What ruler is this?" asked ʿAbdallāh. "Qays b. Saʿd b. ʿUbādah al-Anṣārī." "May Allāh expel Muḥammad b. Abī Ḥudhayfah from His mercy!" said ʿAbd-allāh b. Saʿd, "for he has committed an outrage against his pater-nal cousin[1082] and worked against him, when ʿUthmān had been his guardian and brought him up and done him so much good. But he abused his protection and set upon his governors and equipped men against him until he was killed. Then someone who was worse than himself was appointed over him,[1083] someone to whom ʿUthmān had not granted power over his lands for a year or even a month, because he did not consider him fit for it." "Escape and save yourself, and you won't be killed!" the man told him. So ʿAbdallāh b. Saʿd left and fled until he reached Muʿāwiyah b. Abī Sufyān in Damascus.

[3235]

Abū Jaʿfar [al-Ṭabarī] added, "This report from Hishām proves that Qays b. Saʿd became governor of Egypt while Muḥammad b. Abī Ḥudhayfah was still alive."

In this year ʿAlī b. Abī Ṭālib sent Qays b. Saʿd b. ʿUbādah al-

---

1080. Qurʾān 2:156.
1081. Sent from ʿAlī.
1082. ʿUthmān.
1083. I.e., ʿAlī.

Anṣārī to govern Egypt, and about this we have the following account.

According to Hishām b. Muḥammad al-Kalbī—Abū Mikhnaf—Muḥammad b. Yūsuf b. Thābit—Sahl b. Saʿd:[1084] When ʿUthmān was killed and ʿAlī b. Abī Ṭālib became caliph, he called Qays b. Saʿd al-Anṣārī and told him: "Go to Egypt; I've made you its governor. So go and get ready to travel, and gather your trusted followers to you[1085] and those you want to go with you, so that you arrive there with a force. That will be more alarming to your enemies and more encouraging to your friends. If Allāh wills that you get there, then treat the good doer well and be severe with those you suspect. Be lenient with newcomers and early comers;[1086] leniency brings success." "May Allāh have mercy on you,[1087] Commander of the Faithful!" replied Qays b. Saʿd. "I appreciate what you say, but, as for your advice, 'Go out to it with a force,' by Allāh! If I can enter Egypt only with a force brought from Medina I'll never enter it at all. So I'll leave that force for you. Then if you have need of them they'll be near at hand, or if you want to send them on some mission of yours they'll be there ready for you. I and my household, however, will go on our own. As for your advice about leniency and good treatment, I will ask help for that from Almighty and Glorious Allāh."

[3236]

So Qays b. Saʿd left with seven of his followers and went to Egypt, where he mounted the *minbar*, sat down, and ordered that a letter he had with him from the Commander of the Faithful be read out to the people of Egypt:

> In the name of Allāh the Merciful, the Compassionate. From the servant of Allāh ʿAlī, the Commander of the Faithful, to all Muslims and believers who hear this edict of mine. Peace be upon you! I praise Allāh to you, apart from Whom there is no deity.
>
> After greetings. [I tell you!] Almighty and Glorious Allāh, by the goodness of His actions, His plans, and His

---

1084. Al-Shahrazūrī (U. Sezgin, 123, 226); Caetani, IX, 318 ff.
1085. Reading *ilayka* for *ilayhi*, after Ibrāhīm and IA.
1086. Hinds, "Kūfan Political Alignments," 354.
1087. Polite introduction to a contradiction.

direction, has chosen Islam as His Own religion, that of His angels and of His messengers. He has sent the messengers with it to His servants and has specially ordained for it those of His creation whom He elected. Then one of the things by which Almighty and Glorious Allāh has ennobled this community and singled it out for excellence is His sending Muḥammad to it. In this way he taught them the Book, the wisdom, the ordinances, and the *sunnah*, that they might be guided right. He united them that they might not split into factions, he purified them that they might be clean, and be made life good for them[1088] that they might not oppress. When he had accomplished his mission, Almighty and Glorious Allāh took him, may Allāh's prayers and mercy and blessings be upon him! The Muslims then appointed two leaders as his deputies who were devout and acted according to the Book and the *sunnah*. They conducted themselves well and did not go against the *sunnah*. Almighty and Glorious Allāh then took them also to Himself, and a governor[1089] succeeded them who introduced innovations, so the community found a way to talk against him, so they talked and then criticized and reviled him.[1090] Then they came to me and gave me allegiance, so I pray for guidance from Almighty and Glorious Allāh and ask Him to help me to fear Him. Indeed, I am obliged to you to act according to the Book of Allāh and the *sunnah* of His messenger and to govern you according to His proper manner and to implement His *sunnah* and to be honest with you when you are absent.[1091] 'Allāh is the One from Whom help is sought!'[1092] 'Allāh is sufficient for us; He is an excellent guardian!'[1093] Now I have sent Qays b. Saʿd b. ʿUbādah to you as ruler, so help him, support him,[1094] and assist him

[3237]

1088. Reading *wa-raffahahum* after Ibrāhīm for the text's *wa-raffahum*.
1089. ʿUthmān.
1090. Following the text's *fa-ʿayyarū*, rather than Ibrāhīm's *fa-ghayyarū*.
1091. Cf. Qurʾān 12:53.
1092. Qurʾān 12:18, 21:112.
1093. Qurʾān 3:173.
1094. Reading either *wa-kānifūhu* with the text or *wa-kātifūhu* with the ms.

toward right. I have ordered him to do good to those of you who do good, to be severe with those of you who are suspect, and to be lenient with newcomers and late-comers.[1095] He's among those whose guidance I'm well satisfied with and whose goodness and sincere advice I always expect. So I request for you and for us from Almighty and Glorious Allāh right action and bountiful reward and far-reaching mercy. Peace be upon you and Allāh's mercy and blessings! Written by 'Ubaydallāh[1096] b. Abī Rāfi' in Ṣafar, 36.

Qays b. Sa'd then stood up to make a speech. He praised Allāh and magnified Him, asked Allāh's blessings upon Muḥammad, and said, "Praise to Allāh, Who has brought truth and destroyed falsehood and has prostrated the oppressors. Men! We have given allegiance to the best person after Muḥammad our Prophet we know, so arise all of you and give allegiance over the Book of Almighty and Glorious Allāh and the *sunnah* of His Messenger, for if we don't apply them over you, you won't owe us any allegiance." So the people stood and gave allegiance, and Egypt settled down under his command, and he sent out his provincial governors. However, there was one village there called Kharbitā,[1097] where there was a group that had taken 'Uthmān b. 'Affān's murder very seriously, among them[1098] a man from Banū al-Ḥārith b. Mudlij[1099] from Kinānah called Yazīd b. al-Ḥārith. These sent a message to Qays b. Sa'd: "We shall not fight you, so send out your governors; the land is yours. But let us remain as we are until we see what the people do." Then Maslamah b. Mukhallad al-Anṣārī[1100] of the clan Sā'idah,[1101] one of Qays b. Sa'd's group, rose up and lamented the death of 'Uthmān b. 'Affān and called for revenge for his blood. But Qays b. Sa'd sent a message back to him: "Shame on you! Are you rising up against me?

[3238]

1095. Hinds, "Kūfan Political Alignments," 354.

1096. See *Addenda*, DCXXXIV for the text's 'Ubayd.

1097. See p. 27, above.

1098. "Leading them" (IA).

1099. Caskel and Strenziok, I, 44, II, 310.

1100. Caskel and Strenziok, I, 187, II, 401.

1101. *Thumma min Sā'idah*. Ibrāhīm has *thumma man sā'adahu* "and so did his supporters."

By Allāh! I wouldn't want to kill you even if I were given the rule of Syria as well as Egypt." Maslamah sent back this message: "I shall not fight you as long as you are governor of Egypt."

Now Qays b. Saʿd had resolve and good judgment,[1102] so he sent a message to those at Kharbitā: "I am not going to force you to give allegiance. I will let you be and not fight you." So he made a truce with them and with Maslamah b. Mukhallad and collected the *kharāj* tax[1103] without anyone's resisting him.

It was while Qays was governing Egypt that the Commander of the Faithful went out against the army of the Camel, and he was still in his post when ʿAlī went back to Kūfah from Baṣrah. Because of his closeness to Syria he was Muʿāwiyah b. Abī Sufyān's greatest problem. Muʿāwiyah was afraid that ʿAlī would advance against him with the Iraqi army and that Qays b. Saʿd would advance against him with the Egyptian army and that Muʿāwiyah would be caught between the two.

Muʿāwiyah b. Abī Sufyān therefore wrote to Qays b. Saʿd. At this stage ʿAlī b. Abī Ṭālib was at al-Kūfah, prior to his setting out for Ṣiffīn.

> From Muʿāwiyah b. Abī Sufyān to Qays b. Saʿd.[1104] Peace be upon you! After greetings. If you were resentful against ʿUthmān b. ʿAffān for any preferential treatment you thought he was making, or for whippings he gave, or for verbal abuses against anyone, or for expulsions of others,[1105] or for putting youths in authority, you nevertheless knew—if you know anything—that to take his life was not lawful for you. You have therefore perpetrated a heinous crime and done something shocking.[1106] So Qays b. Saʿd! If repenting for the murder of a believer can have any effect, then repent to Almighty and Glorious Allāh, for you were party to the crime against ʿUthmān b. ʿAffān.

[3239]

1102. He was known as one of the seven *duhāt*.

1103. The land tax, *EI²*, s.v.

1104. Note the absence of a *basmala* here and in the next two letters (but not the fourth).

1105. Like Abū Dharr al-Ghifārī.

1106. Qurʾān 19:89, said of those who say Allāh had a son. The ms. has *amran* for the Qurʾān text's *shayʾan*.

As for your companion,[1107] we have no doubt whatsoever that it was he who incited the people against 'Uthmān and urged them on to kill him until they did so. The majority of your own people are now implicated in his blood. So Qays, if you can join those demanding revenge for 'Uthmān's death, then do so.[1108] Follow our lead, and if I gain the victory you shall be given authority over al-Kūfah and al-Baṣrah[1109] as long as I live. Authority over the Ḥijāz shall be given to any of your close family you wish, as long as I hold power. Ask of me also anything in addition to this you may want. You will not request anything without receiving it. So write and let me know your reaction to what I have written. Peace!

When Mu'āwiyah's letter reached him, he wanted to hold him off[1110] and not disclose his position to him and not to be in a hurry to make war with him, so he wrote to him:

After greetings. I received your letter, and I understand what you say about the murder of 'Uthmān. But I did not commit it, nor was I in any way connected with it. You also say that it was my companion who incited the people against 'Uthmān and secretly urged them on until they killed him. This also I did not witness. You say, too, that the majority of my people are implicated in 'Uthmān's blood, but the very first group to stand up and demand retaliation for him was my tribe. Concerning your request to me to join behind your lead and your offer to me for doing so, I have understood it. It is something I will have to look into and think about. It is not something that should be rushed into. Meanwhile, I will not fight you, and nothing distasteful to you will come to you from my quarter until, Allāh willing, both you and I have considered the matter. Almighty and Glorious Allāh is the One

[3240]

1107. 'Alī.
1108. As a sort of repentance.
1109. *Al-'Irāqayn.*
1110. Cf. the next letter of Qays.

from Whom protection is to be sought. Peace be upon you, and the mercy of Allāh and His Blessings!

When Muʿāwiyah read his reply he realized he was trying pull-push tactics,[1111] and he was not sure that it would not end up as push-deceive.[1112] So Muʿāwiyah wrote to him again:

> After greetings. I have read your letter, but I do not see you making approaches that lead me to recognize you as [offering] peace, nor do I see you distancing yourself in a way that leads me to recognize you as [offering] war. By taking such a position you are like the chin of the camel for slaughter.[1113] Men like myself, who have large numbers of men and fighting cavalry,[1114] do not make up to a deceiver, nor do they incline to a trickster. Peace be upon you!

When Qays b. Saʿd had read Muʿāwiyah's letter and realized that holding off and playing for time would not get anywhere with him, he wrote to him revealing his true intentions:

> In the name of Allāh the Merciful, the Compassionate. From Qays b. Saʿd to Muʿāwiyah b. Abī Sufyān. After greetings. I am astonished how you try to deceive me, how you desire to overcome me, and how you try to make me change my mind for the worse. Are you obliging me to renounce obedience to the most qualified of all people for the leadership, whose words are truest, whose actions are most rightly guided, and whose connections to the Messenger of God are closest? Are you then commanding me to enter into obedience to yourself—obedience to the most unqualified of all people for this rule, most ready of all to speak falsely, whose actions are most astray, and whose connections to Almighty and Glorious Allāh and His Messenger are most distant, a son of those who are astray and those who lead astray,[1115] one of the devil's

[3241]

1111. *Muqāriban mubāʿidan.*
1112. *Mubāʿidan mukāyidan.*
1113. "Moving this way and that to try to trick the slaughterer"?
1114. Lit., "the reins of horses in his hand."
1115. Abū Sufyān, a major opponent of the Prophet.

own devils? As for your statement that you will fill Egypt
with horses and men to fight me, by Allāh! If I do not keep
you concerned with yourself so that your very survival
becomes the most worrying thing for you, you will be
lucky. Peace!

On receiving Qays's letter, Mu'āwiyah lost hope for him; his
being there in Egypt was a big impediment to him.

According to 'Abdallāh b. Aḥmad al-Marwazī—[his father,][1116]
Sulaymān—'Abdallāh—Yūnus—al-Zuhrī: Egypt during 'Alī's
time was governed by Qays b. Sa'd b. 'Ubādah, the holder of the
banner of the Anṣār alongside the Messenger of God. He was one
of those of sound judgment and strong character. Now Mu'āwiyah
b. Abī Sufyān and 'Amr b. al-'Āṣ were making great efforts to get
him out of Egypt and take control of it, but he defended it with
cunning and stratagems. They had neither gained control of him
nor captured Egypt until Mu'āwiyah tricked him through 'Alī.[1117]
When Mu'āwiyah was talking with some tribesmen of Quraysh,
respected for their good judgment, he said: "I never devised a trick
that pleased me more than the one with which I tricked Qays b.
Sa'd through 'Alī while he was in Iraq and Qays was resisting me. I
said to the Syrians: 'Don't speak roughly to Qays b. Sa'd and don't
put out any call to invade him. He supports us; his shrewd advice
comes to us secretly. Don't you see what he has done with your
brothers from the men of Kharbitā who are there under him? He
pays them their allowances and provisions, he gives them securi-
ty,[1118] and he treats any rider well that goes to him from you.
They never find fault with him in any way.' So I made a point   [3242]
of writing to my Iraqi followers about all this," continued
Mu'āwiyah, "so that 'Alī's spies with me here and over in Iraq
should hear it." From them it got back to 'Alī—by Muḥammad b.
Abī Bakr and Muḥammad b. Ja'far b. Abī Ṭālib—and when 'Alī
heard of it he became suspicious of Qays and wrote to him, ordering him to go and fight the people of Kharbitā. The people of

---

1116. Cf. p. 187, below, and *Addenda*, DCXXXV.
1117. By the speech that follows and by a fabricated letter; see p. 185, below.
1118. Lit. "their flocks" (Lane, 1341c), as also in Qays's letter to 'Alī, p. 184,
below.

Kharbitā at that time numbered 10,000. Qays refused to fight them and wrote to ʿAlī.

> They are Egyptian notables and noblemen. Loyal men are among them. They agreed with me, provided I give them security and give them their allowances and provisions, although I am fully aware that their sympathies lie with Muʿāwiyah. So I see no way of maneuvering them that would be any easier for me or for you than what I am already doing with them. Were I to attack them they would be my match. They are lions of Arabs; among them are Busr b. Abī[1119] Arṭāh, Maslamah b. Mukhallad,[1120] and Muʿāwiyah b. Ḥudayj. So let me do things my way; I know how to cajole them.

The only course of action ʿAlī would accept was to fight them, but Qays refused and wrote again to ʿAlī, "If you suspect me, then remove me from your governorship and appoint someone else to it." ʿAlī therefore appointed al-Ashtar ruler of Egypt, but at al-Qulzum[1121] he drank a honey drink and died.[1122] News of this reached Muʿāwiyah and ʿAmr [b. al-ʿĀṣ], and the latter remarked, "Allāh has an army in honey!"[1123] On hearing of al-Ashtar's death at al-Qulzum, ʿAlī sent Muḥammad b. Abī Bakr as ruler of Egypt.

Al-Zuhrī said that ʿAlī sent Muḥammad b. Abī Bakr as ruler of Egypt after the death of al-Ashtar at Qulzum. But Hishām b. Muḥammad [b. al-Kalbī] in his account said the opposite—that ʿAlī sent al-Ashtar as ruler of Egypt after the death of Muḥammad b. Abī Bakr.

1119. *Addenda*, DCXXXV and Ibrāhīm. A bedouin of Banū ʿĀmir of Quraysh and a fiery opponent of ʿAlī (*EI²*, s.v.).

1120. Al-Anṣārī.

1121. The port at the top of the Red Sea (*EI²*, s.v.).

1122. Poisoned by the local *jāyastār*, perhaps at the instigation of Muʿāwiyah (*EI²*, s.v. al-Ashtar). Cf. Hawting, *First Civil War*, 145.

1123. Freytag, I, 10; *EI²*, s.v. al-Ashtar. Cf. Qurʾān—*lillāhi junūd al-samāwāt wa-al-arḍ*. Muʿāwiyah is said to have done this on other occasions, e.g., by means of al-Jaʿdah bt. al-Ashʿath, who is said to have poisoned her husband, Ḥasan b. ʿAlī, for a large sum of money and the hand of Muʿāwiyah's son Yazīd (*EI²*, s.v. al-Ḥasan).

Return to the account of Hishām [b. Muḥammad b. al-Kalbī]   [3243]
from Abū Mikhnaf

When Muʿāwiyah gave up hoping that Qays would comply with
his authority, it made him very anxious, for he was well aware of
Qays's determination and strength of character. So Muʿāwiyah
feigned to the people around him that, "Qays b. Saʿd is on your
side, so say prayers for him to Allāh!" He then read out to them
the letter in which Qays had been compliant and accommodating
toward Muʿāwiyah. He further fabricated a letter from Qays b. Saʿd
and read it aloud to the Syrians:

> In the name of Allāh, the Merciful, the Compassionate.
> To the ruler Muʿāwiyah b. Abī Sufyān from Qays b. Saʿd.
> Greetings! I praise Allāh to you. There is no god but He!
> After greetings. I have considered the situation and I now
> realize that I can no longer support a party that killed
> their imām, a Muslim, unlawful to be killed, who was
> fulfilling his duties and was God-fearing. We therefore beg
> Almighty and Glorious Allāh pardon for our sins and ask
> Him to preserve our religion from error. Here I come in
> peace to you, responding to your call to fight the killers of
> ʿUthmān, the unjustly killed imām of guidance.[1124] So
> ask my assistance regarding whatever money and men
> you would like, and I will expedite them to you. Peace!

At this the news spread among the Syrians that Qays b. Saʿd had
given allegiance to Muʿāwiyah b. Abī Sufyān. ʿAlī b. Abī Ṭālib's
spies conveyed it back to ʿAlī, and when he heard it he was dis-
tressed, shocked, and very surprised. He called his sons and ʿAbdallāh b. Jaʿfar and told them. "What did you think?" he asked.
"Commander of the Faithful," replied ʿAbdallāh b. Jaʿfar. "Leave
what you suspect for what you don't suspect! Remove Qays from
Egypt!" "By Allāh! I cannot credit this from Qays," ʿAlī answered
them. "But Commander of the Faithful," replied ʿAbdallāh b.
Jaʿfar, "remove him! Then, by Allāh! If this news is true he will
not step down for you when you remove him."[1125] They were   [3244]

1124. Reading *imāmi* . . . with Nöldeke (*Addenda*, DCXXXV) and Ibrāhīm.
1125. I.e., if he really has gone over to Muʿāwiyah, he will refuse to give up Egypt
and simply rule it under Muʿāwiyah.

talking in this way when a letter from Qays b. Saʿd arrived, containing the following:

> In the name of Allāh, the Merciful, the Compassionate. After greetings. I inform the Commander of the Faithful, may Allāh ennoble him! that there are men facing me here who are abstaining.[1126] They have asked me to hold off from them and leave them alone until matters between the people have been put in order, at which time we may come to a decision and they may. I therefore thought it wise to hold off from them and not to rush into battle with them, but in the meanwhile to try to win them over. Perhaps Almighty and Glorious Allāh will make their minds more favorable to us and separate them from their error, if He wills.

"Commander of the Faithful!" said ʿAbdallāh b. Jaʿfar. "I'm very afraid that this means he is in fact joining forces with them. Order him, Commander of the Faithful, to fight them!" ʿAlī therefore wrote to him: "In the name of Allāh, the Merciful, the Compassionate. After greetings. Go to these people you mention! If they make allegiance to me as the Muslims have done, all well and good. But, if they do not, then fight them, God willing!"[1127] When the letter reached Qays b. Saʿd and he read it he could not but write back to Commander of the Faithful:

> After greetings. Commander of the Faithful, I was astonished at your order. Are you ordering me to fight people who are holding back from you and leaving you free to fight your enemy? They will support your enemy against you if you go to war with them. Follow my advice, Commander of the Faithful! Hold back from them! Leaving them alone is the best thing to do. Peace!

When this letter reached ʿAlī, ʿAbdallāh b. Jaʿfar said to him, "Commander of the Faithful! Send Muḥammad b. Abī Bakr to rule Egypt! He will take care of it for you. Remove Qays! By Allāh I have heard that Qays says: 'By Allāh! A rule that is only estab-

---

1126. From giving you/me their allegiance.
1127. Cf. the *ḥadīth al-khārij ʿalā imām zamānih kāfir*.

lished by killing Maslamah b. Mukhallad is a bad rule indeed! By
Allāh I have no wish even to rule Syria along with Egypt as the   [3245]
killer of Ibn al-Mukhallad.'"

Now 'Abdallāh b. Ja'far was the brother of Muḥammad b. Abī
Bakr by the same mother.[1128] So 'Alī sent Muḥammad b. Abī Bakr
as governor of Egypt and removed Qays.

Muḥammad b. Abī Bakr's Governorship of Egypt

According to Hishām—Abū Mikhnaf—al-Ḥārith b. Ka'b[1129] al-
Wālibī of Wālibah of al-Azd—his father:[1130] 'Alī wrote a letter for
[Muḥammad b. Abī Bakr] to take to the Egyptians. On his pre-
senting it to Qays, Qays said to him: "What is the Commander of
the Faithful doing? What has changed his mind? Has someone
been saying things to him against me?" "No," replied Muḥammad, "this rule is yours." "By Allāh! Not even for a single hour
will I stay in the same area as you," said Qays. So when 'Alī
removed him from office, he became furious, left Egypt, and
headed for Medina. When he arrived there Ḥassān b. Thābit (who
was one of the 'Uthmāniyyah) came up to him, pleased at his
misfortune, and said: "'Alī b. Abī Ṭālib has dismissed you. You
killed 'Uthmān, and you're still guilty of the crime, and 'Alī
hasn't given you much thanks!" "It's not just your eye that's blind
but your mind as well!" replied Qays b. Sa'd. "By Allāh! If it
wouldn't be the cause of a war between my tribe and yours, I
would break your neck! Get out of my sight!" Qays, accompanied
by Sahl b. Ḥunayf, then left Medina for 'Alī. Qays then told 'Alī
the whole story, and 'Alī believed him. Qays and Sahl later accompanied 'Alī at Ṣiffīn.

According to 'Abdallāh b. Aḥmad [al-Marwazī]—his father—
Sulaymān—'Abdallāh—Yūnus—al-Zuhrī: Muḥammad b. Abī
Bakr came to Egypt, so Qays left to stay in Medina. Marwān and   [3246]
al-Aswad b. Abī al-Bakhtarī[1131] then made Qays fear that he
would be captured or killed. So he mounted his travel camel and

---

1128. Asmā'.
1129. Ibn Fuqaym (U. Sezgin, 206).
1130. U. Sezgin, 151–52.
1131. One of the 'Uthmāniyyah, like Marwān.

went and joined[1132] 'Alī. Mu'āwiyah then sent an angry letter to Marwān and al-Aswad: "The two of you have reinforced 'Alī with Qays b. Sa'd, with his good judgment and with his respected position. By Allāh! If you had reinforced him with a hundred thousand soldiers it would not have angered me more than your expelling Qays b. Sa'd to 'Alī!"

Qays b. Sa'd came to 'Alī and apprised him[1133] of what had happened. The killing of Muḥammad b. Abī Bakr also reached him. All this made 'Alī realize that Qays b. Sa'd had been contending against powerful plots and that those who had urged him to remove Qays b. Sa'd[1134] had been giving him poor advice. So from then on 'Alī listened to Qays b. Sa'd at every turn.

According to Hishām—Abū Mikhnaf—al-Ḥārith b. Ka'b al-Wālibī—his father: I was[1135] with Muḥammad b. Abī Bakr when he came to Egypt and read out his commission to them:

> In the name of Allāh, the Merciful, the Compassionate. The commission of the servant of Allāh 'Alī, the Commander of the Faithful, to Muḥammad b. Abī Bakr on his appointment as ruler of Egypt.
>
> He commands him to piety toward Allāh and obedience personally and publicly; to fear of Almighty and Glorious Allāh regarding things unseen and seen; to leniency toward Muslims and harshness toward the dissolute; to justice toward the *dhimmis*; to establish the rights of the oppressed and to be severe with the oppressor; to forgiveness toward the people and to do good as far as he is able—Allāh rewards those who do good and punishes those who do wrong.
>
> He commands him to call those around him to obedience [to the imām] and to the community [of the imām].[1136] For the final issue and huge reward for them in so doing are incalculable and unfathomable.

[3247]

1132. Reading *fa-ṭamara* or *fa-ẓahara* (cf. Prym's n. *b*); see pp. 5 and 43, above.

1133. Reading *bāththahu* (*Addenda*, DCXXXV).

1134. Like 'Abdallāh b. Ja'far.

1135. Following the correction to the ms. (*kuntu ma'* for *kataba*).

1136. *Ilā al-ṭā'ah wa-al-jamā'ah*; cf. the Prophet's saying *Ilzam al-ṭā'ah wa-al-jamā'ah* (Wensinck, IV, 42a).

He commands him to collect the *kharāj* tax on land at the rate at which it was taxed before, neither to reduce it nor make new amendments to it; then to divide it among its recipients as they divided it before; to be gentle[1137] with them and to treat them equally in his meetings with them and his regard for them;[1138] and to let those near and those distant have equal rights.

He commands him to judge people with truth and to establish equity, not to follow personal desire or to fear the blame of others when following Almighty and Glorious Allāh. For Allāh, may His praise be magnified, is with those who are pious and who give priority to obeying Him and His commands over all others.

Written by 'Ubaydallāh[1139] b. Abī Rāfi', *mawlā* of the Messenger of Allāh, this 1 Ramaḍān/February 21.

Muḥammad b. Abī Bakr then stood up to preach a sermon. He praised Allāh and glorified Him. "The right path of action has been disputed, but praise Allāh!" he said, "Who guided us and you and Who made us and you perceive much the ignorant are blind about. The Commander of the Faithful has placed me in charge of your affairs and has given me a commission, as you have just heard. 'Alī gave me many instructions by word of mouth, and as far as I am able I will never neglect to do what is good for you. 'My success is from Allāh alone; on Him I have relied, and to Him I turn in repentance.'[1140] If you see that my leadership and deeds are in obedience and piety to Allāh, praise Almighty and Glorious Allāh for that, for He is the guide. But if you see any governor of mine governing wrongly and deviating, then bring him to me, and complain to me about him without fear. I prefer it that way, and it is your right. May Allāh through His mercy give us and you success in good works." Then he sat down.   [3248]

According to Hishām—Abū Mikhnaf—Yazīd b. Ẓabyān al-Hamdānī:[1141] On being appointed ruler [of Egypt], Muḥammad b.

1137. Lane, 469b.
1138. Lane, 60b.
1139. *Addenda*, DCXXXV.
1140. Qur'ān 11:88.
1141. Following Prym, Ibrāhīm, and U. Sezgin, 225.

Abī Bakr corresponded with Muʿāwiyah b. Abī Sufyān. He[1142] mentioned this correspondence that had passed between the two of them, but I am loath to detail it because it contains matter that most people could not tolerate.

Now Muḥammad b. Abī Bakr did not even wait a whole month before sending a message to that party that had withdrawn and with which Qays had made an accord. "Men!" he said in it. "Either you enter into obedience to us, or else you leave our territory!" "We will not do that," came their reply. "Leave us alone until we see how our situation turns out, and don't hasten to make war with us!" But Muḥammad insisted, so they resisted him and kept on their guard. They were therefore afraid of Muḥammad b. Abī Bakr at the Battle of Ṣiffīn. But when news came that Muʿāwiyah and the Syrians had held out against ʿAlī, that ʿAlī and the Iraqis had withdrawn from Muʿāwiyah and the Syrians, and that their case had been referred to arbitration, they became bolder toward Muḥammad b. Abī Bakr and openly came out to fight him. Seeing this, Muḥammad sent al-Ḥārith b. Jumhān al-Juʿfī to the men at Kharbitā (among whom was Yazīd b. al-Ḥārith of Banū Kinānah). He fought them, but they killed him. So he then sent a tribesman from Kalb called Ibn Muḍāhim, but [3249] they killed him too. Abū Jaʿfar [al-Ṭabarī] said, "It is said that in this year Māhawayh [Abrāz], the *marzubān*[1143] of Marw,[1144] came to ʿAlī to confirm the peace treaty concluded between himself and Ibn ʿAmir."

The account of this[1145]

According to ʿAlī b. Muḥammad al-Madāʾinī—Abū Zakariyyāʾ al-ʿAjlānī—Ibn Isḥāq—his teachers: After the Battle of the Camel Māhawayh Abrāz, the *marzubān* of Marw, came to ʿAlī b. Abī Ṭālib, confirming peace. So ʿAlī wrote a letter for him to the *dihqāns*[1146] of Marw, to the *asāwirah*,[1147] to the *jundsalārīn*,[1148]

1142. Probably Hishām.

1143. The warden of the march, i.e., the provincial governor (*EI²*, s.v. Marzpān).

1144. The capital of Khurāsān at the time (*EI²*, s.v.).

1145. Ibrāhīm has "The account of those who say this."

1146. The lesser feudal nobility of Sasanian Persia (*EI²*, s.v.).

1147. The heavy mailed cavalry, which constituted the core of the Sasanian army (Morony, 198, 207–8, 528; *EI²*, s.v. Asāwera; I, Humphreys, 80.

1148. An unusual expression, probably meaning officers, corps commanders, local military leaders, or the like, *sālār* being Persian for commander.

and to anyone else at Marw: "In the name of Allāh, the Merciful,
the Compassionate! Peace to those who follow divine guidance!
After greetings. Māhawayh Abrāz, the *marzubān* of Marw, came
to me, and I am satisfied with him."

This was written in the year 36, but subsequently they reneged[1149] and locked the gates of Abrashahr.[1150]

'Alī Despatches Khulayd b. Ṭarīf to Khurāsān

According to 'Alī b. Muḥammad al-Madā'inī—Abū Mikhnaf—
Ḥanẓalah b. al-A'lam[1151]—Māhān al-Ḥanafī[1152]—al-Aṣbagh b.
Nubātah al-Mujāshi'ī:[1153] 'Alī sent Khulayd b. Qurrah al-
Yarbū'ī—some say Khulayd b. Ṭarīf—to Khurāsān.

'Amr b. al-'Āṣ Gives Allegiance to Mu'āwiyah

In this year, 36, 'Amr b. al-'Āṣ gave allegiance to Mu'āwiyah[1154]
and made an agreement with him to fight 'Alī.

The reason for this
According to al-Sarī (in writing)—Shu'ayb—Sayf—Muḥammad
and Ṭalḥah and Abū Ḥārithah and Abū 'Uthmān: When 'Uthmān   [3250]
was surrounded 'Amr b. al-'Āṣ left Medina and headed for Syria.
"By Allāh! People of Medina!" he said. "Anyone who stays here
until this man is killed[1155] will be smitten by Almighty and Glorious Allāh with ignominy. Anyone who cannot help him had
better flee!" Off he then set, accompanied by his two sons, 'Abdallāh and Muḥammad. Ḥassān b. Thābit also left a little later, and
many others followed suit.

According to Sayf—Abū Ḥārithah and Abū 'Uthmān: While
'Amr b. al-'Āṣ was camped at 'Ajlān with his two sons a rider
passed. "Where have you come from?" they asked. "Medina."

1149. Or "disbelieved": *kafarū*.
1150. The arabicized form of Aparshahr, i.e., Nīshāpūr, the district capital of
western Khurāsān (*EI²*, s.v. Abarshahr).
1151. U. Sezgin, 205.
1152. U. Sezgin, 205.
1153. Abū al-Qāsim al-Kūfī, 'Alī's *ṣāḥib al-shurṭah* (U. Sezgin, 205).
1154. I.e., as caliph.
1155. Reading *qatl*, following *Addenda*, DCXXXV and Ibrāhīm.

"What's your name?" asked ʿAmr. "Ḥaṣīrah." "The man[1156] has been besieged,"[1157] retorted ʿAmr. "What's the news?" "I left the man surrounded," replied the rider. "He'll be dead," said ʿAmr. They waited a few days; then another rider passed. "Where have you come from?" they asked. "Medina." "What's your name?" asked ʿAmr. "Qattāl." "The man has been killed,"[1158] retorted ʿAmr. "What's the news?" "The man has been killed," replied the rider, "but nothing else occurred before I left." They waited a few more days; then another rider passed. "Where have you come from?" they asked. "Medina." "What's your name?" asked ʿAmr. "Ḥarb." "It's war,"[1159] retorted ʿAmr. "What's the news?" "ʿUthmān b ʿAffān has been killed," replied the rider, "and allegiance has been given to ʿAlī b. Abī Ṭālib." "I am Abū ʿAbdallāh!"[1160] said ʿAmr. "There will be a war, in which whoever scrapes a wound in it will open it right up! May Allāh have mercy on ʿUthmān. May He be pleased with him, and may He forgive him!" "Men of Quraysh!" spoke up Salāmah b. Zinbāʿ al-Judhāmī. "By Allāh! There was a door[1161] between you and the other Arab tribes. You must take on another door because the first one is now broken." "That's what we want to do," replied ʿAmr, "but the door will be mended only by augers that can drill out the truth from the root of the problem,[1162] so that men will be equal before the law." Referring to the situation ʿAmr then recited:

[3251]

I am heartbroken over Mālik,
> but can grief deflect what has been stored up by divine
> decree?
Is it heatstroke that has felled them?
> If so, I excuse them, or is it that my people are drunk?[1163]

1156. I.e., ʿUthmān.

1157. *Ḥuṣir*, playing on the man's name, as again twice in what follows. The ms. adds, "and has been killed."

1158. *Qutila*.

1159. *Ḥarb*.

1160. Is he reminding those around of his fame and important position?

1161. ʿUthmān.

1162. *Ḥāfiratu al-baʾs*. The image is of something having to be dug out from the hoof of disaster, from the very bottom of a difficult situation.

1163. ʿAmr is referring to the Muslims who did not support ʿUthmān (Mālik in the poem). He would excuse them if it were due to circumstances beyond their

Then he set off on foot, weeping like a woman and saying: "I mourn for 'Uthmān! I lament for modesty and religion!" He went to Damascus, for he had received some information about what was going to happen and acted on it.

According to al-Sarī (in writing)—Shu'ayb—Sayf—Muḥammad b. 'Abdallāh—Abū 'Uthmān: The Prophet had sent 'Amr to 'Umān, and when he was there he heard a prediction from a Jewish scholar. Then, when he saw it come true while he was still there, he sent a message to this scholar: "Speak to me about the death of the Messenger of God, and tell me who will come after him!" "The man who wrote[1164] to you will come after him, but he will only rule for a short time," he replied. "Then who?" asked 'Amr. "A fellow tribesman of his of a similar standing." "How long will he rule?" "For a long time, but then he will be killed." "By assassination or in front of the community?"[1165] asked 'Amr. "By assassination." "Who will then rule after him?" asked 'Amr. "A fellow tribesman of his of a similar standing." "How long will he rule?" "For a long time, but then he will be killed." "By assassination or in front of the community?" asked 'Amr. "In front of the community." "That's far worse," said 'Amr. "So who will rule after him?" "A fellow tribesman of his but behind whom Muslims will not unite and in whose time a fierce civil war will break out. He will then be killed before they can reach agreement about him." "By assassination or in front of the community?" asked 'Amr. "By assassination, and his like will never be seen again." "Who will then rule after him?" asked 'Amr. "The ruler of the Holy Land,[1166] and his kingdom will last a long time. Those who formerly differed and failed to unite will agree about him. He will die a natural death," replied the scholar.

[3252]

According to al-Wāqidī—Mūsā b. Ya'qūb—his uncle: When the news of 'Uthmān's murder reached 'Amr, he said: "I am Abū 'Abdallāh![1167] It was I who killed him, even though I'm in Wādī al-

---

control, but the implication is that they were fully responsible for losing their senses.

1164. Abū Bakr presumably wrote on behalf of the Prophet. Abū Bakr was of Taym.

1165. I.e., will the killer(s) not be afraid to kill in front of everyone?

1166. *Al-arḍ al-muqaddasah*. A Jewish scholar is narrating.

1167. See p. 192, above.

Sibāʿ. Who will succeed to this authority after him? If it's Ṭalḥah, then he's the foremost Arab in generosity.[1168] If it's ʿAlī b. Abī Ṭālib, then I can't see him giving anything more than he will be obligated to. For me he would be the very worst person to succeed."

News then reached him that allegiance had been given to ʿAlī. This was extremely serious for him, so he lay low for a few days to see what the Muslims would do. He then heard of the departure of Ṭalḥah, al-Zubayr, and ʿĀʾishah, so he said, "I will wait and see what they achieve!" But when he was told that Ṭalḥah and al-Zubayr had been killed he became confused. However, someone then said to him, "Muʿāwiyah is in Syria; he doesn't want to give allegiance to ʿAlī, so why not ally[1169] with Muʿāwiyah?" He did prefer Muʿāwiyah to ʿAlī b. Abī Ṭālib. Someone said, "Muʿāwiyah is taking the murder of ʿUthmān very seriously and is agitating for revenge for his blood," and ʿAmr said, "Call Muḥammad and ʿAbdallāh to me."

[3253]

They were called to him, and he said: "You have heard about the murder of ʿUthmān and the Muslims' allegiance to ʿAlī, and Muʿāwiyah's plans to oppose ʿAlī, so what do you both think? As for ʿAlī, there will be no benefit with him. He is a man who takes full advantage of his Islamic precedence. He is not going to delegate any of his authority to me."[1170] "The Prophet died pleased with you," ʿAbdallāh b. ʿAmr replied. "Abū Bakr died pleased with you; ʿUmar died pleased with you. My opinion is that you should not do anything. Just wait at home until the Muslims have agreed upon an imām. Then you may give him allegiance." "You are one of the most important Arab chiefs," said Muḥammad, "so this affair should not be agreed upon without your having a vote or say in it." "What you are recommending[1171] me to do, ʿAbdallāh," replied ʿAmr, "is better for me in the hereafter and safer for my religion. What you are recommending me to do, Muḥammad, is

---

1168. *Fa-huwa fatā al-ʿArab sayban* (*Glossarium*, CCCII). Dots added to the ms. give *nasaban*, "in lineage."

1169. Reading *qārabta* with Ibrāhīm, rather than the text's *qāranta*, "join forces."

1170. ʿAmr became Muslim much later than ʿAlī.

1171. Lit., "ordering"; cf. pp. 48, 51, above, where Ḥasan orders ʿAlī (but is disobeyed).

more glorious[1172] for my life here on earth but worse for me in the hereafter."

'Amr b. al-'Āṣ then left with his two sons and went to Mu'āwiyah. He found the Syrians urging Mu'āwiyah to seek revenge for the blood of 'Uthmān. "You are in the right," 'Amr b. al-'Āṣ said to them. "Seek revenge for the blood of the unjustly killed caliph!" Mu'āwiyah, however, did not pay any attention to 'Amr's words. So 'Amr's two sons said to their father: "Don't you realize that Mu'āwiyah isn't paying any attention to what you say? Leave him for someone else!" But 'Amr did go to Mu'āwiyah, and said: "By Allāh! What you're doing is very surprising. I have given you my support, and here you are ignoring me. I swear by Allāh! If we fight alongside you in revenge for the blood of the caliph, there will still be something that goes against the grain, for we will be fighting someone whose Islamic precedence, virtue, and close relationship to the Prophet you know well. But in fact all we're really after is this world." At this, Mu'āwiyah made up with him and was friendly toward him.

[3254]

'Alī b. Abī Ṭālib Sends Jarīr b. 'Abdallāh al-Bajalī to Call Mu'āwiyah to Acknowledge 'Alī's Authority over Him

Abū Ja'far al-Ṭabarī said:[1173] In this year, as 'Alī was leaving al-Baṣrah for al-Kūfah, having finished with the Battle of the Camel, he sent Jarīr b. 'Abdallāh al-Bajalī to call Mu'āwiyah to give allegiance to him. Now, when 'Alī set out for al-Baṣrah to fight his opponents there, Jarīr had been in Hamadhān[1174] as its governor. 'Uthmān had appointed him to this post. Al-Ash'ath b. Qays[1175] was governor of Ādharbāyjān,[1176] also appointed by 'Uthmān. So, when 'Alī came to al-Kūfah from al-Baṣrah, he wrote to these two men, commanding them to get allegiance to him from their subjects and to come to him. Both then got allegiance and set off to see 'Alī.

1172. *Anbahu* (*Glossarium*, D).
1173. Following the ms.
1174. In central Iran, 48° 31' E, 34° 48' N (*EI²*, s.v.).
1175. Abū Muḥammad Ma'dīkarib b. Qays, a chief of Kindah in the Ḥaḍramawt, d. 40/661 (*EI²*, s.v.).
1176. West of the Caspian (*EI²*, s.v.).

According to ʿUmar b. Shabbah—Abū al-Ḥasan—ʿAwānah: Then, when ʿAlī was looking for a messenger to send to Muʿāwiyah, Jarīr b. ʿAbdallāh said: "Send me, for he likes me. When I get to him I will call him to acknowledge your authority." Al-Ashtar said to ʿAlī, however: "Don't send him! By Allāh! I suspect he's inclined toward Muʿāwiyah." "Let him go," replied ʿAlī, "and we shall see what he comes back to us with." So he sent him and wrote a letter for him to take. In it he informed Muʿāwiyah of the agreement of the Muhājirūn and Anṣār to give allegiance to ʿAlī, of Ṭalḥah and al-Zubayr's going back on their allegiance, and of his war with the two of them. He went on to call him to acknowledge his authority, as the Muhājirūn and Anṣār had done.

[3255] Jarīr therefore set off to see Muʿāwiyah, but when he arrived Muʿāwiyah put him off and kept him waiting. [Muʿāwiyah] then called ʿAmr and asked his advice about ʿAlī's letter to him. ʿAmr advised him to send a message to the Syrian chiefs, implicating ʿAlī in ʿUthmān's blood and so get them to fight for him against ʿAlī. Muʿāwiyah followed his advice.

According to al-Sarī (in writing)—Shuʿayb—Sayf—Muḥammad and Ṭalḥah: When al-Nuʿmān b. Bashīr[1177] came to the Syrians with the bloodstained shirt ʿUthmān was wearing when he was killed, and with the severed fingers of Nāʾilah,[1178] his wife—two with the knuckles and part of the palm, two cut off at the base, and half a thumb—Muʿāwiyah hung the shirt on the *minbar* and wrote to the Syrian garrison towns.[1179] The people kept on coming and crying over it as it hung on the *minbar*, with the fingers attached to it, for a whole year. The Syrian soldiers swore an oath that they would not make love to women or undertake the major ablution[1180] unless obligated by seminal discharge during sleep or sleep on beds until they had killed the killers of ʿUthmān and anyone who might prevent them in any way, unless they should

---

1177. Al-Anṣārī, later governor of Kūfah and Ḥimṣ, a follower of ʿUthmān and then of Muʿāwiyah; killed after Marj Rāhiṭ, 65/684 (*EI*[1], s.v.).

1178. Bint al-Furāfisah of Kalb; she had tried to defend ʿUthmān. Cf. Abbott, *Aishah*, 126, 135.

1179. *Ajnād*. Lane, 470a; *EI*[2], s.v. Djund.

1180. As far as men are concerned, apart from washing the dead, this is only obligatory after ejaculation; Lane, 466c, 2259a; *EI*[2], s.v. Ghusl. It is only *mustaḥabb* or *sunnah* after Friday prayer. The soldiers' oath was urgent—they abjured pleasure, cleanliness, and comfort.

die meanwhile. They remained around the shirt for a year. It was placed each day on the *minbar*; sometimes it was made to cover it and was draped over it, and Nāʾilah's fingers were attached to its cuffs.

According to ʿUmar b. Shabbah—Abū al-Ḥasan—ʿAwānah: Jarīr b. ʿAbdallāh then came to ʿAlī and told him what Muʿāwiyah was doing and how the Syrians had agreed with him to fight ʿAlī. He told him how they were weeping over ʿUthmān and saying that ʿAlī had killed him and was sheltering ʿUthmān's killers and how they would not stop until he had killed them or they had killed him. So al-Ashtar said to ʿAlī: "I was warning you strongly[1181] against sending Jarīr. I told you he was an enemy and a deceiver. It would have been better if you had sent me rather than this man, who stayed with Muʿāwiyah [so long] that he opened every door that [Muʿāwiyah] wanted open and closed every door that [Muʿāwiyah] feared." "Had you been there," replied Jarīr, "they would have killed you. They actually named you as one of ʿUthmān's killers." "By Allāh! If I had gone to them, Jarīr," retorted al-Ashtar, "I would always have found an answer for them, and I would have forced Muʿāwiyah to act before he had time to think. Had the Commander of the Faithful followed my advice[1182] concerning you, he would have thrown you and those like you into a jail you would not get out of until these matters were sorted out properly."

Jarīr b. ʿAbdallāh then left for Qarqīsiyyāʾ.[1183] He wrote to Muʿāwiyah, who replied, ordering him to come to him. The Commander of the Faithful also left and encamped at al-Nukhaylah.[1184] ʿAbdallāh b. ʿAbbās[1185] joined him there, accompanied by a number of Baṣrans who had responded to his call to fight.

[3256]

1181. *Kuntu nahaytuka*; cf. note 1171, above.
1182. Lit., "obeyed me"; cf. note 1171, above.
1183. A town in al-Jazīrah on the left bank of the Euphrates, close to the confluence with the Khābūr (*EI²*, s.v.).
1184. About one days' ride from al-Kūfah for an army.
1185. ʿAlī's governor of al-Baṣrah.

Bibliography of Cited Works

Primary Sources: Texts and Translations

al-Balādhurī; Abū al-Ḥasan Aḥmad b. Yaḥyā. *Ansāb al-ashrāf*. Vol. II. Edited by M. B. al-Maḥmūdī. Beirut, 1393/1973.

al-Dīnawarī, Abū Ḥanīfah Aḥmad b. Dāwūd. *Kitāb al-akhbār al-ṭiwāl*. Vol. II. Edited by I. Kratchkovsky. Leiden, 1912.

Ibn ʿAbd Rabbihi, Shihāb al-Dīn Aḥmad al-Andalusī. *Al-ʿIqd al-farīd*. Vol. II. Būlāq, 1293/1876.

Ibn Abī al-Ḥadīd, ʿAbd al-Ḥamīd. *Sharḥ nahj al-Balāghah*. Edited by M. A. Ibrāhīm. 20 vols. Cairo, 1960–64.

Ibn Aʿtham al-Kūfī, Abū Muhammad Aḥmad. *Kitāb al-futūḥ*. 7 vols. Hyderabad, 1391/1968–71.

Ibn Hishām, ʿAbd al-Malik. *Kitāb sīrat Rasūl Allāh*. Edited by F. Wüstenfeld. 2 vols. in 3. Göttingen, 1858–60. Translated by A. Guillaume as *The Life of Muhammad*. London, 1955.

Ibn al-Kalbī, Hishām b. Muḥammad. *Jamharat al-nasab*. Rearranged and translated by W. Caskel and G. Strenziok as *Ğamharat an-nasab. Das genealogische Werk des Hišām ibn Muḥammad al-Kalbī*. 2 vols. Leiden, 1966.

Ibn Khaldūn, Walī al-Dīn Abū Zayd ʿAbd al-Raḥmān. *Al-Muqaddimah*. Translated by F. Rosenthal as *The Muqaddimah, an Introduction to History*. 3 vols. New York, 1958.

Ibn Khayyāṭ, Khalīfah. *Taʾrīkh*. Edited by S. Zakkār. N.p., 1967.

Ibn Manẓūr, Jamāl al-Dīn Abū al-Faḍl Muḥammad. *Lisān al-ʿArab*. Būlāq, 1301/1884.

Ibn al-Mujāhid. *Kitāb al-sabʿah fī al-qirāʾāt*. Edited by Sh. Ḍayf. Cairo, n.d.

Ibn Saʿd, Muḥammad. *Kitāb al-ṭabaqāt al-kabīr*. Edited by E. Sachau et al. 9 vols. Leiden, 1905–40.

Ibrāhīm. See al-Ṭabarī.

al-Jāḥiẓ, ʿAmr ibn Baḥr. *Kitāb al-bayān*. Beirut, 1388/1968.

al-Masʿūdī, Abū al-Ḥasan ʿAlī. *Murūj al-dhahab*. Edited with French translation by C. B. A. C. Barbier de Meynard and Pavet de Courteille. Vol. IV. Paris, 1865.

al-Shaykh al-Mufīd, Muḥammad b. Muḥammad al-ʿUkbarī. *Al-Jamal, aw al-nuṣrah fī ḥarb al-Baṣrah*. Al-Najaf, 1368/1949.

al-Ṭabarī, Abū Jaʿfar Muḥammad. *Taʾrīkh al-rusul wa al-mulūk*. Edited by M. J. de Goeje et al. as *Annales quos scripsit Abu Djafar . . .* 13 vols. and 2 vols. *Indices* and Introductio, Glossarium, Addenda et emendanda. Leiden, 1879–1901. Edited by M. Ibrāhīm. Vol. IV. Cairo, 1960–69.

al-Thaʿālibī, Abū Manṣūr ʿAbd al-Malik. *Kitāb thimār al-qulūb fī al-muḍāf wa-al-mansūb*. Cairo, 1326/1908.

al-Yaʿqūbī, Abū al-ʿAbbās Aḥmad. *Taʾrīkh*. Edited by M. T. Houtsma as *Historiae*. 2 vols. Leiden, 1883.

Yāqūt, Abū ʿAbdallāh al-Ḥamawī al-Rūmī. *Muʿjam al-buldān*. 5 vols. Beirut, 1374–76/1955–57.

al-Zabīdī, Muḥammad Murtaḍā. *Tāj al-ʿarūs*. Kuwait, 1369/1969.

al-Zawzanī. *Sharḥ al-muʿallaqāt al-sabʾ*. Beirut, n.d.

al-Zubayrī, Abū ʿAbdallāh Muṣʿab. *Kitāb nasab Quraysh*. Cairo, 1953.

Secondary Sources and Reference Works

Abbott, N. "Women and the State on the Eve of Islam." *American Journal of Semitic Languages* 58 (1941): 259–84.

———. *Aishah, the Beloved of Mohammed*. Chicago, 1942; repr. New York, 1973.

al-ʿAlī, Ṣ. A. "Khiṭaṭ al-Baṣrah." *Sumer* 8 (1952): 72–83, 281–303.

al-ʿAqqād, ʿA. M. *ʿAbqariyyat ʿAlī*. Beirut, n.d.

ʿArmūsh, A. R. *Al-Fitna wa-waqʿat al-jamal*. Beirut, 1972.

al-ʿAskarī, M. *ʿAbdallāh ibn Sabaʾ wa ʿasāṭīr ukhrā*. Vol. I. Baghdad, n.d.

Ayoub, M. M. "Dhimmah in Qurʾān and Ḥadīth." *Arab Studies Quarterly* 7 (1986): 172–82.

Biberstein-Kazimirsky, A. de. *Dictionnaire arabe-français*. 2 vols in 4. Paris, 1860.

Brockelmann, C. *Geschichte der arabischen Litteratur*. 5 vols. Leiden, 1937–49.

Burton, J. *The Collection of the Qurʾān*. Cambridge, 1977.

Bury, J. B., H. M. Gwatkin, and J. D. Whitney. *The Cambridge Medieval History*. Vol. II. Cambridge, 1913.

Caetani, L. *Annali dell'Islam*. 10 vols. in 12. Milan, 1905–26.

Caskel, W., and G. Strenziok. See Ibn al-Kalbī.

Conrad, L. I. "Seven and the *Tasbīʿ*." *JESHO* 31 (1988): 42–73.

Donner, F. M. *The Early Islamic Conquests.* Princeton, N.J., 1981.

Dozy, R. P. A. *Dictionnaire détaillé des noms des vêtements chez les Arabes.* Amsterdam, 1845.

Duri, ʿA. *The Rise of Historical Writing among the Arabs.* Edited and translated by L. I. Conrad. Princeton, N.J., 1983.

Freytag, G. W., trans. *Arabum Proverbia.* Vol. I. Bonn, 1838.

Hava, J. G. *Al-Farāʾid: Arabic-English Dictionary.* 3rd ed. Beirut, 1970.

Hawting, G. R. *The First Dynasty of Islam: The Umayyad Caliphate A.D. 661–750.* London, 1986.

———. *The First Civil War: From the Battle of Ṣiffīn to the Death of ʿAlī.* The History of al-Ṭabarī XVII. Albany, N.Y., 1995.

Hinds, M. "Kûfan Political Alignments and Their Background in the Mid-Seventh Century A.D." *IJMES* 2 (1971): 346–67.

———. "The Murder of the Caliph ʿUthmân." *IJMES* 3 (1972): 450–69.

———. "Sayf b. ʿUmar's Sources on Arabia." In *Sources for the History of Arabia.* Vol. 1, pt. 2. al-Riyādh, 1979. Pp. 3–16.

———. "The Banners and Battle Cries of the Arabs at Ṣiffīn (657 A.D.)." *Al-Abḥāth* 24 (1971): 3–42.

Humphreys, R. S. *Islamic History: A Framework for Inquiry.* Minneapolis, Minn., 1988.

———. *The Crisis of the Early Caliphate. The Reign of ʿUthmān.* The History of al-Ṭabarī XV. Albany, N.Y., 1990.

Ḥusayn, Ṭ. *Al-Fitnah al-kubrā.* 2 vols. Cairo, 1959.

Juynboll, G. H. A. *Muslim tradition: Studies in Chronology, Provenance, and Authorship of Early Ḥadīth.* Cambridge, 1983.

Landau-Tasseron, E. "Sayf ibn ʿUmar in Medieval and Modern Scholarship." *Der Islam* 67 (1990): 1–26.

Lane, E. W. *An Arabic-English Lexicon.* 1 vol. in 8. London and Edinburgh, 1863–93.

Lau, L. D. "Sayf b. ʿUmar and the Battle of the Camel." *IQ* 23 (1979): 103–11.

LeStrange, G. *The Lands of the Eastern Caliphate.* Cambridge, 1930.

Levi della Vida, G. "Il califfatto di Ali secondo il *Kitāb Ansāb al-Ašrāf di al-Balāduri, RSO* 6 (1914-1915): 427–507.

Massignon, L. "Explication du plan de Baṣra (Irak)." In *Westöstliche Abhandlungen: R. Tschudi . . .* Ed. F. M. Meier. Wiesbaden, 1954. Pp. 154–74.

Morony, M. G. *Iraq after the Muslim Conquest.* Princeton, N.J., 1984.

Muir, W. *The Caliphate: Its Rise, Decline, and Fall.* Rev. edition by T. H. Weir. Edinburgh, 1915.

Nagel, T. "Ein früher Bericht über den Aufstand von Muhammad ibn ʿAbdallah im Jahre 145 H." *Der Islam* 46 (1970): 227–62.

Nöldeke, T., and F. Schwally. *Geschichte des Qorans.* Vols. I–II. Leipzig, 1909–10.

Noth, A. "Der Charakter der ersten grossen Sammlungen von Nachrichten zur frühen Kalifenzeit." *Der Islam* 47 (1971): 168–99.

———. *Quellenkritische Studien zu Themen, Formen und Tendenzen frühislamischer Geschichtsüberlieferung.* Vol. 1. Bonn, 1973.

Pellat, C. *Le milieu baṣrien et la formation de Ǧāḥiẓ.* Paris, 1953.

Petersen, E. L. *ʿAlī and Muʿāwiyah in Early Arabic Tradition: Studies on the Genesis and Growth of Islamic Historical Writing until the End of the Ninth Century.* Trans. P. L. Christensen. Copenhagen, 1964.

Schacht, J. *The Origins of Muhammadan Jurisprudence.* Oxford, 1950; repr. Oxford, 1975.

Sezgin, F. *Geschichte des arabischen Schrifttums.* Vol. I. Leiden, 1967.

Sezgin, U. *Abū Miḥnaf: Ein Beitrag zur Historiographie der umaiyadischen Zeit.* Leiden, 1971.

Smith, G. R., trans. *The Conquest of Iran,* The History of al-Ṭabarī XIV. Albany, 1994.

Spuler, B., editor. *Wüstenfeld-Mahler'sche Vergleichungs-Tabellen.* Wiesbaden, 1961.

Watt, W. M. *Muhammad at Medina.* Oxford, 1956.

Wellhausen, J. *Skizzen und Vorarbeiten.* Vol. 6. Berlin, 1899.

Wensinck, A. J., et al. *Concordance et indices de la tradition musulmane.* 8 vols. Leiden, 1936–69.

Wright, W. *A Grammar of the Arabic Language.* 3rd ed. 2 vols. London, 1962; repr. Cambridge, 1977.

Index

Included are names of persons, groups, and places, as well as Arabic terms that recur often in the text or are discussed in the footnotes. An asterisk (*) indicates a figure who is mentioned in the text only as a transmitter. Entries that are mentioned in both text and footnotes on the same page are listed by page number only. Finally, the Arabic definite article al-, *the abbreviation* b. *(for* ibn, *"son of"), the word* bint *("daughter of") and all material in parentheses have been disregarded in the alphabetizing of entries.*

A

Abān b. ʿUthmān 44, 67
ʿAbbād b. ʿAbdallāh b. al-Zubayr* 139
al-ʿAbbās b. Muḥammad* 145
ʿAbbās b. Sahl al-Sāʿidī* 175
ʿAbd al-Aʿlā b. Wāṣil* 156
ʿAbd Khayr al-Khaywānī 93, 94
ʿAbd al-Majīd al-Asadī* 21, 145
ʿAbd al-Malik b. Abī Sulaymān al-Fazārī* 1, 5
ʿAbd al-Malik b. Muslim* 156
ʿAbd al-Qays 15, 64, 69, 72, 77, 78, 86, 90, 96, 106, 115, 120, 121, 133, 136, 142, 144
ʿAbd al-Raḥmān b. Abī Bakrah 46, 77, 168
ʿAbd al-Raḥmān b. ʿAttāb b. Asīd al-Qurashī 45, 55, 67, 71, 123, 132, 135, 139, 140, 142, 147, 163, 170
ʿAbd al-Raḥmān b. al-Ḥakam 159

ʿAbd al-Raḥmān b. al-Ḥārith b. Hishām 71, 123, 132
ʿAbd al-Raḥmān b. Jundab* 14
ʿAbd al-Raḥmān b. Jusham b. Abī Ḥunayn al-Ḥamāmī 144
ʿAbd al-Raḥmān b. Sulaymān al-Taymī 117
ʿAbdallāh b. ʿAbbās 2, 20, 22–24, 32, 37, 46, 53, 54, 84, 87, 88, 95, 96, 102, 103, 122, 169, 197
ʿAbdallāh b. ʿAbd al-Raḥmān b. Abī ʿAmrah* 42
ʿAbdallāh b. Aḥmad* 141, 151, 153, 156
ʿAbdallāh b. Aḥmad al-Marwazī* 7, 183, 187
ʿAbdallāh b. Aḥmad b. Shabbawayh* 171
ʿAbdallāh b. ʿĀmir al-Ḥaḍramī 37, 39, 40, 43
ʿAbdallāh b. ʿĀmir b. Kurayz 20, 21, 40, 56, 160